Cruising Guide

Jim Aeby

Also by Brian M. Fagan

Cruising Guide to Southern California's Offshore Islands

Staying Put, The Art of Anchoring

CRUISING GUIDE

San Francisco to Enseñada, Mexico

Brian M. Fagan

Caractacus Corporation Santa Barbara, California

Published by Caractacus Corporation
Santa Barbara, California.

Typeset and Book Design by
Iris Studio.
Imagesetting by Chroma-Litho.
Printed in U.S.A. by Gilliland Printing.

Photography Credits:
James T. Aeby, cover
Pat Leddy, back cover
Lesley Newhart, author portrait

Caractacus Corporation
132B Harbor Way
Santa Barbara
CA 93109

Library of Congress Cataloging in Publication Data:
Fagan, Brian M.
Cruising Guide: San Francisco to Ensenada, Mexico
Includes Index
1. Boats and Boating - California - Mainland and Channel Islands - Guide-books
2. California coast - Description and Travel - Guide-books. I. Title.
Library of Congress Catalog Card Number 94-68035
ISBN 0-9634635-1-9

Courtesy Bancroft Library, University of California, Berkeley.

Fremont's California Battalion enters Monterey in 1846.

DISCLAIMER

This book, along with the accompanying charts and illustrations, is not to be used for navigation, but for reference purposes only.

The contents have been carefully prepared. They are based on personal inspection, official publications, and other data deemed reliable, with the objective of making the cruising skipper's voyage more enjoyable. Every reasonable effort has been made to achieve up-to-date accuracy; but the infinite complexities of personal observation and a constantly changing world render total accuracy impossible.

Only governments, with their vast resources of money, personnel, and vessels, can achieve such reliability. Accordingly, all sailing information and directions in this book must be checked against the latest available charts, publications, and notices to mariners whenever a cruise is undertaken.

Every skipper is responsible for the safety of his or her crew and vessel, and he or she must plot the course.

The Author and Publisher must therefore both specifically disclaim any and all personal liability for loss or risk, to persons or to property or both, which might occur, either directly or indirectly, from any person's use or interpretation of any information contained in this book.

ACKNOWLEDGMENTS

Patrick Short

This book is a collective effort. Dozens of sailors have contributed to this book over the many years of its preparation. They include commercial fishermen and divers, people who cruise the coast under sail and power, Naval officers and park rangers. I am very grateful to these many friends, and apologize for not being able to name them all individually. I owe a particular debt of gratitude to Jim Aeby and Pat Leddy, who designed the book and saw it through production, and to Bob Kieding, who was a wonderful partner in the enterprise.

Thanks are due to the following for permission to use their photographs in this Guide. Individual credits appear with each picture:

Toni Abbott

Jim Aeby

Jeff Barnhart

Gene's Photo and Rock Store, Avalon

Geri Conser

Peter Howorth

Pat Leddy

Lesley Newhart

Graham Pomeroy

Patrick Short

O COMMANDER JAMES ALDEN, USN, GEORGE DAVIDSON, and the many other government surveyors of the US Coast Survey, 1848-1859, who first charted the California coast.

88
88

Contents

Veil clouds over Santa Ynez Mountains. Peter Howorth

This cruising guide began as a series of ideas about passage making in California formulated during a quarter century of sailing off the West Coast. These ideas lurked in the back of my mind for years, helped me plan cruises as far afield as Finland and Greece, and to survive the shallow waters of the Bahamas. In 1981, I published *California Coastal Passages* (Capra Press, Santa Barbara), a short guide to sailing from San Francisco to Ensenada now long out of print. The success of that book and persistent requests for a revised version have resulted in a new and more comprehensive sequel.

I have sailed in many cruising grounds, but few of them rival the California coast for sheer diversity and spectacular scenery. You can eat in some of the finest restaurants in the world, berth in the largest marina on earth, or enjoy island anchorages as remote and unspoiled as they were a century ago. California is a paradise for the cruising family, whether under sail or power. *Cruising Guide: San Francisco to Ensenada, Mexico* describes the most challenging coastal waters, from central California in the north to northern Mexico, in the south.

If the early adventurers and discoverers made their explorations in small crazy vessels, with wretched and unworthy instruments and methods, it is no less true that the first Coast Survey parties made theirs with inadequate funds, and under difficulties and privations that the well-housed Californian of to-day can never fully appreciate.

George Davidson,
Directory for the Pacific Coast
of the United States, 1858.

One school of thought among California sailors believes that you can find your way around very nicely by leaving the Golden Gate and literally "turning left at the lights." Well, you can, but you may have many frustrating moments and sleepless nights. This guide is designed for people like me who worry about longer passages, and want to know what they are likely to face beyond the traffic lights. To judge from the many cruising seminars I have attended, there are far more of us than perhaps would admit it.

This cruising guide consists of seven chapters, which introduce California waters. I describe suitable yachts and essential equipment,

Pacific Coast Highway 1 Trestle. © Geri Conser, 1994

brief you on the weather, and provide a historical background for your cruise. Chapter 7 outlines basic passage-making strategies for making longer voyages, the strategic framework for any cruise you plan. These seven chapters are by way of being the appetizer. The remainder of the book is the entree. Eight more chapters describe the coastline from San Francisco Bay southward to the Mexican border and just beyond. These chapters are sailing directions, designed and laid out to be used on deck and on passage. So I wrote this book both to enlighten and to entertain, also to guide you from landmark to landmark as you sail to distant waters.

Back in the 1850s, surveyor George Davidson compiled the first set of sailing directions for the California coast. He fixed the position of major headlands like Point Conception and spent days on end in small boats and camped on windy promontories in the process. I wrote this book over a period of more than twenty years, during more passages up and down the coast than I care to remember, in everything from glassy calms to 45-knot northwesters and driving rain. My notes are weatherbeaten and coffee stained. Some pages even bear a light brown tinge of after-dinner brandy. I have combined these staccato notes with material from many sources. The *US Coast Pilot, volume 7* is the official directory to the coast, an invaluable, if generalized description designed for commercial vessels. The Pilot's measured paragraphs provided a backbone, but are just the beginning. I delved into historical archives, consulted nineteenth-century directories and charts, read George Vancouver, Richard Henry Dana, and many other early travelers. Good sailing directions use official sources, but go much further to satisfy the smaller vessel's needs. My descriptions draw on official sources, but most important of all, on the collective experience of generations of sailors, including my own. For example, no one has written a better description of a California northwester than Richard Henry Dana, while George Davidson's directions for entering San Diego harbor under sail have no rival.

I believe that practical sailing directions are used in combination with the relevant NOAA charts. An up-to-date set of charts provides accurate information on lights and navigational aids, which change almost daily and, inevitably, make small details in these pages outdated. You lay out courses on charts, develop Dead Reckoning plots, use your courses and bearings to assess strategies for the hours ahead. What these directions do is to add background information, strategic detail, and, above all, impressions based on practical observation and experience. For instance, the remarks about rounding Point Conception northbound come from indelible lessons learned when trying to beat against howling northwesters off the point.

This book gives qualitative impressions, discusses ideas and strategies which have enabled me to make successful passages along the coast in a wide variety of weather conditions. I stress the word impressions, for good seamanship is based on impressionistic judgments about local conditions and ever-changing circumstances of wind and weather. You may end up disagreeing with my judgments, but then conditions may be different when you are in the same place. I try to give you the general outline and major landmarks, as well as ideas about favored courses, currents, and so on. The harbor descriptions assume you have the large scale chart plan aboard. I aim to get you safely into

Courtesy Bancroft Library, University of California, Berkeley

Drawing of Monterey waterfront in 1846, by Lt. J.W. Revere, U.S. Navy, grandson of Paul Revere, Revolutionary War hero.

port and to tell you where to got to find a berth. I make no attempt to list all the excellent private marinas and other facilities in California harbors, which change constantly. A call to the local harbormaster will give you information ahead of time, or you can rely on advertising-supported publications, which specialize in such data. This is a book about getting there safely and enjoying yourself along the way.

A word on electronic navigation is appropriate here. Any sailing directions must assume you have no such aids aboard. GPS, Loran, and radar are so reliable they have taken all the guesswork out of coastal pilotage, even in fog. Such devices are wonderful monuments to late twentieth-century technology, but they can go wrong at the worst moments. I take a conservative position and describe our waters from the perspective of someone without electronic aids, on the argument that the information provided is essential for preparing Dead Reckoning plots, which every responsible skipper keeps anyhow, and for identifying landmarks when you have fixed your position. This is a navigator's book, not a push-button sailor's concession to responsible pilotage. I wager you may need much of the seemingly irrelevant detail in these pages one day.

This book has a companion volume, *Cruising Guide to Southern California's Offshore Islands* (Caractacus Corporation, Santa Barbara, 1992). The *Cruising Guide* offers a detailed description of the many anchorages at the Southern California islands for those planning a leisurely stay in these magical waters. The descriptions in the present book cover only the major anchorages, such as one might use on a short visit, or while on passage to other mainland destinations. Space precludes comprehensive sailing directions for the Channel Islands here.

The pages which follow are as accurate as I can make them at the time of publication. Conditions are changing all the time, and despite every care, some errors or inaccuracies may have crept into the book. Interested readers are encouraged, even urged, to bring changes, errors, or different strategies to the attention of the author, c/o Department of Anthropology, University of California, Santa Barbara, California 93106.

Brian Fagan

Important Warning

This book expresses numerous opinions about anchorages and ports along the California coast and about cruising conditions in these waters generally. If anything, these opinions are on the conservative side. Realize that these are the opinions of the author, and that your judgement as to whether to use an anchorage, make a passage, or pursue some other course of action may differ according to weather and other conditions at the time.

In the final analysis, safe cruising comes down to sound judgements on the spot—and I cannot make these for you.

Conventions

Certain arbitrary choices had to be made when writing this book, basic conventions that are carried right through the text. You should be aware of these as you use this volume.

Direction of travel in this book is from north to south. To use the sailing directions to journey from south to north, use them in reverse!

Points of the compass and directions are not all written out in full, i.e., North, South, Northwest, etc., but often given in letter form: NW, SSW, etc., except when referring to a landmark (Northwest Anchorage) or a weather phenomenon (northwester).

Bearings are given in degrees magnetic (1994). Most sailing directions use true bearings, but I felt magnetic headings would be less trouble for small craft fitted with magnetic compasses. Check the variation for the year you use this book, and remember to convert true bearings from other publications, where appropriate.

Distances are in nautical miles (2,000 yards), including land distances; or they are stated in yards or feet.

Depths are in feet, and, in the context of anchorages, usually give a range, i.e., 25-30 feet. All soundings are to mean lower, low water. In other words, calculate your tidal depths from our base line soundings. Note that NOAA charts sometimes give depths in fathoms (one fathom equals six feet). We sometimes use fathoms here, especially in passage-making and offshore contexts. Government charts will convert to metric soundings in the next few years. Please be alert to the pending change.

Lights: I have made every effort to make this book relatively timeless, but navigational aids, especially lights, change constantly. The light characteristics in this book are accurate as of September 1 1994. Check later editions of charts and light lists, also Local Notices to Mariners for updates. GPS and radar have made radiobeacons somewhat of an anachronism. I have omitted them from the sailing directions in this book, but they can be found on the relevant NOAA charts.

Light characteristics follow chart conventions, i.e., Gp. Fl. W.R. 5 sec. 200 feet 29 miles (Group flashing white and red every five seconds, light exhibited at a height of 200 feet, and visible (theoretically) for 29 miles). HO Chart 1, Chart Symbols explains all the abbreviations. I strongly recommend having a copy aboard.

Anchorages: I have visited every anchorage in this book, spent the night in most of them, and used many of them in different weather conditions. The experience taught me the folly of trying to rate anchorages like movies or hotels. Cruising is not like visiting restaurants or staying in motels. Everything depends on your judgment of prevailing conditions when you are in the vicinity of a cove. Ratings in these sailing directions might bias your judgements. I prefer to give you general advice rather than rating symbols. Nor do I give you coordinates or other data which you can easily obtain from the chart folio you have aboard. There is far more to these waters than merely plugging in a GPS or Loran. I feel they need more respect than merely unthinking use of electronic gadgetry. In other words, one day they will go wrong!

Generally, the anchorages described in these pages are suitable for vessels of all sizes from 80-feet to under 20-feet overall. Some Channel Islands anchorages are too small for larger yachts, but I do not cover them here. Again, you must judge local conditions for yourself.

Anchoring in harbors is a controversial subject, especially in San Diego. As a general rule, the authorities discourage the practice, partly because of safely considerations, also because a small number of boat owners consider in-port anchorages permanent residences. Check with local harbor offices before anchoring in an area under their jurisdiction. As a general principle, it's getting harder and harder to anchor safely anywhere south of Santa Monica, or even at Catalina, where moorings now clutter most coves. You can do it, but the exercise may tax your ingenuity.

Marinas and Port Facilities, Activities Ashore. I wrote this *Cruising Guide* to get you from place to place, and into port safely. Harbor facilities and marinas change constantly, especially those under private ownership. At the time of writing, few new marina developments are under way in California, so the situation has stabilized somewhat. As a guiding principle, I describe marina and berthing facilities in general terms, give details of public facilities, and relatively little information about privately owned marinas. It's not that I have anything against them, quite the contrary. My considerations are space and ever-changing detail. Most visitors to a strange harbor call in at the harbormaster's office, where up-to-date information on berthing and transient slips is always available. The harbormaster will always know which marinas have space, which do not, and the reservation policies and rates governing each. If you want advance information, do not hesitate to give the harbor office a call. I give telephone numbers for each port. You can sometimes obtain information from advertising-supported publications and magazines, but a call to the local harbor office will elicit up-to-date information just as quickly.

California is not like the Mexico, South Pacific Islands or New Guinea, where towns, stores, and fuel are rarities.

Every mainland port has adequate fuel, provisioning, and water facilities, and most repairs can be undertaken even at smaller ports like Monterey, Santa Cruz, or Santa Barbara. For this reason, I have not dwelt on these basics, except for indicating where you may need to rent a car or hire a cab to reach a supermarket. Again, the harbor master's office or local yacht club will be glad to give directions and assistance.

This book is light on shore attractions, which, in most cases, are the subject of innumerable guidebooks. To dwell on things to do ashore would double the size of this volume. Everyone, including non-Californians, knows, for example, that Disneyland can be reached from Newport Beach or Alamitos Bay, or that Monterey has a world-famous aquarium. Indeed, many crews organize their cruises around visits to these destinations. Nor do I endorse any restaurants, chandleries, boat yards, or other commercial establishments, for the patronizing of these is, also, a matter of personal judgement, taste, and the depth of an individual's pocket. For further information on local tourist attractions, festivals, and cultural events, contact the local tourist information office or chamber of commerce.

Fair winds and smooth passages!

—Brian Fagan

Part One

California Passage-Making

E by NE about fifty leagues; then ENE in the general direction of the Ladrones; through Los Volcanes or the higher Ladrones NE by E to thirty -one degrees latitude and longitude twenty-eight and a half east of Manila; ENE to thirty-six or seven degrees in longitude forty; thence to the region of Cape Mendocino, SE to thirty-five degrees latitude without sighting land; SE to the landfall at the island of Cenizas in thirty degrees, or at the island of Cedros a degree and a half lower at the entrance to Sebastian Vizcaìno Bay...

Sailing directions for Spanish galleons traversing the Pacific from the Phillipines to California and New Spain by pilot Cebrera Bueno.

Toni Abbott

CHAPTER 1

Coastal Passages

It was a beautiful day, and so warm that we wore straw hats, duck trousers, and all the summer gear. As this was midwinter, it spoke well for the climate..."

Richard Henry Dana,
Two Years Before the Mast, 1840

One boisterous day, I was sailing well reefed down before a 20-knot breeze, tacking downwind to keep the coast in distant sight off the Big Sur coast. A low overcast hung over the yellow cliffs, casting a slight chill on the air. This was before the days of GPS (Global Positioning Systems) and Loran. My cruising companion, John kept a dead reckoning plot on the chart as Susan, the third member of our trusty crew, kept peering into the gloom for white lighthouse buildings ashore.

We had been forewarned by Santa Barbara sailors about the evils of Point Conception, a regular boiling nether region where pitiless headwinds would be our fate. Our doomsaying friends had painted the passage northward in the direst terms, as if we were to pass through the Gates of Hell. John, Susan, and myself had set out literally trembling in our deck shoes, with few words of encouragement except from one oil boat skipper, who urged us to just go.

"Watch the weather," he advised. "Use the foggy hours, and wait for headwinds to blow out at sunset."

We did just that. As the wind piped over 20 knots close to Conception, we sheltered in Cojo Anchorage where the occasional freight train lumbered along the railroad embankment back of the open roadstead. By 2200, the wind had died, leaving a glassy calm. We started our faithful auxiliary and motored northward a safe distance offshore against a lumpy sea, straining our eyes for Point Arguello: Much to our relief, its welcome flashes duly appearing on schedule as we motored on through the gloom.

Peter Howorth

Occasional porpoises playing around the bows, cast streams of bioluminescence in the opaque sea. As dawn turned night into murky grey, a slight morning breeze came from astern. We stopped the diesel, then drifted under main, and genoa. Our foghorn sounded its forlorn sound into the dense fog. I alternated between hatchway and the chart table, checking our log for boat speed. John updated the Dead Reckoning plot, estimated our position since the fix on Arguello. I trusted him completely, having sailed all over Southern California in his company, ever since we met in a harbor-side bar a few weeks after I arrived in Santa Barbara. He knew every rock, every anchorage in the south, but had never been north of Conception. Though an experienced sailor, with that calm, competent air that comes with years at sea, this was a first trip north for Susan, too. She was John's girl friend of many months. (They're married now with a growing family, but, since then, we have lost touch.)

Susan guessed we were close to Morro Bay. We were nearing a rapidly shelving coast frequented by occasional tankers and numerous fishing boats. The three of us were contemplating options. When suddenly a fishing boat burst out of the fog, going at full speed: She passed close to our starboard side and vanished before any of us could shout. I tensed, held my breath, feeling vanquished and alone, listening to condensation dripping from the boom. My sailing companions felt lost in the fog, too.

"So much for the bar admirals in Santa Barbara." Susan stood quite apart from where I stood, staring into the blank of a seaman's nightmare.

I had never been in so thick a fog before. All the years of book learning passed before me. Though we were close to Morro Bay, with no currents to worry about, I knew to steer inshore was to invite disaster. There was nothing to do but plot depth meter readings, look for the 10-fathom line, and hope we could anchor in relatively shallow water to wait out the fog.

Eighteen fathoms, sixteen fathoms, twelve: The bottom slowly shallowed. Then just as we reached the 10-fathom line, like a miracle, the fog lifted and Morro Rock stood out like a signpost three quarters of a mile ahead. Our fears evaporated. A bright ray of sunshine bathed the Rock in a momentary yellow. In a surge of relief, we motored into the harbor entrance, then secured at Morro Bay Yacht Club. How we celebrated! John and Susan cooked up a mountain of eggs, bacon, and hot coffee, which we consumed amidst the warm laughter of friends who joined us from shore.

Five days later and with a strong sense of achievement, we sailed through the Golden Gate. Our feelings must have been similar to even those Spanish captains of a century and a half ago. I remember reading how a captain of a Spanish treasure galleon, bound from Monterey to the Golden Gate in 1776, had elected to make a long board offshore instead of making short tacks close inshore. Such was the ship's drift to leeward, the captain ended up tacking northward when on the latitude of Point Loma and San Diego Bay. He took three

Morro Bay © Geri Conser, 1994

weeks to reach Point Reyes before sailing southward into the Gate. Now we were sailing home in the arms of the very winds we had been warned about, sailing a coastline that the Bostonian, Richard Henry Dana of *Two Years Before the Mast* fame, once took northward past Big Sur in a clumsy square rigger.

The wind was blowing a steady 25 knots. John steered us down a larger swell than usual. He told me not to worry, it would be clear and we could see for miles. Our speed increased, some hazy rays of sun shine hit the nearby cliffs. I took a turn at the wheel, drinking innumerable cups of coffee.

"Thank heavens for diesel engines. I'd hate to beat against this." Susan said.

"Amen," John murmured, as a gust caused us to surf down the face of another large swell. Then the sun came out as John predicted and the peaks of the Santa Lucia mountains stood out above the gray. We hurried past Pfeiffer Point, the ship light on the helm flicking ahead as if eager to reach home. The conversation turned from inept skippers to passage planning. John started it, all our talking about the passage north, undertaken with trepidation during ten days of June fog, and how much more enjoyable it would have been if we had some small boat sailing directions to guide us.

"What about a cruising guide for the coast?" He asked, as we jibed offshore, leaving the Point Sur light far astern off the port quarter. At the time, the idea of writing a cruising guide went in one ear and came out the other. I was more interested in the lore of passage making. Since we had motored most of the way up the coast, and mainly at night, I had been taking advantage of the period of near-total calm by reading George Davidson's *Directory for the Pacific Coast of the United States*. And as it often happens at sea, the conversation shifted to Davidson's book. He wrote it in 1858, after eight years of arduous mapping and survey work. Much of the work was done in open sailing and pulling boats. The early pilot books based on his *Directory* reveal a marvel of elegant engravings, that compared accurately with the foggy headlands we saw inshore. The early surveyors operated in what were effectively uncharted waters. The seamanship of these tough young men came from local knowledge, from fishermen and merchant skippers who knew every nook and cranny of the California coast. Until then, clipper ship captains navigated with pages torn from school atlases and by word of mouth.

It was the Morro Rock episode and John's question of the return passage that prompted me to write this book. At the time, I had just finished writing the *Cruising Guide to Southern California's Offshore Islands,* a minute, anchorage-by-anchorage description of the Santa Barbara Channel and its well-traveled waters. During our cruise in the San Francisco Bay area, many Northern California sailors had asked me about the Channel Islands. They were just as afraid of headwinds and Point Conception as us southerners. The Morro Bay experience reminded me forcibly of just how little I knew about coastal passage making strategies north of Conception. As we rounded the point, enjoying a final sun-filled spinnaker run back home, I played with the idea of writing a companion guide for passage making. When I mentioned it to friends in Santa Barbara and Los Angeles, a surprising number of them confessed how uneasy they feel about cruising outside their regular stamping grounds.

"It's fine to talk about the joys of Santa Cruz Island or the Sacramento Delta," a friend complained, "but we're apprehensive about the open water passage from Marina del Rey to the islands, or to San Francisco. What about the weather and rough seas?"

About once or twice a month, a complete stranger from Los Angeles or San Diego would call, asking questions about Point Conception and the passage north. "How do we make progress to windward?"

"What about anchoring in San Simeon Bay?"

I began to receive letters from people planning trips to our waters from the San Francisco Bay area, even as far as the Pacific Northwest. They asked the same questions: "Isn't Point Conception too dangerous for small yachts?"

Now I receive Fax or E-mail messages on the Internet, all asking if I plan to write a sequel to the Channel Islands book telling them what to expect when cruising the northern Bay area and around Point Conception. The portrait of a companion book began to take shape after I met one distinguished 35-year member of the Santa Barbara Yacht Club, who had never visited San Miguel Island, a mere 40 miles away! Stan was a superb racing sailor, with an uncanny ability to win against the stiffest competition. He had sailed to the familiar coves of Santa Cruz Island dozens of times, but never ventured into the windier waters of the western Channel. Convinced that Stan, and many others had missed something, I started collecting notes and reading Davidson more thoroughly.

The result, a year later, was *California Coastal Passages* (Capra Press, Santa Barbara, 1981). Because sailors from all over California continue to seek advice about rounding Point Conception, the tides and winds of San Francisco Bay, even about anchoring oil barges in rocky streams in northern Alberta, I decided to write the successor to the long out of print *California Coastal Passages.*

The new book, *Cruising Guide: San Francisco to Ensenada, Mexico,* is a distillation of many peoples' ideas, of classic and lesser known writings about the California coast, a mix of stories and solid navigational data. The ancient Greeks had a good word for such a book: a *Periplus,* a "sailing about." Perhaps the most famous in the scholarly world is *The Periplus of the Erythraean Sea,* sailing directions for the Indian Ocean and its coasts compiled by an anonymous Greek sea captain, who lived in Egypt in the second century AD. The *Periplus* is a mixture of a trade directory and a British Admiralty Pilot that describes the East African Coast: "Where there are anchorages, extended for six courses towards the south-west." The reader is treated to a little navigation, then more description of "small boats sewn and made from one piece of wood, which are used for fishing and catching marine tortoises." Later on, the reader learns that the inhabitants of this East African coast are "piratical" and trade in ivory and gold.

My book might well be called *The Periplus of the Western Coast,* for it is designed as a "sailing about," for cruising Central and Southern California.

The *Cruising Guide* is divided into three parts. Part I is a general account of passage-making along the California coast, of yachts, equipment, electronics, and planning strategies. We discuss, among other things, weather, anchors, GPS, swells, and history. Parts II and III are concerned with more detailed sailing directions, with the specifics of passage-making and cruising from the Golden Gate to Point Conception, and from there along the Southern California coast to Ensenada, Mexico. Each part is long on passage-making strategies, on coastal descriptions, less detailed on minor anchorages and ports, since the main purpose of this book is to help you complete safe passages along the coast. But there is enough information to enable you to enter the larger harbors and better-known anchorages, even in rough weather. Both Parts II and III draw on the rich experience of others, of sailors as diverse as George Vancouver, Richard Henry Dana, and George Davidson, to say nothing of twentieth-century seamen.

The mix of sailing directions, pilotage, and general reading is a deliberate one, born of many quiet hours off-watch, where you have nothing to read, yet need to escape that slight sense of apprehension that gnaws at even the most experienced sailor. You know the feeling, one born of uncertainty about what the next few hours will bring. Perhaps the wind will pipe up, or fog descend at dusk. You are short of water or fuel, the engine is proving erratic. That's when it's comforting to realize that others have been there before you, and had just the same feelings, and lived to write about them. Though William Buckley, the well-known conservative commentator, travels in a style and luxury under sail that few of us can afford, he writes brilliantly about cruising under sail. Of a long passage, he writes: "The ocean and the sky and the night are suddenly alive, your friends and enemies, but not any longer just workaday abstractions. It is most surely another world and a world worth knowing."

How right he is!

I have been frightened at sea many times: Once on that memorable occasion off Morro Bay in fog and a flat

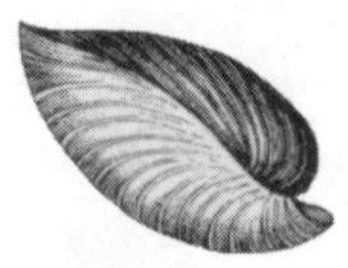

calm, and when I was caught on a lee shore at Santa Barbara Island in a 50-knot Santa Ana wind, another time when I was knocked on my beam ends off Point Conception, to mention only three instances of many over the years. I have become less afraid of admitting to my fears, and I suspect this is half the battle of a sailor's life.

Years ago, I sailed from England to France with an aged, retired Royal Navy Admiral, who was legendary for his small boat seamanship. The wind was freshening from the east as we rowed out to his mooring and his gaff-rigged 30-footer glistening in the light rain. We were silent as we clambered aboard, both preoccupied with the rough passage ahead. Hours later, the skies cleared and the new moon shone high ahead on a smooth sea in mid-Channel. As we changed watches at midnight, I asked the Admiral if he was ever afraid at sea. "Of course, my boy," he rumbled. "I'm always scared when I start out. The game wouldn't be worth it otherwise." Every time I leave harbor, I remember his words. The sea, a hard task mistress, is intolerant of human frailty, merciless with those who ignore the warnings it provides ahead of time. Those who are cavalier about safety precautions, tides, and landfalls eventually learn the hard way or pay for their carelessness with their lives. We feel frail and puny in the ocean's presence, awed by the Pacific's great swells as they pound the rocks of Point Reyes, sending spray high over the lighthouse perched by humans 265 feet above sea level. Sailors wrestle with corkscrewing seas that wrench our stomachs as they lump in on a southeasterly breeze, sit helplessly becalmed in fogs so dense that one cannot see the bow from the pilothouse, worrying about the unseen steel juggernauts which lurk in the gloom. Small wonder we feel apprehensive when setting out offshore, for unknown coasts and anchorages. Our apprehension is entirely human, and the sailor's a liar who does not have such feelings, not once, but again and again. But we can alleviate our fears by **prudent seamanship, thorough preparation,** and **adequate safety precautions:** three basic principles of safe cruising and enjoyable passage-making.

Pat Leddy

Contrary to popular belief, California cruising is not just harbor-hopping or short weekends at Drake's Bay or among the offshore islands of the Santa Barbara Channel. California has magnificent passage-making waters, rich in history and with enough navigational challenges to satisfy the most hardened offshore sailor. Her busy waters have been traversed by hundreds of yachts large and small each year. Crews on once-in-a-lifetime cruises to Mexico and the South Pacific pass through here. While many California skippers, preferring to stay closer to home, will explore the Channel Islands. The West Coast between San Francisco and Ensenada offers a remarkable constellation of cruising grounds: from the lowlying Sacramento Delta to the sheltered but windy reaches of the Bay area, or from the remote offshore islands to the urbanized, marina-oriented Southern California mainland. However, to reach any of these cruising grounds sailing one to another, you are bound to make a longer passage, either close along the coast, or far offshore. Such journeys can be as short as 30 miles, or as long as several hundred, with some distances out of sight of land. Either way, you will have to plan at least two longer passages to and from your chosen cruising ground, even if you are staying within California waters.

Whether bound to or from Mexico and the South Pacific, or just coastal cruising, the prospect of rounding Point Conception, the notorious "Cape Horn of the Pacific," or passage-making along the rugged Big Sur coast, gives many people the shivers. With good reason, for these waters can be rough, demanding, and downright dangerous. Point Conception is the big barrier, a remote headland poking far into the Pacific, a place "where the sailors say it begins to blow the first of January and blows until the last of December." Richard Henry Dana took 20 days to sail from Santa Barbara to San Francisco against the summer northwesterlies. He writes in *Two Years Before the Mast* of a gale off the Central California coast, which pummeled his ship for days from a clear sky:

> ***"All this time there was not a cloud to be seen in the sky, day or night; no, not as large as a man's hand. Every morning the sun rose cloudless from the sea, and set again at night in the sea, in a flood of light. The stars, too, came out of the blue one after another, night after night, unobscured, and twinkled as clear as on a still frosty night at home, until the day came upon them. All this time the sea was rolling in immense surges white with foam, as far as the eye could reach on either side..."***

Dana was aboard a square-rigger with a poor windward performance, staggering against 35-knot northwesterlies. With no diesel engines, certainly no electronics, and an inefficient rig, he had no option but to stick it out and beat every mile of the way in the face of relentless winds. The ship tacked inshore for the Golden Gate when halfway to Hawaii. These are the images sailors carry in their minds as they contemplate a passage around Point Conception and upwind along the Big Sur Coast. And such a passage is inevitable if you plan to visit either the San Francisco Bay area or Southern California. Small wonder many skippers hesitate, forgetting they have many advantages over their hardy predecessors. They have powerful diesel engines, efficient masthead rigs which enable them to point as close as 30 degrees to the wind, then use sophisticated electronic navigational instruments, and time-honored, efficient anchors. Not only that, but a benevolent government provides not only lighthouses, buoys, and navigational satellites, but constant and readily accessible weather forecasts. Even moderately experienced sailors can cruise in almost complete safety along our coastline provided they watch the subtle signs of changing weather.

On the face of it, there are few incentives for Southern Californians to head north against the prevailing winds. North of Point Conception, these winds blow harder, the waters are cooler, and the iron-bound coast is open to the fetch of thousands of miles of open Pacific. A passage up or down the Central California coast is a different proposition from battling 30-knot winds in the sheltered waters of San Francisco Bay or crossing the Santa Barbara Channel. But anyone sailing out under the Golden Gate Bridge is faced with a full day's open water sailing even to reach Drake's Bay to the north, or Pillar Point Harbor to the south. To the novice, a passage down to Point Conception and beyond can seem as lengthy as an ocean voyage. Just the thought of rounding Point Conception puts off even experienced sailors. Bar stories about this historic promontory abound in every yacht club between Vancouver and Ensenada. Transpac racers, who sail to Point Conception's windy vicinity to practice heavy weather sailing and sometimes return with sails in tatters, have not helped its reputation.

Even within a relatively homogeneous area like Southern California, there are important variables of weather, wind, and passage timing to be taken into consideration. Whenever cruising people gather in the north or south, they ask the perennial questions:

"What's the best time of year to sail north past Point Conception?"

"Should I stay inshore, or tack far out of sight of land, then head inshore toward the Bay?"

"When racing to Catalina Island from the Bay, should I stay inside the Channel Islands or outside?..."

"Are there land breezes at night along the Big Sur coast?"

As we explore the shoreline, we'll examine these questions and many others, using information gleaned from nineteenth-century pilot books, local knowledge acquired from casual conversations with cruising people, divers, and fishermen, and from my first hand experiences as a sailor and a scientist cruising our coast for more than a quarter century.

I once tried to sail northward against a 30-knot summer wind. We rounded Point Conception after a leisurely breakfast, beating easily into a fine 10-knot breeze. Half an hour later, the boat was pounding into a rapidly rising headwind, with two reefs in the main and the storm jib. Our stomachs rebelled. A steep, vicious sea pushed us to leeward, ever closer to land. After twenty minutes we had had enough and ran thankfully back to the welcome shelter of Cojo anchorage in the lee of Conception. Dana and his contemporaries had to keep going under these conditions, sailing far offshore under close reefed topsails. With no option but to do so, Dana's square rigger would be helpless in calm conditions.

California waters may be more congested than in Dana's day, and urban sprawl now mantles much of the coast, but conditions at sea are little changed. Like Dana, sailors are still confronted with prevailing winds which blow from N to S with monotonous regularity along the California coast in summer. Sailing vessels were often faced with a long slog to windward, even on a 20-mile passage. We can still experience those windy days when Dana and his fellow sailors spent hours aloft, reefing topsails, their ship staggering against a fierce headwind. Even so, they could rejoice in the warmth of the storm, in the dry air, pausing now and then to admire a horizon so clear the sea met the horizon in a sharp line, even at midnight. Even today, sailors can still wear shorts at sea in mid-winter and experience those days when a 35-knot breeze blows out of a clear sky of which Dana wrote:

"When you can see a cloud to windward, you feel that there is a place for the wind to come from; but here it seems to come from nowhere."

But all is not overwhelming headwinds! Days on end off California shores can be calm, when flat conditions at night and during the morning hours will enable you to power to windward in comfort. You will never have to take three days to beat from Ventura to Santa Barbara, as our nineteenth-century, engineless forebears did.

Then there's those fogs, the seemingly endless dreary early summer days like my memorable dawn off Morro Bay, when sky and horizon merge into gloom and you can see less than quarter of a mile if you're lucky, and 100 feet if you're unlucky. You conjure up visions of fast-moving tankers bearing down on you, with the watch officer asleep on the bridge, oblivious to your radar reflector. Fog: The cruising sailor's equivalent of the stealthy shark's jaws bearing down on the scuba diver. Sensible precautions will minimize the risk. Wise sailors steer clear of shipping lanes in those conditions and make their way into shallow water if possible. Rare are the days when you cannot see in front of your face. The quixotic nature of our climate, if it's really thick, visibility will lengthen to a few hundred yards in pretty short order.

I got caught in a bank of near-zero visibility fog in the middle of the Santa Barbara Channel once. There I was with a defective engine in a flat calm. I had no Loran or GPS, just a rough dead reckoning in my head. Fortunately, I was well clear of the shipping lanes. The fog soon lifted enough for me to be seen by others, but the radar reflector aloft was scant comfort.

Perhaps the greatest danger in our waters is being lulled into a false sense of security.

In summer, the morning fogs and afternoon winds come and go with monotonous regularity. You settle into a comfortable routine, one where the wine glasses appear in the cockpit as the watch changes before dinner and you forget that Neptune may have one up his sleeve for you, like the memorable occasion when I anchored at Sacate anchorage by Point Conception. It was a perfect summer's evening at high tide,with the moon high overhead. Happy to be snugged down for the night, I never bothered to check the depth or weather forecast. The next morning an early wind came in from the southeast. It was a little stronger than usual, as the ship swung inshore to

Lesley Newhart

the edge of the breaker line, I had a few anxious moments like the time off Morro Bay. The boat was rolling wildly in steep wind waves moving in toward the breaker line, less than a hundred feet away, the anchor line jerking at the bow. I shortened in the line, then broke out the anchor from the bottom with the engine on the very bottom of the tide. Before we sailed clear, I felt suitably chastened. Reanchoring for breakfast at Cojo Anchorage to the west, I resolved to be more careful in future. At sometime, inevitably, your guard goes down.

The only thing predictable about our weather is it can be unpredictable, especially when it blows off the land. When the famous Santa Anas blow into Southern California from high deserts far inland, the wise skipper stays in port. It's a fool's venture to go past Point Conception or sail off the Big Sur coast at the height of a winter gale.

One January day, 60 mph winds were reported from oil rigs off Point Arguello. Though there are none of the 28-foot tides of northern France or Nova Scotia, nor the deadhead timbers of the Northwest, nor hurricanes, ice, or pirates to plague the California coast, we do have powerful winds and big seas. But a careful skipper with a well-prepared ship has nothing to fear in passage-making off California.

Many cruising fears stem from unreliable information. A century-and-a-half ago, surveyors like George Davidson compiled charts and pilots for low powered steamers and often clumsy sailing craft which worked close inshore. Davidson and his colleagues knew what it was like to dodge kelp close inshore, to shelter behind Pfeiffer Point when it was blowing 40 knots outside, your anchor placed on a patch of sandy bottom. The sailing directions commonly refer to the availability of firewood and water supplies in remote coves, to the need for sailing vessels approach from south to approach inconspicuous San Simeon Bay with "short tacks inshore, or they will assuredly miss it." Now these priceless sailing directions of the 1850s, lie hidden away in obscure academic libraries. Modern-day official charts and sailing directions cater to larger commercial ships following well-defined shipping lanes, often further offshore. They stop only at larger ports and have no use for information on refuge anchorages along the Big Sur coast or at the Channel Islands. The small boat sailor's knowledge, akin to that facing the windjammer skipper in the 1850s must rely on charts, lighthouses, and electronics. However, with GPS'

Peter Howorth

almost fiendish accuracy and a reliable diesel engine, you can explore the most obscure anchorages with greater confidence than even ten years ago.

I wrote this *Cruising Guide* for the cruising family who wants to make passages to windward in comfort and not thrashing about in pursuit of a racing trophy. I wrote it especially for people who use calm, grey days and fog cycles to slip north past the Cape Horn of the Pacific under power, easing their way along the cloud-shrouded Big Sur coast while the north-westerly sleeps. I designed the book for northern sailors planning a trip to the Channel Islands, or to Cabo San Lucas, the Sea of Cortes, perhaps the Marquesas and far beyond. The *Cruising Guide* will get you there and back, navigating from headland to headland, with now and then a stop to enjoy a comfortable port or a spectacular anchorage along the California coast.

Lesley Newhart

CHAPTER 2

Navigators

We sail in historic waters. People have lived and worked along the California coast for at least 10,000 years in quiet anonymity, leaving nothing but the more durable of their artifacts behind them. The written history of the coast begins with Spanish explorer Juan Cabrillo in 1542, but archaeological sites and oral traditions take the story back deep into the past, to a time when much of North America was frozen under vast glaciers and Pacific sea levels were much lower than today.

This Punta de la Concepción is a high headland, very white, rugged and cut down toward the sea, and on the top of it are some black spots which are dry grass...To the N is a regular bay which I named La Purísima Conceptión...This is where we anchored and took on water with complete ease. If one succeeds in sighting this point at sunset and the wind remains calm, one can anchor in the aforesaid bay, for it is protected from the winds from the 4th quadrant.

Spanish pilot Juan Pantoja of Cojo anchorage, Point Conception, August 2/3, 1782. From Richard Whitehead, *The Voyage of the Frigate Princesa to Southern California in 1782* (Santa Barbara: Santa Barbara Mission Archive-Library, 1982, p. 64).

The Native Americans

The first native Americans entered Alaska from Siberia across the Bering Strait at least 12,000 years ago. Within 2,000 years, their descendants had settled in Central and Southern California, along a coastal homeland of uncertain rainfall and starvation ever present. Ice Age sea levels measured 100 feet lower 10,000 years ago. Low lying continental shelves extended out from modern shorelines, making the Santa Barbara and San Pedro Channels narrower than today. The San Francisco Bay area was a deep estuary. Archaeological sites which chronicle pioneer Indian activities lie underwater. Occasional artifacts resurface in fishing nets. While some, notably stone bowls, may have dropped overboard from canoes, a few finds collected by divers may well represent early human settlement at a time when California coastal groups hunted and foraged inland, visiting the coast when sea mammals and fish were plentiful.

Between about 6,000 and 1,000 B.C., when the ancient Egyptians built the Pyramids by the Nile, and Stonehenge in southern Britain was a revered Bronze Age temple, the peoples of the California coast had settled in greater numbers near the shoreline. They collected plant foods, and became increasingly expert fisherfolk. Sea levels continued to rise until about 4,000 B.C., drowning productive coastal plains which yielded rich stands of edible grasses. As the Pacific rose and coastlines stabilized, so the people turned to fishing and fall acorn harvests for their subsistence. Population density grew in local areas where both sea and land resources were plentiful, and, above all, predictable.

Central and Southern California's coastal populations, remarkable for their intensive hunting, fishing, and gathering activities, continued to increase. After 3,000 B.C., the coastal climate, essentially similar to today's, generally warm and dry, but with unpredictable rainfall, challenged survival. Every local group had to depend on its neighbors. For thousands of years, coastal and inland groups bartered with one another—exchanging dried fish for acorns, deer meat and hides for soapstone from offshore islands, sea shell beads for turquoise from the distant Southwest. By the time the Spanish arrived, well-trodden trade routes linked the Southern California coast with the Southwest, the San Francisco Bay area with the Central Valley and the high mountains. Cooperation with other groups, linked by kin ties, became the key to survival.

We know about the coastal people from hundreds of archaeological excavations from Point Reyes to San Diego, from scattered historical accounts, translations of ancient languages, and anthropological studies. California coastal archaeology carefully samples enormous, grey colored shell heaps, "shell middens," which are shellfish discards of centuries of coastal foraging. Such middens stand out from the surrounding terrain, and are easily spotted from the ocean, because of their light grey soil. Take a close look at the exposed layers of a prehistoric shell midden and you'll discern thin layers of charcoal, shell, and occasional artifacts. Such unspectacular evidence makes up the priceless scientific records the

© Geri Conser, 1994

Peter Howorth

archaeologist uses to reconstruct the history of the first seafarers and fisherfolk to live in our waters. Please do archaeology a favor and leave the shell middens undisturbed! They can easily be destroyed by eager souvenir hunters.

What we know about the native coastal American hinges upon an elaborate hunting and foraging society. About 2,000 B.C., people from the interior had settled in the rich and diverse environment of the San Francisco Bay region. They lived off the fish, shellfish, and waterfowl around and in the Bay, in the Monterey region, and along the central coast. Many settlements lay close to freshwater streams and marshlands, where the people could ocean fish and harvest nuts, hunt game, and exploit other land foods. As time went on, the first settlements in the most favored areas hived off new ones. Eventually, smaller hamlets surrounded each larger community. Each territory had their own leaders.

Santa Barbara Museum of Natural History diorama.

Reconstruction of Chumash village life: (Above left) Chumash baskets.

After A.D. 1400, coastal villages proliferated dramatically. Local leaders, who ruled, participated in ceremonies and gift exchanges, as well as warfare with their neighbors. Intervillage trade exchange used clam shell disks as informal "money" over a large area of the coast. The Santa Barbara Channel, home of the Chumash Indian thousands of years ago, represents one of North America's most elaborate hunting and foraging societies. By the time Europeans arrived in California, an estimated 15,000 Chumash lived along the mainland coast and on the Channel Islands. Well-built, dome-shaped grass and reed dwellings housed as many as 1,000 people in large communities. Each village had a sweat house, a nearby cemetery protected with a wooden stockade. The largest Chumash villages served as political "capitals" over several lesser settlements. Chumash political life, always in a state of flux, could erupt at any time, over food supplies and territory, over blood feuds, wives, and perceived insults. Intervillage warfare flourished in an exceptionally rich environment, as neighbor quarreled with neighbor over food supplies and territory.

Each autumn, the Chumash harvested acorns from local oak forests inland, hunted every kind of animal imaginable year-round. The people ate large quantities of dried fish and seaweed from November to March, ranging inland for fresh plant foods in spring. Fishing improved with warmer weather. Peaking in late summer and early fall, huge schools of tuna and other fish swarmed in open waters. Chumash fishermen rarely ventured far offshore, for, in season, they could harvest thousands of anchovy feeding on phytoplankton upwelling from the cold waters deep in the Pacific. One Spanish missionary wrote of the Chumash: "It may be said for them, the entire day is one continuous meal." But the Santa Barbara Channel was no paradise, with its highly variable rainfall. Periodic El Niños brought violent storms, caused fish to move away from the coast, and uprooted inshore kelp beds. Much of the time, Chumash lived on the edge of starvation. Their skeletons show clear signs of malnutrition and dietary stress. Occasional combat wounds inflicted by clubs and arrows during battles contradict any notion of Eden.

However, the Chumash were superb seamen. Their specialized fishing technology made life on the Pacific possible. They used plank canoes (tomols) about 25 feet long. Master canoe builders constructed each tomol from driftwood planks, painstakingly adzed and fitted together to form light, carefully ballasted canoes with distinctive "ears" at bow and stern. When loaded, the stable tomol could move with swiftness on the water, easily propelled by four men or more using double-ended wooden paddles. These remarkable sea craft were used for fishing. They were used also to trade with people on the islands, or to carry passengers along the shore. Since they leaked constantly, one of the three-person crew would bail constantly with an abalone shell. Tomols required almost daily caulking and repair.

The Chumash launched their canoes from open beaches. They would carry the tomol into the water until she was just afloat. While the captain held her bow into the waves, passengers and cargo were positioned aboard. Then the crew scrambled in, while a fourth man held the canoe. He gave her a sharp push offshore as the paddlers worked her beyond the breaker line. A skilled crew kept up a steady pace all day, paddling to a canoe song repeated over and over again.

A reconstruction by Travis Hudson and Peter Howarth of a plank canoe (tomol), used by both the Chumash and Gabrieliño groups for fishing.

Boat speed depended on the wind direction. With a following wind and swell a modern replica canoe could make 6 to 8 knots. But if the same 8-knotter blew from ahead, the tomol made no headway against wind and waves. Almost certainly, the Chumash seafarers made their island journeys and fished offshore during calm weather and during morning hours. Average passage speeds of 7 knots to and from the offshore islands were probably not uncommon in smooth conditions.

Further south, the Gabrileño occupied the Pacific coast areas now under the urban sprawl of Los Angeles and Orange County. This particular group controlled valuable soapstone deposits on Catalina Island. Soapstone is soft and ideal for making stone griddles and pots. The Gabrileño traded such vessels widely along the coast and into the interior. Even further south, the Luiseño and nomadic bands of Diegueño peoples moved seasonally between coast and interior harvesting acorns, seeds, also shellfish and marine mammals. They fished as well in estuaries and close inshore.

The Spaniards

On June 27, 1542, two poorly outfitted ships under the command of Spanish mariner Juan Rodrigues Cabrillo sailed northward along the Baja coast to explore the unknown shoreline beyond Cabo San Lucas. After three weary months of battling headwinds, Cabrillo reached landlocked San Diego Bay on September 28. He obtained firewood and water, then coasted northward in pleasant weather, anchoring on October 10 off what is now the Rincon near Carpinteria in the heart of the Santa Barbara Channel.

View of Cuyler's Harbor, San Miguel Island.

by George Davidson, 1850

A large Chumash settlement of large, circular thatched huts named Skuku lay close to shore. Now partially buried under the modern freeway, US 101, the village was densely populated. But Cabrillo's two ships were blown offshore by a strong headwind off Point Conception to Cuyler Harbor on San Miguel Island.

There he waited for favorable winds. Then scudding northward before November gale-force winds past the Big Sur Coast, he made landfall on the rocky shoreline near Fort Ross, 75 miles NW of the Golden Gate. His battered ships turned southward before a strong northwester after furious winds drove them far offshore, and entered the Gulf of the Farallones. They beat to and fro, failing to see the narrow Golden Gate entrance. Since they could not make their way into the sheltered water behind Point Reyes, now known as Drake's Bay, the exhausted ships coasted south, wintering at Cuyler Harbor, where Cabrillo died as a result of injuries suffered in an accident. Pilot Bartolomé Farrelo now took charge. Again he forced his way northward to the vicinity of Fort Ross, but at the last minute had to retreat once again in the face of the prevailing northwesterlies. He never returned.

The windswept California coast offered few attractions to gold-hungry conquistadors. It would have to be by another route before the Spaniards explored again in Cabrillo's footsteps. But the same winds could be used to an ocean-going skipper's advantage. After the discovery of a return trans-Pacific route to the New World from the Philippines in 1565, Spanish ships regularly sailed south along the California coastline after making landfall on Point Mendocino. Some galleons took refuge under the lee of Point Reyes, using a set of jealously guarded sailing directions, which fell into the hands of English privateer Francis Drake when he captured two Spanish ships off Nicaragua in April 1579. By June of that year, Drake had sailed north, hoping to intercept a treasure ship. He refitted his leaking *Golden Hinde* in the bay under Point Reyes, which bears his name, building a stone fortification to protect his crew against local Indians. He visited the Farallones and wrote:

> ***"Not far without this harborough lye certain islands...hauing on them plentifull and great store of Seales and birds, with one of which we found such prouision as might completely serue our turne for a while."***

Drake never saw the Golden Gate, but his exploits prompted the Spaniards to explore the coast more thoroughly for harbors of refuge. The galleon *San Augustin* under Sebastian Rodriguez Carmeño was ordered to survey the coast to the south of his landfall, during his return voyage from the Philippines. She made land near Point Reyes and was promptly wrecked in Drake's Bay. In one of the most extraordinary, and unsung, small boat voyages of history, many of the crew sailed south to Acapulco in two small boats, a distance of about 2,150 miles.

Serious exploration began with the explorer Sebastian Vizcaìno in 1602. Vizcaìno sailed through the Santa Barbara Channel, where he admired Chumash tomols. He wrote:

> ***"A canoe came out to us with two Indian fishermen, who had a great quantity of fish, rowing so swiftly that they seemed to fly...After they had gone***

> ***five Indians came out in another canoe, so well constructed and built that since Noah's Ark a finer and lighter vessel with timbers better made has not been seen. Four men rowed, with an old man in the center singing...and the others responding to him."***

At the time, thousands of Chumash lived on the offshore islands of the Santa Barbara Channel. Vizcaìno describes in his journal, how the Indians were

> ***well formed and of good body, although not very corpulent."***

His small squadron battled its way north past Point Sur and into Monterey Bay, where he anchored in "the harbor that is called Punta de Pinos." The port was named Puerto de Monte-Rey in honor of Don Antonio de Mendoza, Count of Monte-Rey, then Governor of New Spain. Vizcaìno reported:

> ***"There is a great extent of pine forest from which to obtain masts and yards...oaks for shipbuilding and this close to the seaside in great number."***

Vizcaìno was the first to map the Gulf of the Farallones, but he also missed the Golden Gate because of strong headwinds and the dangerous waters around the Farallones themselves. For years, Spanish ships with their poor sailing qualities kept outside these rocky islands, lest there be too little water between them and the mainland.

For many years, Vizcaìno's reports and simple maps were the only information on the coast. Sailing directions were guarded jealously, passed from navigator to navigator. Often career seamen who served on ocean-going ships, they were a small group of colorful men, who received special pay and privileges. The Spaniards kept their navigational information under lock and key, since local knowledge had vital strategic importance. By the mid-eighteenth century, the California coast was relatively well known to them, even if there were no permanent settlements or ports of refuge. The situation changed after the land-based Gaspar Portola Expedition explored the coastline between San Diego and San Francisco in late summer, 1769 and winter, 1770.

The Portola expedition was efficiently organized and set out from San Diego to assess the potential of the coast. Portola and his entourage spent several weeks in the Santa Barbara Channel, when Father Juan Crespi, a priest in the party, observed the Chumash carefully. He visited a large village known as Syuhtun, a settlement of 60 houses with a good stream and fertile soils nearby. Crespi decided this was a good spot for a mission. Seventeen years later, the Santa Barbara Mission was founded on the higher ground above a Royal Presidio erected near Syuhtun in 1782.

Portola traveled north into central California inland from the Big Sur Coast. Crespi wrote:

> ***"We encountered the Sierra Santa Lucia which is a very high range, white, rough, and very precipitous toward the sea."***

Governor Portola mapped Monterey with its lagoon and stream, which ran close to the Spanish camp. From there, he marched northward along the coast. Exhausted and running short of food, he discovered an *"estero,"*

> ***"a great arm of the sea, which extends inland at least eight leagues; its narrowest part is three leagues wide, and in its widest stretch it will not fall far short of four. In a word it is an extremely large and most famous port, which could not only contain all the navies of His Catholic Majesty, but those of all Europe as well."***

This was the *"port of San Francisco,"* with a narrow entrance that would, Portola felt, be deep enough for large ships to enter.

On a second expedition, Portola founded the Presidio and Mission of Monterey on June 3, 1770. In 1774, Captain Don Fernando de Rivera y Moncada, commander of Monterey, climbed to the summit of Point Lobos at the mouth of the Golden Gate. He and his party set up a standard of the Holy Cross on the outer, rocky summit of the headland.

A year later, the supply ship *San Carlos* under Lieutenant Juan Bautista de Ayala was ordered to take soundings in the Golden Gate. She arrived off the Gate on August 5, 1775 and sent a small launch in on the afternoon flood tide and wind. Evening set in and the boat did not return, so the *San Carlos* felt her way in the failing light. Ayala used moonlight to find safe anchorage off the south shore, somewhere near the present site of the Presidio. Next day, he moved across to a safe berth off what is now Sausalito, where he found abundant water and fuel. For forty days, he explored every corner of the great estero, a piece of sheltered water so large some navigators called it a Mediterranean Sea. A year later, Lieutenant Colonel Juan Bautista de Anza explored the Bay during an 18-day foray from Monterey, deciding on the locations for a fort, presidio and mission. The latter was dedicated on October 8, 1776.

The first visiting navigator to describe the fledgling settlement was the British explorer George Vancouver, who anchored off the Presidio on November 14, 1792. He was received warmly by the Commandant and his wife, and toured the unfinished fort, "about two hundred yards long, enclosed by a mud wall, and resembling a pound for cattle." Vancouver inspected a chapel at the south end of the open plaza, which was destroyed in the great earthquake of 1812. By the time F.W.Beechey, Royal Navy, surveyed the Bay in 1826, the Presidio was in a dilapidated condition, equipped with three rusty cannon.

The Golden Gate itself was originally named "La Boacana de la Ensenada de los Farallones" by Pedro Fages in 1772, "the large entrance from the Gulf of the Farallones." His name did not stick. In June 1846, J. Charles Fremont presented to the U.S. Senate a formal "Geographical Memoir" in which he referred to the "Golden Gate" for the first time. The narrow strait has been called Golden Gate ever since, appearing in the Coast Pilot of 1857 and on all subsequent coastal charts. Fremont took the name from the harbor entrance of Classical Byzantium which was called Chrysopylae or the Golden Horn. He said: "The form of the harbor, and its advantages for commerce...suggested to him the name the Greek founders of Byzantium used."And, on the same principle, Fremont named the San Francisco Bay entrance; The Golden Gate.

The Surveyors

California was ceded to the United States by Mexico on May 30, 1848. At the time, ships operating along the West Coast relied on rough sketch maps, many of them compiled from Spanish sailing directions, on atlases, and informal word of mouth. The Federal Superintendent of the Coast Survey

The first United States Government survey of San Francisco Bay was carried out by Commander Cadwalader Ringgold, USN, in 1850. He mapped the entrance and approaches, compiling a 45-page pamphlet and accompanying charts. This rare publication was an instant success, with skippers from many lands clamoring for more.

stepped in during the fall of that year, organizing the first survey parties from experienced mappers working on a systematic survey of the Atlantic Coast. For nine years, Commander James Alden, USN, worked up and down the coast in small ships, refining early reconnaissances, and making recommendations for lighthouse sites. His survey parties worked from small schooners under every kind of weather condition imaginable. Alden started work at the height of the Gold Rush, which made it almost impossible to retain a crew. His colleagues included a young man named George Davidson, an unsung hero to California seamen, who devoted the rest of his life to mapping and geographical work on the West Coast.

Meanwhile, George Davidson fixed the precise latitude and longitude of Point Conception in the same year. Working from small rowing boats and sailing craft, often wind-bound for days on end, Davidson and his colleagues recorded tidal data and magnetic variation, then triangulated prominent landmarks from Puget Sound to San Diego. Davidson alone traveled between 50,000 and 60,000 miles in small boats, which gave him a close up view of the smallest indentations along the coastline. He spent days on end with lead and line in hand. Davidson remarked:

> ***"When seeking for an anchorage, drifting with currents, or on boat duty, I have invariably kept it going from my own hand."***

Few people have ever acquired such a thorough knowledge of our waters. *George Davidson's Directory for the Pacific Coast of the United States* first appeared in 1858. A true labor of love as well as an official publication, it became an instant best seller in the marine world, Davidson's short work forms the basis of the *US Coast Pilots* of today.

In some respects, the *Directory* is more useful than its modern descendants, for it caters to the small boat sailor. For instance, we read that the outer edge of the kelp along the western shore of Point Loma, San Diego,

> *"marks the line where the depth of water suddenly changes from 20 to 10 fathoms."*

I checked this observation myself some years ago and found it is a useful pointer in thick fog for anyone in a small boat. Only someone working close to the water would record such a detail. Or read the directions for entering San Diego Bay itself. They are a model of clarity for a small sailing vessel:

> *"Round up gradually until Ballast Point is brought in range with the easternmost house of La Playa (distant one mile from Ballast Point and on the same side of the bay), and be careful not to open more of the village, as the shoal called Barros de Zuniga stretches south from the east side of the entrance..."*

You can imagine a sunburnt Davidson and a handful of silors slipping into the bay on a warm summer's day, with no diesel engine to speed them on their way.

Even more fascinating are some of the statistics quoted in the Dirctory's pages. We learn that 13 vessels arrived in San Francisco from Australia in 1857, with an average passage of 81 1/2 days. We learn also, that beef was plentiful in the Bay.

> *"Fine fat bullocks, weighing from 400 to 500 pounds, hide included were purchased for $5."*

At Monterey, *"Landing on the beach is generally disagreeable."*

Peter Howorth

Along the shores of the Santa Barbara Channel, ***"Crayfish of a very large size are found in great numbers"***

Many of the passage making strategies and navigational ideas presented in the Companion have been gleaned from the talented, hardworking nineteenth-century surveyors who worked under very harsh conditions and in all weathers to chart our coasts for the first time. Some of these men have been commemorated in small anchorages and by rocky headlands and hills overlooking the waters where they labored. When they packed away their theodolites and compasses, a string of powerful lighthouses marked a thoroughly mapped coastline. We use the fruits of their arduous labors to this day. So much of the lore in this volume goes back more than a century, to the days when everyone navigated the coast under oars and sail.

Lesley Newhart

CHAPTER 3

Weather Essentials

Don't worry too much about predicting the weather; people have been at it for years with little success. Rather, be ready for all kinds of weather—the sure prediction is that they're all coming your way sooner or later—and be prepared to keep her going through their endless variety.

Roger Taylor
The Elements of Seamanship.

Any sailing directions for the California coast begin with the weather, for the vagaries of the coastal climate govern all our passage-making. Richard Henry Dana hated the passage up the California coast, the inexorable northwesterlies, which blew day after day without respite during summer months, the interminable slatting around in oily calms during quiet night watches. Even in our modern diesel power yachts and sleek cruising boats capable of pointing as close as 30 degrees to the wind, we dread passage making to windward along our shores. Sailing downwind on the wings of the prevailing winds can be a nerve-racking experience, keeping in touch with the fog-crowded coast to port, tacking inshore and offshore to avoid a dead run, the inevitable corkscrew motion from seas on the quarter, and unexpected jibes. Yet, with careful planning, you can miss these traumatic experiences, taking advantage of the predictable and not-so-predictable weather cycles of the California coast.

The key to successful passage planning in California is understanding the weather, the many factors that cause 35-knot headwinds to blow in your face or days of flat calm to bedevil your long-planned fast passage south from the Bay to the Channel Islands.

Sources of Weather Information

Compared with sailors in many parts of the world, we live in an information-rich environment, which brings us weather data at every turn. Television, radio, telephone tapes, newspapers, even Weatherfax for those with deeper pockets: There's a wealth of warnings and recommendations at your finger tips, quite apart from the lore of weatherbeaten fishermen, experienced cruising people, and competitive sailors with years of winning under their belt. They smile wisely, look sagely at the distant horizon with wizened faces, as they contemplate the vital signs—a veil cloud, a pearly line of haze, a line of foam in the breakers. They utter mellifluous predictions, which are seeming magic, frequently all too correct, and sometimes completely different from official forecasts. I always feel intimidated by such people and their euphemistically named "local knowledge." I shouldn't be. They are merely using their powers of observation, honed by years on the water, and, in the case of fishermen, making their living in conditions when pleasure sailors would not venture out of harbor. Such knowledge is easy to acquire by making daily observations of the weather, even when not afloat, by learning the basics of weather map reading (not covered here), and by knowing the fundamental forces which shape local and coastal weather.

Rough seas in Windy Lane.

Peter Howorth

Our predecessors, and many mariners around the world, still make passages on the basis of their long-term experience with the weather, their knowledge of winds, clouds, and swells. Our industrial society has such sophisticated communication systems that we almost swim in weather information. The secret is not so much acquiring information as using it effectively.

Weather forecasting is still an art as well as a science, for all the awesome predictive power of modern computers, the seeing eyes of satellites high in space, and virtually instantaneous weather observations from all corners of the Pacific. Most experts agree forecasts are correct about 75% of the time. So there is some consensus on the point. Over the years, I have listened to, and copied down, thousands of marine weather forecasts, as have other cruising sailors. Forecasting marine weather is far harder than that on land, for observation points are far and few between. The situation is improving as far as California is concerned with the placement of permanent weather buoys along the coast. Each observation station is, of course, a reflection of existing local conditions. The best forecasts depend, of course, on information drawn from many more sources, such as weather satellites high in space and data on jet streams.

National Weather Service marine forecasts predict weather conditions on the high seas and in coastal waters about 24 to 36 hours in advance. Though slowly changing conditions may reflect up to 72 hours of future weather, when listening to such forecasts, bear in mind they are somewhat generalized. Because they must be short and to the point for transmission, they cannot reflect your precise local conditions. For instance, you can be certain that a 20-knot northwesterly off the coast will be stronger as the wind funnels through the Golden Gate. And local conditions of Point Conception can bring much stronger gusts and considerably higher seas than those in the marine forecast.

Always assume marine forecasts are for open waters, away from distorting land features.

Using weather forecasts is the art of monitoring trends, using both the conditions you are experiencing, say, ten miles off Morro Bay, and broadcast information. For example, I was once anchored in Cuyler Harbor on San Miguel Island at the western end of the Santa Barbara Channel. The noon forecast spoke of an approaching, fast-moving front, which would bring strong SE winds to the offshore islands by mid-afternoon. The skies were clear, a light westerly blowing, with no signs of clouds streaming across the sky, signs of an impending frontal passage. Cuyler Harbor is dangerous in a southeaster, so we made a fast downwind passage to the north shore of Santa Cruz Island and anchored in Fry's Harbor, a fine all-weather anchorage, just as a wild, cloudy sunset and backing winds gave further warning of the approaching storm. By monitoring changing weather signs, local conditions, and future trends, we had made sensible, strategic decisions. We spent a comfortable night despite the wind howling high ahead as torrential rain pelted the decks.
Marine weather forecasts come in three categories:

High seas forecasts cover areas more than 250 nautical miles from shore, while offshore forecasts cover waters between 250 and 60 miles out.
Coastal forecasts cover a strip from 60 miles offshore to the coast.
Inland forecasts cover San Francisco Bay, the Sacramento Delta, and other sheltered waters.

What kinds of information can you expect from a broadcast forecast? On the largest scale, high seas forecasts always give the positions of high and low pressure centers. Coastal forecasts focus mainly on wind speeds and sea state. Occasionally information on approaching fronts and expected rainfall forecasts a trend. Track it for several days before your planned passage. This way you have a picture of the next 24 hours. These longer term trends will affect your passage planning more than anything else.

One final point: The most important element in any forecast is how to use the information. For example, a 50-foot diesel trawler with an experienced skipper can easily handle a summer windward passage along the Big Sur coast against 30 knots of northwesterly and accompanying swell. A forecast of 20- to 25-knot winds in Windy Lane (the notorious patch of rougher water off the north coast of Santa Cruz Island in the Santa Barbara Channel) would give cause for thought to even an experienced owner of a 25-foot inboard-outboard fishing boat. The forecast will give you an educated guess at local conditions. Only you can decide whether the intended passage will be hazardous to your boat and your crew. As the skipper, your limitations are based on, firstly, your experience, secondly, the design and capabilities of your vessel, and, lastly, prevailing wind and sea conditions.

Warnings

We cruise along a coast where powerful gales and very strong winds have been known to batter our relatively benign shores. The National Weather Service issues wind and storm warnings under three categories:

Small Craft Advisories. Winds of 21 to 33 knots, either with or without 10-foot or greater swells. SCAs are commonplace occurrences throughout California waters, especially in the San Francisco Bay area and off Point Conception, and in the offshore island waters of Southern California.

Gale Warnings. Winds of 34 to 47 knots and severe sea conditions. Avoid passage making in these conditions if you possibly

can. If caught out, keep well clear of the coast, heaving-to if necessary.

Storm Warnings. Winds of 48 knots and greater. Sailors take up golf. If caught out, you are probably going to have to heave-to under bare poles or run before the storm. Fortunately, such conditions are rare south of the Bay area, although Santa Ana winds and other local phenomena can achieve storm force velocities.

NOAA Broadcasts.
VHF-FM broadcasts are available 24 hours a day, 365 days a year and are updated every six hours, at 0200, 0800, 1400, and 2000 Pacific Standard Time, sometimes more often. They can be picked up on almost any battery-operated FM receiver and on most, if not all, VHF marine radios.

The frequencies are:
Weather 1 (WX1): 162.55 MHz
Weather 2 (WX2): 162.40 MHz
Weather 3 (WX3): 162.475 MHz
Weather 4 (WX4): 161.650 MHz

Television and Radio Broadcasts.
Television and commercial radio forecasts reach, for the most part, people living on land. Television weather maps can give you a general impression of highs, lows, and weather fronts. Keep them in mind when you listen to NOAA broadcasts. Most commercial radio stations use canned forecasts, like the classic "Point Conception to the Mexican border, winds light to variable night and morning hours, westerly 10 to 15 knots in the afternoons." Some radio stations do make a point of broadcasting marine forecasts, especially on the weekends, but NOAA makes them superfluous.

Newspapers.
Many newspapers publish satellite maps, synoptic charts, and weather forecasts broken down into many local areas. The Los

Angeles Times and San Francisco Examiner both do an excellent job. You can use several days' papers to track changing weather patterns. Inevitably, newspaper weather is a little outdated, but is useful as general background.

Telephone.
You can call National Weather Service offices for information, a service which is invaluable if you are planning a long passage up or down the coast between Southern California and the Bay area. I have found both the Redwood City and Santa Maria NWS offices extremely helpful:

> Redwood City Forecast Office **415-364-7974**
> (24 hours/day)
> Santa Maria **805-925-0246**
> (0600 to 1500 weekdays only)

Weatherfax is invaluable for obtaining forecasts and synoptic charts, but few pleasure craft except larger vessels and some ocean racers carry such expensive equipment. I wish I could afford it!

No official forecast, or even local knowledge, is a substitute for your own experienced eye and careful observation of local weather conditions. Become an expert on clouds and troughs of low pressure, on ridges and pressure gradients. Your assessment of weather will gradually become sounder through experience. Confidence in passage-making strategy comes with this practice.

The best way to make your educated assessments is to be to be familiar with long-term weather patterns, listen to experienced local mariners, who have an enormous reservoir of anecdotes from years at sea, and compile your own data by direct observations. Many years ago, I anchored in a sheltered cove on the northern coast of Santa Cruz Island. Only one other boat was in the anchorage, a battered fishing boat. With the warm weather, perfect visibility, and wind absolutely calm, we enjoyed a glass of wine before dinner. A gentle popple set into the anchorage, making us rock slightly. A few minutes later, the fishing boat got under way. We rejoiced at having the cove to ourselves for the night. As the fishermen passed close by, the skipper yelled at us. "Best get out now! The Santa Ana's coming in. It's already blowing on the mainland." Over the protestations of my hungry crew, I followed his lead. We ate dinner in open water, then beat and motored our way to the mainland. Back in port, we learned a fierce Santa Ana had come in soon after dark, turning all the anchorages along the north coast into vicious lee shores. Some days later, I met the fisherman by chance and thanked him for his timely warning.

"How did you know the Santa Ana was coming," I asked.

"Simple," he said. "They had wind warnings on the radio for campers and trailers on Interstate 5 and then the waves came in from the northeast."

Though official weather forecasts had talked about "strong winds below canyons and passes," we hadn't listened to the radio, talked to experts, and paid attention to subtle weather signals. If it hadn't been for the old battered fishing boat and her skipper, we would have been in big trouble.

General Factors Affecting California Coastal Weather

The California coast boasts of being one of the few Mediterranean climates in the world with plenty of sunshine, near-perfect temperatures, and markedly seasonal rainfall. We share this distinction with parts of the Mediterranean, the Cape of Good Hope in South Africa, portions of Chile, southern Australia, and New Zealand. Our wonderful sailing waters experience weather shaped by global weather factors, and local phenomena.[1]

The Pacific High

The Pacific High usually sits about 400 to 600 miles off the California coast, a huge dome of air which exercises a profound influence on sailing conditions in- and off-shore. The movements of this vast high pressure zone vary from season to season. When the High is in its usual position, low pressure systems are deflected from the California coast. When it is weak, or displaced further south or west, high pressure weakens along the shore and lows approach, and pass over, coastal California.

High pressure varies seasonally. In December and January, the Pacific High is at its weakest, located about 30 deg. N and 137 deg. W. Storms now move into the Pacific Northwest, their fronts sweeping through California, bringing rain to the parched coast. By March, the High begins to strengthen, to shift northward along the coast. High pressure blocks storms, as the landmasses of Mexico and the extreme southwestern United States warm up. Onshore winds increase, as cool, moist air moves inland to replace hot, rising air from inland valleys.

Between June and September, the Pacific High sits offshore, blocking storms from our cruising ground. Strong winds blow clockwise around the high, bringing strong northwesterlies to the coast. Weather expert Kenneth Lilly has likened the summer high to "a giant balloon," whose shape and orientation causes the wind and weather to vary through the summer months. For example, when the Pacific High moves further offshore and extends a ridge of high pressure into the regions north of San Francisco, the high temperatures found east of the coastal mountains flow over the coast, bringing 100-degree temperatures and unaccustomed heat waves.

Come October, the Pacific High weakens gradually and weather patterns become more irregular. The first storms edge into California, ushering in the wet season and the winter months. The fall is a transitional season, where much depends on the intensity of the Pacific High. In drought years, for example, the High can stay far north, blocking storm after storm far to the north, to the point that several years can pass with well below average rainfall.

Keeping track of the vagaries of the Pacific High is vital when planning long passages along our coast.

Air Masses

Both continental and maritime air masses pass through our cruising grounds and exercise a profound effect on our weather.

Maritime air masses originate far out in the Pacific. Most of those reaching the California coast come from cool, moist air, more northerly latitudes offshore, which accounts for our generally cool and equable coastal climate. Warm maritime air masses reach southern California regularly from the tropics or subtropics during the summer, occasionally affecting areas as far north as San Francisco Bay and northern California. Winds tend to be light, the air extremely muggy and humid, and large swells from distant tropical disturbances can pound south-facing beaches.

Continental air masses are usually dry, for they originate over the interior of North and Central America. The hot desert areas of the Great Basin, Southwest, and Mexico bring intense heat to the coast during late summer and fall, while cold and dry air in winter comes from Canada and subarctic regions. When higher pressure is N and NE of the Bay, continental air enters Central California. An enormous dome of chill, arctic air forms in the lower atmosphere in the north. Then N to NE winds bring the cold through gaps in the Rocky Mountains, causing temperatures to plummet in California ports.

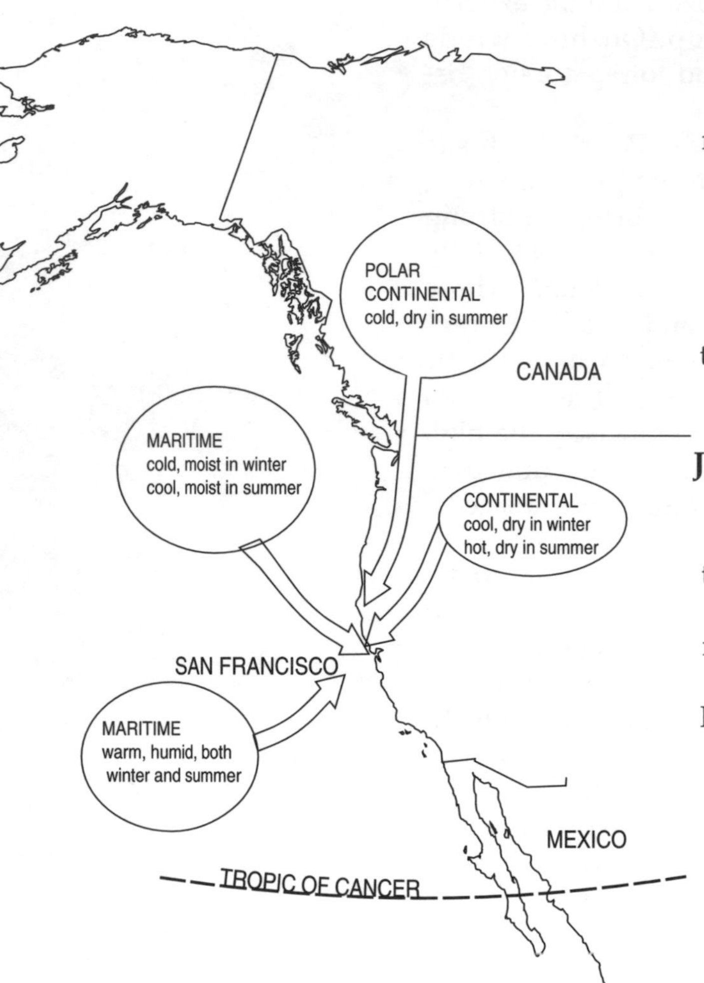

Air masses affecting the California coast. (After Kenneth Lilly, 1985)

Jet Streams

Jet streams are like rivers, but high in the atmosphere. They separate cool and warm air masses, are several hundred miles wide, and lie at altitudes between 18,000 and 40,000 feet. The Northern Hemisphere jet stream flows in a generally west to east direction, speeding up and slowing down, changing direction as days and weeks pass. Not that the direction is constant, for it contorts into ridges and troughs, configurations that bring about major changes in coastal weather. High pressures tend to develop under the influence of high altitude ridges, while lows form on the surface in areas where troughs form. The jet stream is strongest during the winter months, from September through early June. During these months, the movements and configurations of the jet stream determine the development of storm systems approaching the California coast.

Really intense low pressure systems, with readings below 960 millibars, are unknown along our coast. Low pressure systems tend to mature off the Oregon and Washington coasts, having originated far away in the tropics. They move northeastward up the coast, the fronts ahead and south of them sweeping through California. The volatile mixing of tropical and polar air when subtropical and polar jet streams meet results in strong winds and rain. The high swells associated with these storms radiate outward from the center of the low and can batter coastlines hundreds of miles away.

Low pressure systems and their associated fronts approach the California coast from SW to NW. The weather they bring depends a great deal on the course and strength of the jet stream. The stronger the jet stream and the closer it is to the coast, the worse the storm.

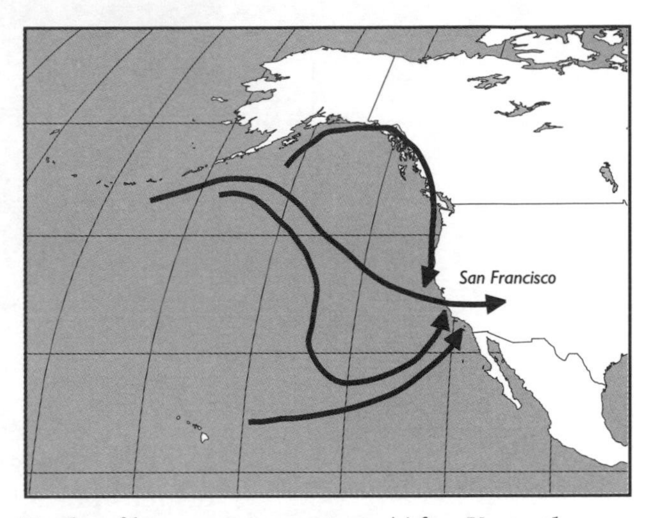

Tracks of low pressure systems (After Kenneth Lilly, 1925)

Ocean Temperatures

We cruise in waters that are hardly tropical. No one in California experiences the Bahamas' 87-degree water temperatures, for even Southern California waters warm up no further than the mid- to lower-70s. Our old friend the Pacific High causes complex changes in water temperatures near the coast. By late summer, the persistent high offshore and the regular northwesterly winds along the coast cause warm surface water to move offshore. Much colder water from the depths of the Pacific rises to the surface. Such massive, but irregular, upwelling, especially off steep coasts and south of major headlands like Point Conception, enriches the fertility of the marine environment. Upwelling constantly replenishes the surface layers of the ocean with nutrients. In turn, these nutrients foster plant growth and cause unicellular algae - phytoplankton - to flourish. A submerged peninsula running SE from Point Conception, of which Santa Rosa and San Nicolas Islands form a part, intensifies the upwelling process near the Santa Barbara Channel. Before the days of modern commercial fishing, billions of spawning sardines fed on the nutrients and zooplankton lying near the surface close offshore. The sardines moved inshore in summer, where pelicans and larger fish fed on them, as did native Americans. This regular food supply encouraged many prehistoric coastal groups to live in permanent settlements.

Water temperatures play a major role in coastal weather. For example, San Francisco Bay waters warm up

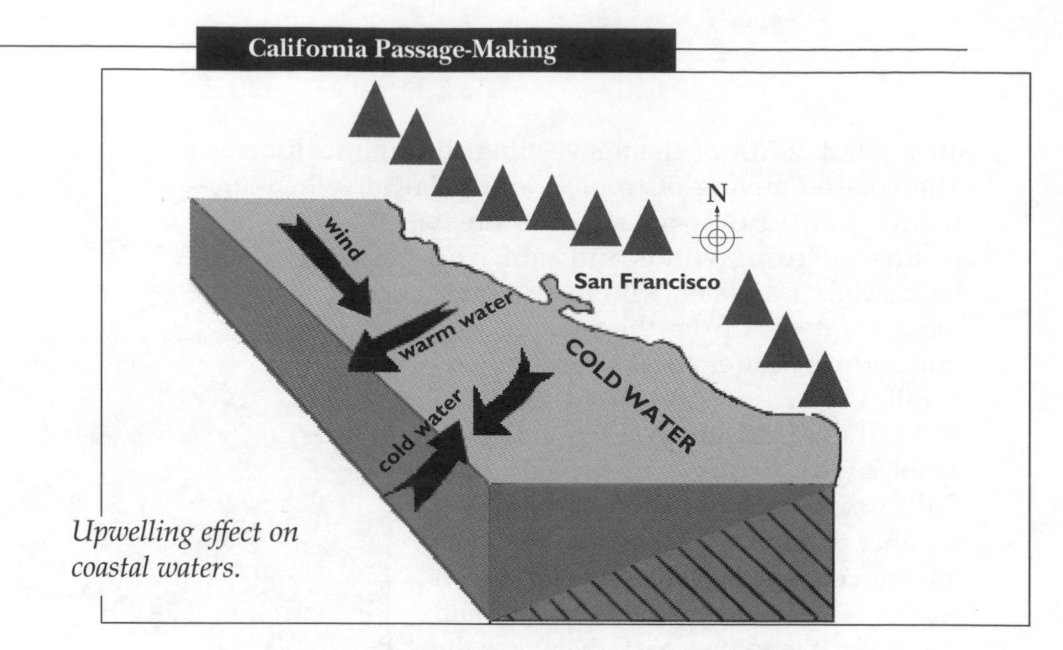

Upwelling effect on coastal waters.

to over 65 degrees in the height of summer, while 54 degrees prevails in the coastal waters outside the Golden Gate. The constant summer northwesterlies, which pass over this water, become cooled from below. As cooler air sinks slowly from aloft in the high pressure, it is warmed by compression, causing a temperature inversion. If the air is moist enough, dense sea fogs develop, which blow through the Golden Gate on the afternoon sea breeze.

One of the great thrills of California sailing is to run at high speed through the Gate, spinnaker drawing in the strong afternoon wind, with the red bridge high above mantled in fog. The last time I entered the Gate, the gray lay a few hundred feet above the ocean, masking the summit of Point Bonita, the bridge uprights, and the white buildings high on the southern cliffs. Fog horns sounding on the wind, we sailed under the Golden Gate Bridge, picking up the afternoon traffic high overhead, the flooding tide rushing beneath our keel. Suddenly, the fog parted like a curtain, revealing the entire Bay skyline and San Francisco in a blue panorama ahead. The massive high rises of San Francisco rose from a cascade of densely packed streets and houses, white, futuristic cruise ships moored along the harbor piers at the city's feet. The Presidio, Fort Mason, the Saint Francis Yacht Club: All the familiar landmarks swept into view as we shaped a course for Oakland and Alameda deep into the Bay. Off in the distance we could hear the sea lions barking at Pier 39. Our passage from Santa Cruz Harbor had been a fight against strong headwinds all the way. But I will never forget our dramatic entrance into a world of brilliant blue, chasing whitecaps, seemingly a universe away from the gray world outside. Now and then, grey stratus clouds blew further inland to Alcatraz Island. The warmer water caused the surface gloom to lift and form a high fog. The temperature inversion aloft, kept the trapped fog from dispersing completely into the warmer atmosphere.

Fogs

A rugged coast, backed by steep coastal ranges that plunge almost directly into the Pacific, plays a vital role in our weather. Because the mountains limit the routes by which marine air can pass inland, this coastal topography determines the routes taken for entering the Bay area. The only sea level defile is the narrow Golden Gate. Adding to the precipitous nature of the narrow passage are the inevitable fogs, the thickest lying in the Gate itself as far inland as Alcatraz. Keeping summer temperatures low, the fog hangs around, sometimes for weeks at a time.

Patrick Short

Monterey Bay, famous for its prolonged summer fogs, sucks the gray inland as far as the Salinas Valley and mantles Carmel in a foggy gloom. Further south, along the Big Sur Coast all the way down to Point Piedras Blancas, where the Santa Lucia Mountains rise steeply from the ocean, the fog tends to stay on the seaward side. Between Piedras Blancas and Point Conception, where most of the coastline is lowlying, the fog spreads inland to San Luis Obispo, and more persistently, to Santa Maria, which also tends to stay foggy in summer.

Pat Leddy

Persistent fog exists in summer southward of Point Conception, along the shores of the Santa Barbara Channel and Channel Islands. It covers the low lying coastal plain of the Los Angeles Basin. The Santa Ynez Mountains act as a barricade, keeping the fog close to the coast in the Santa Barbara-Ventura area, while the southern shores of the Channel Islands can be sunnier than the northern coasts. Summer temperature differences between coast and interior can be as much as 30 to 35 degree. The marine air flowing inland heats rapidly as it passes through gaps in the coastal mountains: The Berkeley Hills or Avila Bay rarely bringing cooler temperatures inland.

Marine Layers

Peter Howorth

The *"marine layer"* contrasts sharply with the warmer air which lies at higher altitudes over the coast. The transition zone between the marine layer and the warmer air above it is known as the "inversion layer." The intensity of this inversion layer depends on temperature differences between the cold and warm air. The inversion serves as a lid which suppresses vertical air movement. Cooler air tends to stay inside the layer, because it is too dense to rise into warmer zones. The dense fog and low stratus clouds so familiar to California sailors tend to form under *"marine layer"* conditions.

The fog is intensified when the marine layer and temperature traps water vapor between the ocean surface and the base of the inversion, especially when the warmer air is less than 1300 feet above water.

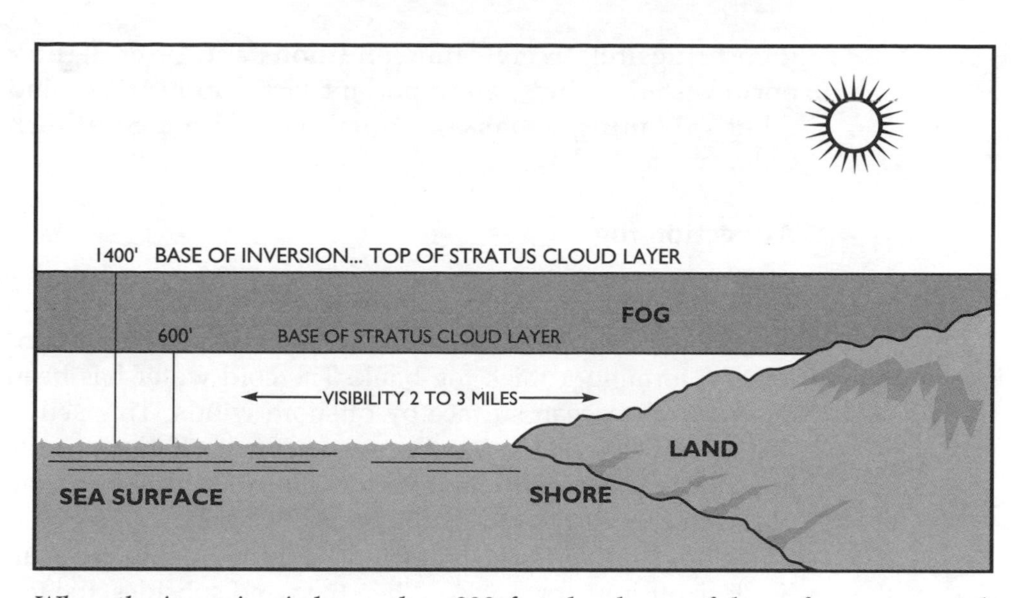

When the inversion is lower than 800 feet the chance of dense fog over coastal waters increases.

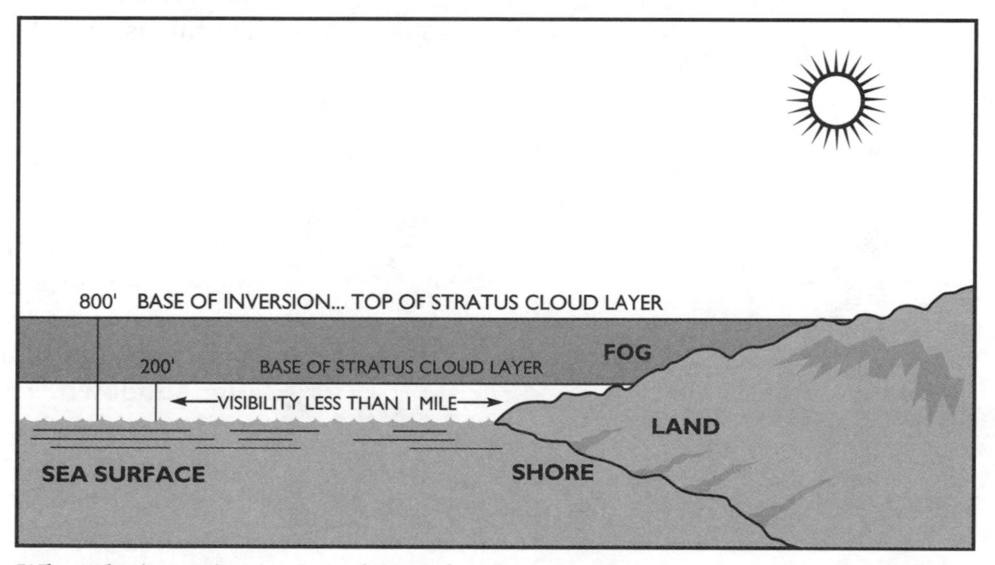

When the inversion is around 1400 feet, low clouds rather than fog form over coastal waters.

Meteorological expert Kenneth Lilly quotes studies by Dale Leipper of the Naval Postgraduate School in Monterey, which find that coastal fogs often form in ten-day cycles. The inversion layer gradually descends, reaching its lowest point on the fourth and fifth days, giving prolonged periods of visibility of less than a half-mile. Then the inversion layer gradually lifts, eventually rising above 1300 feet, when the fog disperses. Leipper's researches intrigue me. He corroborates what I have sometimes watched, how the fog thickens then gradually disperses over ten days or so in Southern California. The fog then brings relatively calm conditions and often lighter northwesterly winds, an important factor to bear in mind when planning a passage northward from Southern California to the Bay area.

Advection fog

Advection fog develops when warm, moist sea air blows inshore and strikes cold water near the coast. The air condenses, forming a thick fog bank. The cold water has been drawn to the ocean surface by offshore winds. This action disperses the warmer water seaward. Such offshore winds are frequent between Gaviota and Point Arguello, at the northern boundary of the Santa Barbara Channel, where cold upwelling and warm Pacific winds form fog banks that can lie close offshore for weeks. When the wind subsides, the fog drifts inshore over the coast. Sea fog like this is prevalent between May and July.

Brian Fagan

Radiation fog

Radiation fog, sometimes called "ground fog," forms as the land radiates heat after sundown. The warm air rises, drawing in colder air just above the ground. The air cools, condenses, and rapidly forms a fog bank that usually burns off by midmorning. Radiation fogs are most common between September and January.

Coastal fog and low clouds tend to be thickest during the night and morning hours. As the air near the land surface warms up during the day, lower air layers reach a temperature similar to the air above the inversion and the fog dissipates into hazy afternoon sunshine. Since both land and sea fogs vanish when a strong wind gets up, an alert skipper can sometimes find stronger wind on the edge of a fog bank.

Pressure Gradients and Santa Ana Winds

We coastal sailors usually enjoy moderate temperatures, despite great temperature variations between coast and interior. Temperatures only climb to extreme levels when the Pacific High moves over to cover part of Oregon and northern California. Then pressure builds inland, causing northeasterly winds to blow over the California coast, sweeping extremely hot interior air out over the Pacific. The glassy calm conditions can leave you panting for air in an open cockpit or stuffy deckhouse. When a heat wave hits San Francisco and Monterey, edging temperatures into the 90s or even higher, a sailor can get caught becalmed for hours. Once on a downwind passage from the Bay area in September, I was expecting a wonderful, boisterous spinnaker run. Instead, I found myself motoring in a flat calm. We sailed for a total of 4 hours the entire way, and the wind never rose above 8 knots. Air temperatures were in the 80s.

In fall and winter, a build-up of high pressure in Utah and Nevada often follows the passage of a front inland through northern California. The pressure difference between coast and interior can be as much as 2.5 millibars, bringing strong northeasterly winds to southern California. As the winds move into the region, they sweep over the coastal mountains via the passes, being heated at a rate of about 5.5 degrees F/thousand feet by compression. These are the notorious Santa Ana winds, which can gust for hours at speeds in excess of 40 to 60 knots, turning anchorages on exposed coasts like the northern shores of Catalina and Santa Cruz Islands into death traps. Santa Anas are most common between September and January, although similar conditions can develop at any time of year when high pressure in the interior bring dry NE winds and high temperatures to the coast.

Santa Ana conditions usually last from four to six days. As the high weakens inland, the marine layer reforms. Coastal cloud and fog return to the coast. If the descending winds are warmer than the marine air, as is usually the case, then the "warm" Santa Anas will stay confined to passes and to areas below coastal canyons. "Cold" Santa Anas are far more intense and dangerous. Under these conditions, the descending, heated air is cooler than the air overlying the coastal plain. A cold Santa Ana pushes inshore marine air out to sea and sweeps over the coastal plain with tremendous velocity, often causing property damage, leaving small craft battered and strewn ashore.

Major segments of Southern California affected by Santa Anas are shown in the accompanying illustration: The Palmdale, Point Mugu, Anacapa, eastern Santa Cruz Island areas, and the eastern shores of Catalina and Santa Barbara Island are affected, areas that should be avoided during Santa Ana conditions. Ironically, some of the most beautiful of California days are among the potentially most dangerous.

Santa Anas, and other offshore winds, are hard to forecast, except in most general terms. Because they often occur following frontal passages along the sea coast, vigorous Santa Anas and down-canyon winds are often associated with strong northerly jet streams. Unlike low pressures and many passing fronts, Santa Anas and their equivalents give little advance warning, especially at the Chan-nel Islands. The wise mariner avoids passage making when pressure is high inland. The weather will be hot, dry, and crystal clear, with signs of impending downslope winds in the form of slight wave movement from NE.

In Southern California, stay in port when radio broadcasts warn of restrictions on trucks and high-sided vehicles on Interstate 5! Santa Ana conditions are blowing or are imminent. If berthed in an exposed anchorage, be

Santa Ana at Avalon Harbor — Gene's Photo and Rock Store, Avalon

prepared to leave at very short notice. You may find yourself anchored on a lee shore in gale force winds, as dozens of yachts did at Santa Cruz Island over Thanksgiving, 1977. Many boats were driven ashore to become total losses.

You can experience highly localized downslope winds in many places at any time of year, especially off prominent headlands like Point Reyes or Point Conception. I have been knocked on my beam ends by a sudden squall off the latter headland in late summer. Luckily, we were well reefed down against such a contingency, but that did not prevent dinner from flying off the stove into the navigator's berth! A pound of tomato-flavored spaghetti sauce gave the galley a startling decor.

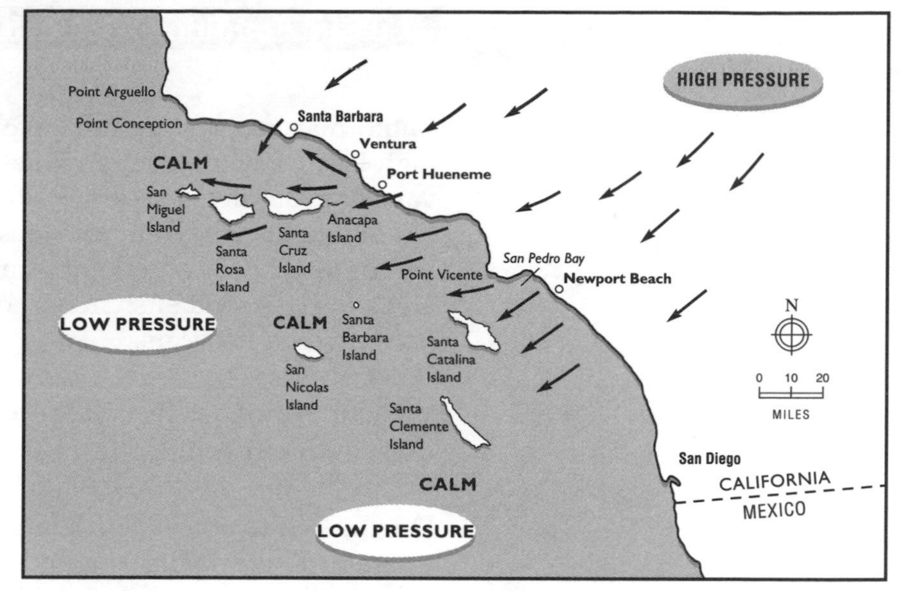

Wind patterns in severe Santa Ana conditions in Southern California.

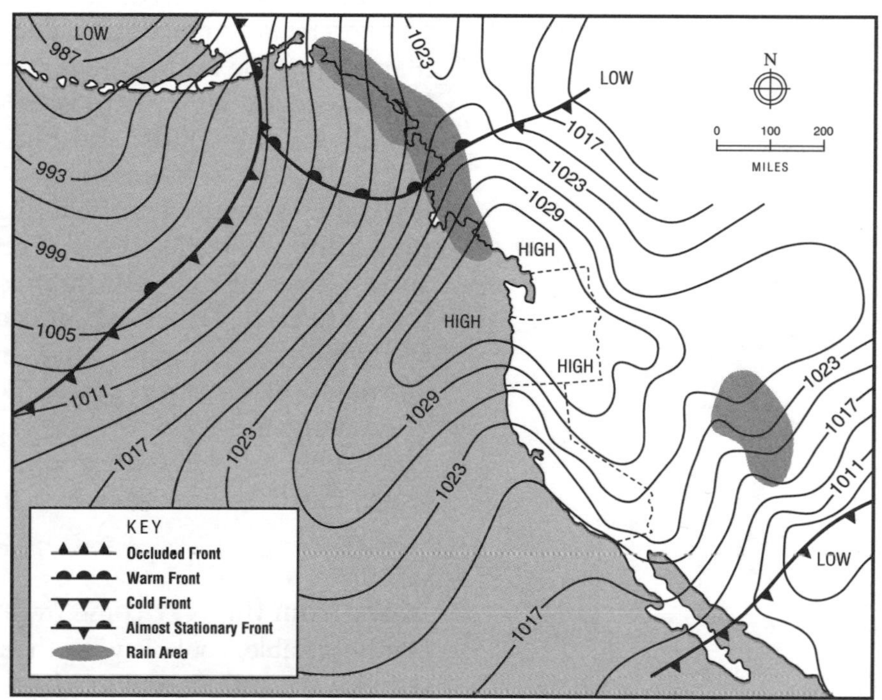

Santa Ana conditions over the California coast. November 19, 1956.

Coastal Conditions through the Year

California's cruising grounds have hundreds of different, high local climates, where rainfall and wind velocity may vary dramatically in areas but 10 miles apart in the course of a single day. The composite description which follows is based on years of observations at meteorological stations along the coast and offshore. In some places the records go back as far as 114 years.

Winter Months: Southeasters and Northwesters (November through March)

During winter the Pacific High tends to weaken and migrates to the south. Fog and low clouds are still common during periods of dry, stable weather. Weakening and southern movements of the anticyclone allow large Pacific storms to approach the coast. Many more such low pressure systems pass through northern and central California than they do through the south. Such storms are usually carefully tracked by the National Weather Service long before they reach the coast.

The air circulates around the low center in such a manner that the leading edges, or "fronts," caused by mixing warm and cold air masses create the turbulence of clouds, shifting winds, and rain to develop southeasters. These "fronts" seldom strike without warning and are tracked by satellites far offshore. As the storm approaches, prevailing westerlies die out and dark cumulus clouds gather. The water close inshore is usually turbid, but now begins to clear. The clouds appear to settle, squalls occur, followed by steady rain. After several hours, the SE wind decreases. As the storm passes, skies begin to clear and the wind shifts to NW or W, depending on your location. If you intend a passage during a period of stormy weather, watch the direction from which the lows arrive.

Lows from the NW come from the Gulf of Alaska. They bring unstable, cool air with them. The SE winds associated with the system will gradually veer round to W as the rain and gusty winds pass through. As the skies clear, the winds can blow up to 50 knots. Avoid passage-making under these conditions.

Above all, do not be tempted to ride the SE condition northbound unless a safe port is close at hand. You will encounter gale force headwinds within a few hours.

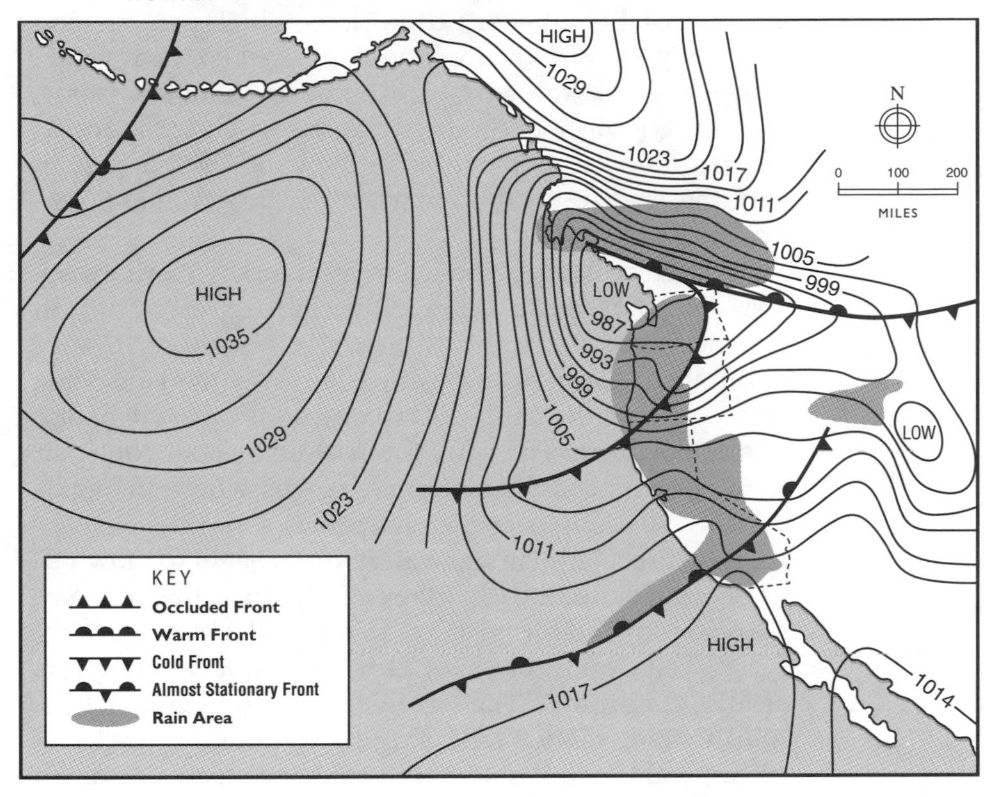

Frontal system passing over the California coast. December 29, 1956.

If you must sail, radio ahead for a weather check at your destination first.

Lows from the W are often associated with a broad area of low pressure extending over the latitudes of the east Pacific.: Such conditions can bring a whole string of rain-filled storm systems to northern California. The entire state enjoys a relatively prolonged period of wet and stormy weather. Your chances of having some longer periods of SE wind are somewhat improved under these circumstances, but do not be tempted to take on a lengthy passage.

Lows from the SW often bring the heaviest rainfall. Massive cloud banks precede the storm, the winds shift to SE, and then to WNW as the bad weather clears relatively slowly compared with NW lows. Temperatures remain more constant. You may have more warning both of approaching SE conditions and of post-frontal winds with SW lows.

The greatest danger with low pressure systems lies in the unstable, blustery conditions which can develop after they have moved on. Violent squalls, heavy rain showers, even waterspouts are not uncommon. I have been caught offshore on days like these, when the winds are so strong the kelp dances in the wind. Best to stay in port and enjoy a good book when the post-frontal northwesters howl.

Southeasters become less common by April. Gusty NW gales now pose a dangerous hazard, especially in Northern and Central California. An onshore flow of moist air displaces rising warmer air over the land Then night falls and the land cools to nearly the same temperature as the ocean. The wind drops close inshore. Moist air condenses on coastal mountain ranges where the air is coldest, especially near the low passes. Once the air temperature is cooler than the water, winds begin to blow offshore, usually until early morning. By noon the next day, the onshore wind fills in again, to repeat the same cycle.

Veil clouds, or cloud caps, are valuable indicators of NW conditions. They are easily recognized: white, solid-looking clouds that cling to mountain passes and ridges, and to the W end of the offshore islands. At dawn or dusk, veil clouds may resemble an enormous wave breaking over the mountains. As the wind picks up and the land warms, the huge cloud breaks up into spinning "cotton balls," sometimes called "puff clouds." The clouds usually disappear by late morning and reappear after sundown. Here are some pointers on northwesters and veil clouds:

- **The extent of the clouds is determined by the amount of wind that formed them in the first place.**

- **The more clouds present in the early morning, the stronger the wind will be.**

- **If other clouds are present as well, the northwester will last only a few hours.**

Veiled clouds over Santa Ynez mountains. Peter Howorth

If the other clouds disappear and the veil clouds remain, plan on a three to five-day gale. These longer blows are commonest in the spring months.

Severe Northwesters often strike the northern coastline before the south.

Listen to weather reports from Point Pinos and Piedras Blancas on the Big Sur coast. Point Arguello and San Nicolas Island reporting stations in Central and Southern California also lie in the direct path of the strongest northwesterlies, and provide a valuable check on cloud indicators.

Summer Weather (April to October)

The Pacific High dominates the weather map off the California coast during the summer months. This creates a common condition where a long-lived high pressure system lies off the coast, while low pressure sits in the interior. These conditions create a pressure differential that maintains an air flow in from the Pacific over the coast. As this air passes over the cool waters of the coast, a relatively cool "marine layer," is formed. The pressure gradient between the high and low zones dominates weather patterns over the coast and creates a prevailing NW air stream parallel to most of the California coast. This wind blows almost parallel to the coast until it reaches Point Arguello, where the shoreline turns east. A wind of between 25 and 35 knots now fans out both offshore toward San Nicolas Island and inshore along the east-west mainland coast.

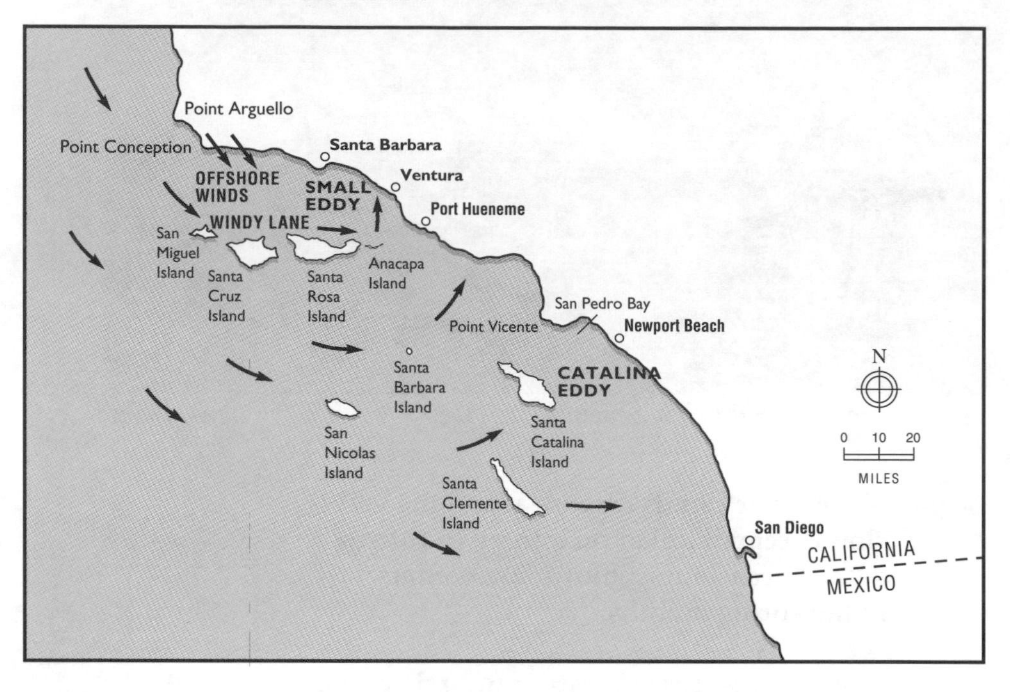

Catalina Eddy conditions in Southern California.

Pat Leddy

When the wind blows from NW at 15 knots or more along the outer Channel Islands, it slows as it fans towards shore, sometimes changing direction. The NW wind backs to W past San Nicolas Island, then SW as it approaches Catalina Island. The eddy forms when the breeze approaches the shore, loses strength, then comes out of the S and SE. By this time it has reversed its original direction, forming a characteristic eddy. This "Catalina Eddy" is often accompanied by fog and low clouds at the coast. If San Nicolas reports clear skies and NW winds over 15 knots, the Eddy is probably in effect.

During summer months, the North Pacific High strengthens and migrates northward, with its eastern edge off the coast of Oregon and California. Cold water that flows southward along the coast maintains cooler temperatures and assists in chilling the overlying air and causing the inversion, bringing stable weather conditions along the coast. Low pressure systems passing across the Pacific are diverted N far away from California.

May, June, and July are usually the foggiest months from Ventura northwards. Thick, grey overcast days can persist for days, even weeks. Such conditions reduce visibility at sea but are often the best weather for making passages to windward. In other words, a yacht wanting to cruise to San Francisco may have excellent conditions for the passage between May and July.

If a thermally induced low pressure center is created in southwestern Arizona, then the sea breeze tends to strengthen along the coast during the afternoons, increasing the strength of the prevailing NW winds. This can cause strong headwinds N of Point Conception, and less favorable passage conditions.

California summer weather tends to be foggy from May through mid-July, with muggy, hot conditions prevailing from mid-July to the middle of September. Hot, dry days are more common from then until October, or even January, the season when dry, hot NE winds can blow. Such conditions often occur in fall and winter when a front has moved inland through Northern California and is followed by a high pressure build up over the Pacific Northwest and the Great Basin.

Strong, onshore NW winds can sometimes bring cool sea air into land basins near the coast. When the NW breeze drops, the trapped air heated by the land sweeps out of the basins down the coastal canyons. Such winds are sometimes called "Sundowners," since they are most common at dusk.

Occasionally, maritime tropical air invades Baja and Southern California during the summer, bringing hot, humid weather and thunderstorms to the coast. The winds are light and sailing tends to be unpleasant. Extremely rare tropical storms have been recorded in Southern California, in which case you should be snug in port. Even distant Mexican storms can generate 6 to 8-foot swells that radiate from storm centers hundreds of miles away. These can arrive in S-facing anchorages without warning in sets of half a dozen or more swells that could throw you up on the beach. Your best guard against these "sneakers" is to monitor the VHF weather channels that track the course of tropical storms off Baja. Heavy, sudsy foam close inshore can be a sign of heavy surge, and you should watch S-facing beaches carefully for this condition when tropical storms are reported, usually between June and early October.

Weather Signs

Our description of coastal weather is necessarily impressionistic, for there is no substitute for first-hand observation. Intelligent tracking of changing weather is a skill you can develop on land, even out of an office window! You will soon develop your own tell-tale signs of different weather conditions on land and at sea. Here are some passage-making pointers which I have found useful over the years. Perhaps they will provide a foundation for your own arsenal of weather signs:

- You will probably encounter settled, and predictable, weather conditions when fog and low clouds persist nights and mornings. To make sure, keep a check on the position of the North Pacific High on your local newspaper or TV station weather map. Dewy conditions are often a sign of settled weather and last about ten days.

- Good visibility, hard grey profiles of distant land formations, and constantly changing, grey cloud banks may indicate an approaching frontal system. Postpone your departure until conditions settle down.

- Clear skies, brilliantly crystal visibility, and billowing white clouds streaming from mountain tops and island summits offshore are probable signs of strong winds. Veil clouds are reliable indicators of strong NW winds.

- Clear, cool weather with snow on the mountains can mean cold, unstable conditions offshore.

- Cumulo-nimbus clouds over the mountains or turbulent clouds in the same area: Summer showers and squalls from SW are likely.

- Hot, dry, and very clear conditions, with dry decks and flat calm are clear signs of an offshore wind condition. So are layers of smog blown offshore from the Bay cities or Los Angeles. Downslope winds blowing offshore are likely, sometimes blowing with great violence, especially below canyons and mountain passes.

For weeks on end, our weather patterns are settled and predictable, making California a sailors' paradise. You soon learn to use the changing rhythms of our coastal climate to your advantage, just as the Chumash and the conquistadors did centuries ago.

Endnote

1. In writing this chapter, I have relied heavily on Kenneth Lilly's admirable *Marine Weather Handbook: Northern and Central California*. Paradise Cay Yacht Sales, Sausalito, 1985.

Photos by Patrick Short.

Chapter 4

Boats, Boats

Recently, I attended a Catalina Owners' Rendezvous at the Isthmus on Catalina Island. More than 200 owners attended with their yachts, ranging in size from 22 to 50 feet, all suitable craft for California coastal cruising. Though the Rendezvous was an informal seminar on the subject of messing about in boats, there were a couple of days when opinions thickened the air. Sail or power; I have been around boats most of my life. My opinions on suitable cruising vessels are admittedly full of unashamed biases, acquired with sweat and blood. I have spent hours at sea in bad weather and in good, anchored in remote anchorages, berthed in crowded ports, at anchor in remote anchorages, testing the qualities and disadvantages of various boats. As Kenneth Grahame's Rat says to the Mole, "whether in or out of em, it doesn't matter, that's the charm of it." There's something fascinating about boats, the feel of them under sail or power, or simply paddling along in a quiet river, just being busy or sitting contentedly at anchor, or varnishing brightwork; for plain contentment, a day spent afloat pays off in dividends that have nothing to do with budgets, mortgages, and disposable income.

> *There is nothing - absolutely nothing - half so much worth doing as simply messing about in boats...or with boats...*
>
> Kenneth Grahame
> *The Wind in the Willows*

For better or worse, we live in a world of mass-produced yachts popped out of fiberglass molds by the dozen. A crowded southern California anchorage on Labor Day often resembles a serried row of white-hulled Clorox bottles, in which the only thing to distinguish one family boat from another will be the name painted on the hull. Mass-produced fiberglass yachts, while strongly built and designed with sedulous care, have opened up California waters to thousands of people who have never ventured to sea before, making our coastal area one of the greatest concentrations of pleasure craft in the world. The very existence of the popular, mass-produced 30-foot cruising yacht has led to a revolution in marina facilities, in harbor construction, and in navigational aids. Crowding along the California coast has ironically made it safer. Because there are so many boat owners, they have become a significant political voice in Sacramento and Washington. Every boat owner should join BOAT/US. A powerful lobby in Washington, BOAT/US fights retrogressive legislation such as confiscatory luxury taxes on boats and federal boat use taxes.

At the Catalina Rendezvous, seminars and presentations by experts covered such esoterica as marine electronics, diesel maintenance, and knot tying. Catalina designers and management mingled freely with the owners, exchanging ideas, listening to gripes, showing people the latest designs. Much of Catalina's success as a leading yacht manufacturer comes from the constant interaction with owners. Interaction had led to design improvements, even to industry-wide adoption of ideas like the transom swim ladder and the deck anchor locker. Even so, there are still those yacht owners who crave individuality, who want something out of the ordinary, either built by themselves or constructed with loving care by one of the handful of small boatbuilding concerns which flourish, against all odds, in the world of the 1990s. I wager even a short island cruise in southern California will yield a few sightings of truly exotic megayachts, or of lovely schooners like Errol Flynn's Sirocco, still sailing a half-century after her original owner's death. For those of us who enjoy "messing about

© Geri Conser, 1994

in boats," there will always be a choice: of classic yachts to restore and love, old tug boats to convert into sinfully comfortable motor yachts, wooden ChrisCraft to remind us of the carefree, pre-fiberglass 1950s. There's no denying it, Kenneth Grahame is right. Messing about in boats is far more than owning one. It's looking at, and enjoying, other people's.

Yachts for Coastal Cruising

The Chumash Indians could have taught us a thing or two about seamanship, for they knew even the most subtle of weather signs. They also had a strong sense of the limitations of their watercraft, something we sometimes forget. You can see all manner of weird craft wending their way to Catalina Island on a summer's weekend, everything from wind surfers to small racing shells. Summer conditions are so predictable that even the zaniest vessels arrive safely. That is not to say that their skippers are good seamen, for to cross the San Pedro Channel in such fragile boats without an escort is inviting disaster, perhaps even from a passing ship's wake.

The first lesson in choosing a boat for serious cruising in our waters is to know your sailing limitations, and to have some idea of what you intend to do with your boat. If your ambitions are regular day sailing and occasional weekends at Catalina, that's one thing. If you plan to sail from the San Francisco Bay area to San Diego on a regular basis, that's quite another. Whatever the weather and your cruising ground, for any serious California cruising, you need a well-found yacht with adequate waterline length, covered decks, and strong rigging.

Let's look at some of the options.

Brian Fagan

The size of your boat depends on the depth of your purse, your experience, and long term cruising plans, as well as available crew.

Trailer Yachts

I like trailer yachts, especially the new breed that are unashamedly designed for trailing. Without resembling a compressed, box-like version of a larger cruising boat, these latest designs are a dream to rig. The Santana 2023, for example, is designed to be launched and sailed away, fully rigged, in a mere seven minutes. This, and other designs by manufacturers like Catalina and Hunter, now feature water ballast, which simply drains away, leaving you with a manageable weight for the family car. Their performance can be positively lively, although they tend to be skittish in a lumpy sea.

You can trail a yacht as long as 27-foot overall, with an all-up weight of about 9,000 pounds. Boats like the well-known Nor'Sea 27 are proper little cruising yachts, with comfortable accommodations for four, inboard diesel engines, full galley facilities and a head. The Nor'Sea 27 has crossed oceans. Dozens of owners regularly trail them to the Pacific Northwest, to Cabo San Lucas, and much further afield. You can take a trailer yacht like this anywhere.

Other trailer yachts are designed for young families with modest budgets or people whose main interest is camping, gunkholing, and day-sailing. The Santana 2023 is unashamedly aimed at people who decide on impulse to go sailing for the day or the weekend. They can be packed and off to the launching slip within minutes, the notion being that nothing, but nothing should interfere with sailing away as soon as possible. Such yachts have rudimentary accommodations and a sketchy galley, although many boast of a head compartment. Basically a camping yacht, the 2023 is somewhat rudimentary for island cruising, or fast-running tides in the Golden Gate. Where they come into their own is for beach cruising, where you sail from sandy bay to sandy bay, nosing onto the sand to camp at day's end. Similar day cruising for camping purposes can be found on Lake Powell or the Delta, but not along the Pacific Coast, where ground swells and wind waves make landing a jostling, difficult experience even on calm days.

Trailer yachts like the Santana are fine for Bay sailing and for summer conditions in Southern California, but I do not recommend them for long passage-makers, except in very experienced hands—and those hands would probably prefer something larger.

Choices of Coasting Yachts

Make no mistake, the California coast is deep water country. Twin-bilge keels, leeboards, and centerboards are popular in the Chesapeake, Florida Bay, and in the northeast, but shallow draft confers little advantage along our shores, unless you are exploring the Delta or the upper waters of some estuary. Aficionados argue that shallow draft boats allow you to anchor where deeper draft yachts fear to secure. In most California harbors you cannot anchor. Few mainland or island anchorages have extensive patches of tidal flat or shallow water where you'll find yourself anchoring in a few feet: Deep draft sailing yachts rule on our Pacific waters.

Theoretically, you should be able to sail any standard 25-foot or larger, deep keel production yacht anywhere between San Francisco and Ensenada. However, many well-known designs manufactured in California or

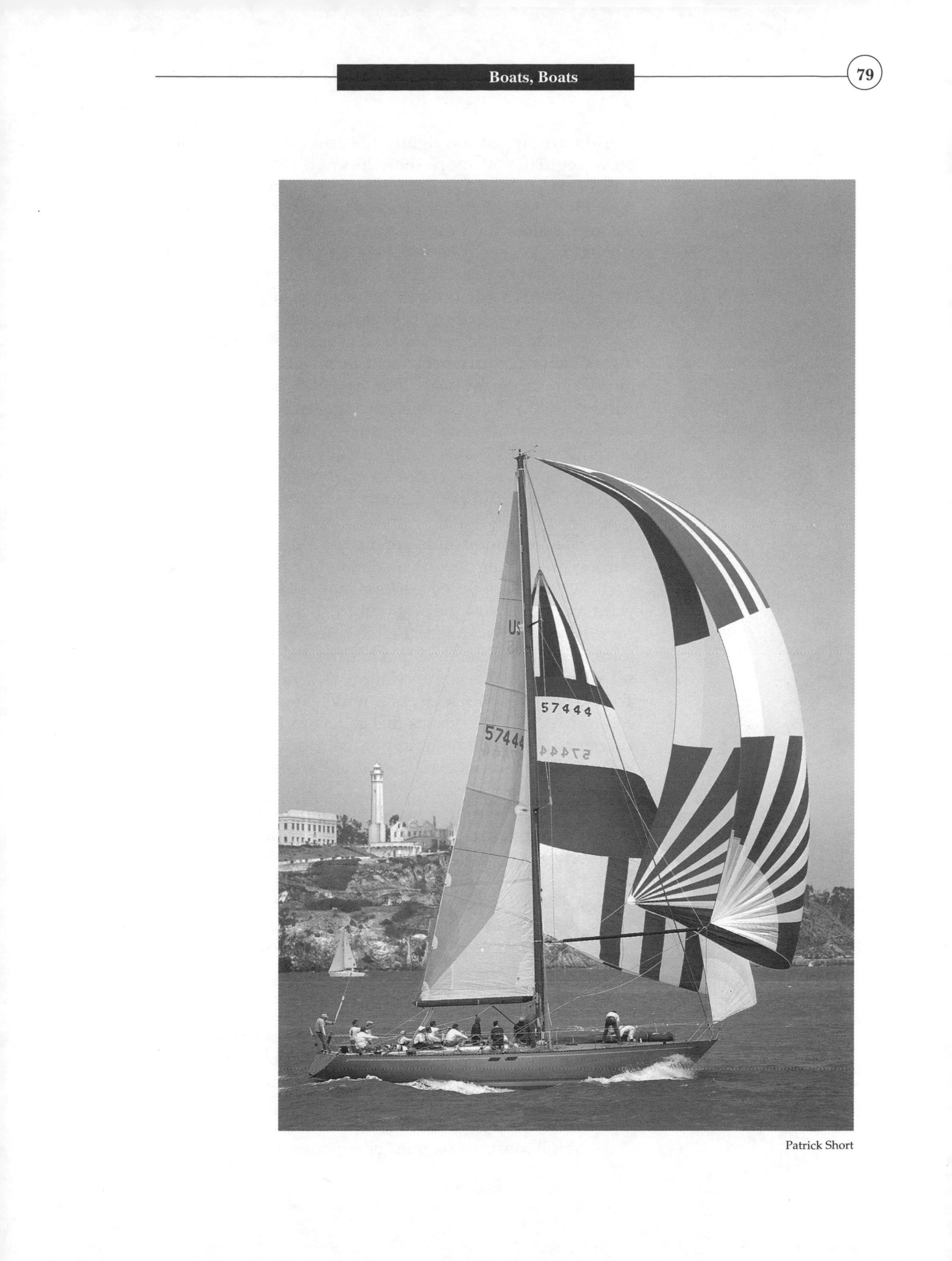

Patrick Short

Florida are rigged too lightly for areas where the winds blow regularly at more than 25 knots. Many Southern California yachts have extra high rigs to compensate for their local, prevailing light conditions, while San Francisco Bay area sailors add heavy-duty stays, and sometimes even stronger mast sections for their windy summer sailing weather. Serious coastal cruising, you will be caught one day and have to ride out gale-force winds and seas in open water. Ship out with the strongest rig possible.

Many people react to an offshore passage by choosing as heavy displacement yacht as possible. "Traditional" heavy displacement boats look gorgeous but they sail to windward like the proverbial cow against even small, steep wind waves. They end up motor sailing for long dreary hours while their lighter brethren enjoy a smooth and rapid passage upwind. The enjoyable part of any offshore passage is to have fun getting to one's destination as fast as possible.

California offshore conditions include a high proportion of light air days. A moderate to light displacement yacht with good light air performance, and superior windward abilities makes the best cruising boat for our offshore conditions. A decade ago, the offshore sailor wanting performance was condemned to a narrow, uncomfortable vessel with minimal accommodation that sailed on her ear. Today, you can choose from a wide range of supremely comfortable offshore yachts that sail as well as their racing ancestors. Besides, a night in port gained by a fast passage is far preferable to an extra period of darkness, usually in a flat calm, in the open sea.

When choosing a vessel for offshore passage-making in California, you should select one with the following features:

- Adequate waterline and overall length to handle ocean swells and wind waves up to 10 feet or more, and winds of up to 60 knots in an emergency.

- Moderate to light displacement with fin, or modified fin keel hull design, with superior windward performance and good tracking ability downwind. Beware of some well-known racing designs that have a reputation for squirrelly performance when running. Hull construction must be superior quality.

- A rig of adequate strength to survive full gale conditions at sea and repeated knockdowns in severe conditions. I have a strong bias towards a single mast rig, on the grounds that it is far simpler to operate when shorthanded. Most California production boats have masthead sloop rigs. Ideal for offshore work where frequent sail changes may be needed, is a cutter configuration. Useful, too, is a roller furling jib. But you should be able to set a separately rigged storm jib if need be.

- A diesel engine of sufficient power to move the yacht to windward against a bumpy swell at 5 to 6 knots.

- Sufficient number of comfortable berths for each member of the crew to have a bunk to themselves. For serious open water passages these bunks must be fitted with canvas or wooden leeboards. A passage berth is quite different from what may be an ideal bunk in port. You must be able to jam yourself into it with comfort when going to windward in a rough sea. Many production yachts that claim to sleep six in fact offer about two passage berths, if that. Double berths are wonderful in port, but impractical at sea, especially when the yacht heels over.

- Gimbelled cooking facilities that can be used even under the severe conditions.

- Adequate navigation space, including a strong chart table.

- The minimum number of highest quality through-hull fittings.

- Interiors must be designed for passage-making rather than marina living. Include a permanently secured chart table, adequate handholds below, and superior ventilation.

- Decks must be protected with fore and aft pulpits and overstrength double lifelines.

- Navigation lights must conform to Coast Guard and international rules of the road.

According to the depth of your pocket book and if pressed for an ideal sailing yacht for California waters, I would opt for a semi-fin keel design, in the 30 to 40-foot range, equipped with a diesel capable of running her against prevailing swells at about 6 knots. My ideal rig would be a cutter, which gives you a smaller foretriangle. Provided I have adequate winches, I could live comfortably with a masthead sloop configuration.

Power Boat Choices

I am not a powerboat man. My hours of conversation with experienced power boat owners, I must confess, have reinforced my envy of my friends, when I hear how they forge easily to windward in the comfort of a cozy pilot house against a headwind, while I am wedged into my cockpit at a 15 degree angle, or perhaps more. Some years ago I had the opportunity to motor up the Sir Francis Drake Channel in a superb, 46-foot air-conditioned power cruiser against a 25-knot headwind, sipping beer and enjoying the sight of a veritable fleet of bareboats beating their brains out against the boisterous Virgin Islands trades. Even better, we snagged a prime anchoring spot off the Bitter End, and I could rent a Laser for two hours of wild planing, while the fleet of bareboats were still battling the same wind. Safe, economical motor yachts can be a supremely comfortable way of cruising our coast.

The basic designs for many of today's seagoing motor yachts were developed after World War II in Northern California and the Pacific Northwest. Experienced sailors of such vessels will argue that a seaworthy power yacht is the only way to go in California.

Outboard runabouts or the sleek sport yachts shown on the covers of the glossier powerboat magazines won't do for the passage-making experiences this book talks about. In every passage-making experience, the skipper has a great deal to do with the boat's capability. The most popular power yachts seen on the West Coast are the so-called trawler designs, which come in every shape and size from 30 foot to 60 foot and more. Calling pleasure craft "trawlers" is a misleading, loosely classified rubric that has little to do with the seagoing fishing boats from which they allegedly are descended. Early trawler yachts did, indeed, originate in commercial fishing boat designs, as did the well-known Fisher motor sailors. Inspired by North Sea fishing boat lines, they are popular in European waters. A distinctive type of their own, the Fisher was designed to carry their crews from A to B at moderate speed with reliability and comfort.

Few trawler yachts make really long ocean passages, which are commonplace for sailing yachts. Equipped at great expense for the job, trawlers have the range and seaworthiness to make long coastal passages of several hundred miles. However, they do not necessarily have the 2400-mile range for a 60-day cruise and storage space for supplies needed for a crossing to, say, the Marquesas. The so-called light trawler type like the well known Grand Banks designs have ranges of 900 to 1500 miles, more than adequate for California purposes.

20-knot headwinds are a fact of life on the West Coast. Vessels in the 28-foot to 32-foot waterline length range should be able to maintain normal cruising speeds of between 6 and 10 knots in headwinds up to 15 knots when they will have to slow down. Even if stabilizers are fitted, motion and behavior in rough seas are an important factor in small power yacht cruising. Yachts in the 36-foot to 42-foot waterline length range should be able to maintain normal cruising speed in at least 20 knots of headwind. A larger yacht of this kind is ideal for serious coastal cruising under power in California. However, you must consider other factors such as docking fees, higher insurance premiums, maintenance, and running costs. But the 36- to 42-footer can be handled easily by two people and is capable of sustained passages in considerable comfort. The longer yacht allows you plenty of living and entertainment space. Its length also permits the pilothouse, galley, and living areas to be concentrated amidships or a trifle aft, where the motion is felt least. As a general rule, the longer the waterline length, the greater speed and comfort.

For years, California skippers have been content with trawler yachts which cruise under 10 knots. Now people have talked to sport fishermen and sailors and realize the advantages of quick passages and so they want speed. In response to such expectations, Grand Banks recently introduced a line of high speed cruising yachts that can cruise at normal speeds over 15 knots. Other manufacturers are already following suit. Boat speed has become an important factor not only in the sport fishing, but in the cruising marketplace.

Brian Fagan

To summarize, here are some desirable characteristics of a power yacht for serious coastal cruising:

- Sufficient waterline, if possible in the 36 to 42-foot range, to allow one to sustain cruising speed in the face of moderate to heavy winds and seas on the bow.

- A range of up to 1,000 miles at cruising speed, to allow sustained passages not only in California, but in Mexican waters.

- A displacement/length ratio from about 160 to 220, a design which uses considerable power to sustain speed with reasonable fuel economy, while not compromising too much on range.

- An enclosed pilothouse, with living accommodations, galley, and navigation area amidships or slightly aft, with a flying bridge and adequate sun shading.

- Stabilizers (if appropriate), or some method of reducing rolling at sea such as flopper stoppers.

- A bowsprit for handling anchors and a stern platform.

- Adequate guard rails and bow and stern pulpits or stout bulwarks.

- Some means of protecting large window areas in extremely rough weather (sustained open water cruises only).

- Some means of hoisting a dinghy on deck, and adequate stowage for the tender out of harm's way. Options include a derrick and chocks, davits over the stern, or even canting the boat up on the diving platform, not an option I prefer.

Golden Gate entrance to San Francisco Bay, from NW. © Geri Conser, 1994

- Adequate lighting and other safety features similar to those for sailing craft.

For economy, I would recommend diesel power, although properly vented and installed gasoline engines are cheaper to purchase. You will have to run a lot of hours to recover the price differential. If you can afford it, buy a yacht with twin engines, for ease of maneuvering at close quarters, and for insurance at sea. But modern diesels are so reliable that a single engine makes very good sense, especially in yachts up to 40 feet.

A trawler yacht for many people, especially more elderly couples, makes eminent good sense. I've always wanted to make a long passage in a trawler, but the chance has never come along. It's a pity that so many of them sit idle in their marina slips when they could be making really challenging voyages. All too often, they are used for short weekend cruises.

Whatever yacht you choose for our waters, think long and hard before making the plunge. Charter a boat like the one you crave for a weekend cruise. You will learn more from such a trip than any number of test sails. Above all, think ahead and be utterly realistic about the kind of cruising you have in mind. Does it make sense, for example, to incur the enormous expense of buying a 42-foot trawler or 40-foot cutter if all you plan to do is to sail to Catalina Island occasionally or just explore San Francisco Bay? Have you plans to voyage further afield in a few years? Do you want to make a series of passages up and down the coast to and from the Channel Islands or to Mexico? Think in a time frame of at least five years and tailor your purchase plans accordingly. Finally, keep it simple and avoid festooning your boat with unnecessary gadgets and electronic gear. I don't know about you, but expensive navigational devices have a habit of smiling and dying when I come along. Maybe it's my face, but, almost invariably, I would have been better off without. More about gear and electronics in the next chapter.

Patrick Short.

CHAPTER 5

Equipment

Let's turn from boats to gear and equipment. What are the essentials for a cruise in California waters? I must confess to an inherited bias born of sailing in engineless yachts in my youth, which means the fewer electronics and associated gadgets the better. But even modest-sized yachts ship out with such goodies as radar these days, which is fine if you can afford the initial cost, the maintenance, and know how to use the equipment. This chapter is addressed to skippers who are concerned with concerned with what is essential for responsible seamanship, basics rather than luxuries.

> ***Think out all the possibilities of the proposed passage, not only what one proposes to do under favorable conditions but also what one would do in the event of bad weather, fog, or rain sufficiently heavy to prevent one seeing buoys or marks.***
>
> Claud Worth
> *Yacht Navigation and Voyaging*
> (1929)

A Reliable Diesel Engine

This section is addressed to sailors!

Why a diesel engine? Because of the long hours of flat calm weather: A reality in our cruising grounds. Few of us can spare the two or three days of precious vacation time to work our way to windward from, say, Ventura to Point Conception, or from Morro Bay to Big Sur under sail alone. We sail in congested waters, far more crowded than those of even a generation ago. Coastal shipping passes up and down our coast along well-defined routes, sometimes through legally established traffic separation zones such as operate in the Golden Gate and Santa Barbara Channel, and in the San Pedro Channel. In the days of ever more sophisticated radar, these ships steam at cruising speed even in dense fog, and often cannot pick up small yachts in wave clutter. Engineless and becalmed in the middle of a shipping lane in a summer fog is suicidal. It's like stalling in a Honda Civic when being tailgated by a semi at 65 mph. You haven't a hope. Engine trouble in the middle of a busy shipping lane, with tankers bearing down on you from two different directions isn't exactly fun either. Pleasure cruising in our waters without a reliable engine underfoot, even if you are a purist in its use, is downright dumb!

Commercial shipping apart, the sheer congestion of popular yacht harbors like Berkeley, Santa Cruz, or Marina del Rey makes an engine

Brian Fagan

imperative, if nothing else as insurance against ignorant skippers who insist they have the right-of-way at the height of the Sunday afternoon rush hour back into port in high summer. I have actually been driven aground in harbor by aggressive boats oblivious to speed limits or the rules of the road. The mind boggles at the thought of sailing into port under such maniac conditions, when everyone is returning to port at the same time.

Lighter displacement yachts can achieve miracles to windward under virtually zero wind conditions, and can tack on a dime in harbor. Nevertheless, they should carry some form of auxiliary power, if only an outboard motor, both for emergencies and for use in shipping lanes when becalmed, especially in crowded harbor entrances. It is downright irresponsible even for a small yacht to tack back and fro across a crowded fairway. Sailing without an auxiliary engine is a safety hazard, simply because too many people are on the water for anyone in a boat larger than a day sailor or dinghy to have the luxury of sailing back into port.

Boats longer than about 25 foot overall should have an inboard engine for passage making and harbor hopping. Such installations are more expensive, but they are a sound investment for any crew interested in completing open-water passages within a reasonable time. You may enjoy flopping around at 3 knots under outboard engine at 0200, but I would rather have the inboard and be bedded down and asleep at anchor!

The diesel versus gasoline debate seems to have been settled in favor of lightweight diesels in recent years, but there is no reason why a well ventilated and properly installed gasoline engine will not satisfy your needs. Many older yachts still use gasoline Atomic 4s, to the extent they have become a minor cult.

Sails

Again, this section is addressed to sailors!

In these days of jiffy reefing and sophisticated roller furling genoas, sail inventories tend to be much smaller than a few years ago. Assuming you have a roller system, here's a minimal inventory for enjoyable, safe coastal cruising:

- **Mainsail,** with two rows of reef points and jiffy reefing, also preferably a rod vang for good sail control. I swear by fully battened mainsails with lazy jacks for both control and ease of reefing while under way.

- **Roller furling 150% genoa,** with ultra-violet protective strip on the exposed edge when rolled up. You need adjustable tracks for moving the sheet cars when the jib is partially rolled up. A bearing out spar/spinnaker pole is essential. Some people prefer hanks and a wire forestay so they can change jibs without a roller furler, but modern systems are so reliable they are ideal for coastal cruising.

- **A heavy weather jib.** Such a sail is essential for peace of mind, especially north of Point Conception, during strong northwesters, and in San Francisco Bay's summer wind. Consider investing in a heavily constructed, flat cut 80% to 90% jib with a short hoist and a sail area between 115 and 215 sq. feet, depending on boat length. These sails are a perfect partner for a single- or double-reefed mainsail.

- **A cruising spinnaker,** or genniker, makes downwind passages doubly enjoyable. Most come with easy-furl socks, which seem to work well, even in relatively heavy weather.

Brian. Fagan

Rolling furling gear

You can add light weight drifters and other specialized sails, but there is no substitute for a well built basic inventory. When passage-making, carry lengths of batten stock in case you have to replace some, also a sailmaker's kit and ripstop tape for quick repairs.

Safety Gear

Anyone sailing offshore in California waters should assume that they will meet rough weather one day, and that, in an emergency, they may have to fend for themselves for a considerable time before help arrives. Coast Guard and offshore racing requirements are minimal yardsticks for serious cruising.

Here's a list of essentials:

Whether under sail or power, you should carry:

- **Adequate ground tackle** including two anchors of sufficient weight to hold your boat in relatively exposed anchorages during a full gale. (More on anchoring and ground tackle below and in Chapter 6)

- **Life jackets** of USCG approved design for every member of the crew, equipped with lights and whistles.

- **A "Transpac" pole,** U-shaped life ring, Xenon overboard light, drogue, and die canister, all mounted on the stern pulpit.

Many skippers now sail with a Lifesling installation or with a Man Overboard Module, a package which automatically deploys when thrown overboard.

Whatever man overboard gear you carry, be sure you and your crew know how to use it instinctively in an emergency. Incidently, it's interesting to note just how few power yachts carry man overboard gear ready to deploy off their sterns. I suppose they assume everyone will be in the deckhouse in bad weather. But what happens if some gear breaks loose in a rough sea and you have to be on deck, or someone slips and falls over board on a calm, but lumpy night?

- **Deck safety harnesses** for all members of the crew.

I think every power and sail boat should carry safety harnesses. By the same token, you should have consistent policies as to their use. One skipper I know makes everyone on deck wear them in winds over 20 knots in daytime, and at all times after dark. Many racing crews are notably casual about safety harnesses, sometimes on the grounds they get in the way, which strikes me as courting disaster.

European sailors, sailing as they do in cold waters, use safety harnesses routinely, even in moderate weather. Only rarely do you see California yachts with safety harness jackstays rigged along the side decks from bow to stern, so you can hook on and move forward without unhooking. Such installations are routine on European yachts, and should be on any California boat venturing offshore, especially north of Point Conception.

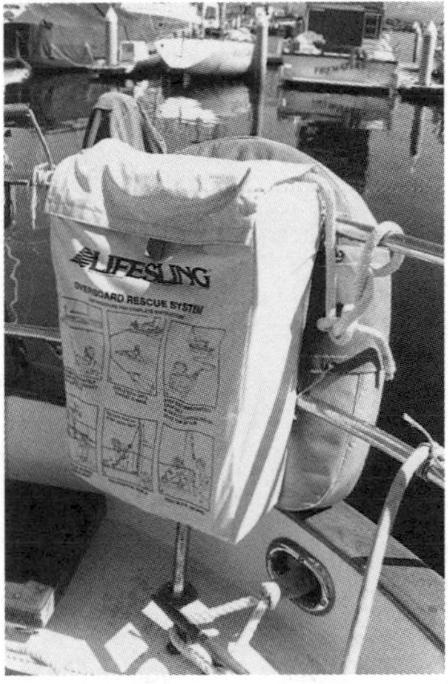

Brian Fagan

A Sea Sling

- **A radar reflector,** preferably mounted permanently, as high in the rigging as possible. Great debate surrounds the most effective designs. Consult your local marine supply store for advice.

- A set of **day and night flares** in excess of USCG requirements.

- At least **two manual bilge pumps,** one mounted in the cabin, the second operable from the cockpit. These are in addition to any automatic electric bilge pumps aboard. What happens if a rogue wave, or a sudden knockdown when your hatches are open floods your batteries?

- A minimum of **two fire extinguishers,** one near the engine room and galley, the other readily accessible in the cockpit.

- **A Freon horn** and a backup manual foghorn.

- **A permanently mounted compass,** swung for deviation. Make sure you have a bearing compass aboard as a back-up. Each

A mounted compass Brian Fagan

compass should be adequately lit. If your main compass is an electronic one, be sure to have a backup magnetic installation. Wooden plugs for emergency repairs for through-hull fittings.

A sharp knife and a pair of **heavy duty bolt cutters** close to the cockpit for clearing away after a dismasting. The latter do not come cheap, but when you need them, you need them badly. Be sure to keep them well greased, so they do not rust when in storage. **A VHF radio** with channel 16, the emergency frequency.

A GPS (see under electronics, below).

An Emergency Position Indicating Radio Beacon (EPIRB), mounted near the cockpit. Remember to check the batteries of this, and other battery-operated equipment, regularly. These self contained battery-operated transmitters, when activated emit signals that are picked up by satellite, then relayed to a shore station. A Category I 406 type is best for our waters.

A waterproof first aid kit, with supplies to cover fractures, and other shipboard accidents. You will also need a simple first aid manual. There are several good ones on the market, written by emergency physicians with sailing experience. One of the best investments you can make of a winter's evening is a Red Cross first aid and CPR course, offered free of charge in many communities.

Like engines, safety gear is expensive, but it is worth every penny on those rare occasions when you really need it. It's a sobering thought, but over the years in California, I have used every piece of safety equipment aboard at least once. Fortunately, the situation has never been life-threatening.

Finally, make sure that every member of the crew, even children, know where fire extinguishers, life jackets, and other safety essentials are kept. Can you locate your through-hull plugs in less than 15 seconds when you spring a leak with Point Conception half a mile to leeward in a 20-knot wind? I tried last week in harbor and it took 2 minutes for me to find them...

The Question of Life Rafts

All the safety gear listed above assumes either that someone falls overboard, or that some mishap like a dismasting or the collapse of a through-hull fitting needs emergency attention. But what about the remote chance you might have to abandon ship in deep water, some distance from land, say, 20 miles off Monterey or Dana Point? If you lose your ship, perhaps through fire or by hitting an underwater obstruction at speed (which happens more frequently than you might imagine), you may have only a few minutes, or even seconds, to abandon ship. In equipment terms, what are your options?

Some cruising yachts, and many fishermen, carry survival suits, which are designed to keep the wearer warm while staying afloat for many hours. Such suits are expensive and bulky, but are certainly effective if you have time to put them on.

Many skippers go on passage with their rubber dinghies half inflated and the dinghy pump close to hand, assuming they will have enough time to blow up the remaining compartments in an emergency. This option is probably adequate enough in benign coastal waters, and is commonly used in the Santa Barbara Channel. Some cruising people carry CO_2 bottle installations for emergency inflation: a nice solution, but you must check the bottle regularly and stow it out of the sun. Inflatable dinghies like the Avon or Zodiac do not really make very satisfactory lifeboats, for they flip in strong winds, and are difficult to board in rough seas and strong winds. Nor are they easy to right or row in anything but calm weather. Inflatables with rigid bottoms are even harder to control, for, while heavier, they offer more windage.

The ultimate, and most expensive, solution is an inflatable, packaged liferaft. Nearly every European cruising yacht, whether power or sail, carries such a raft as a matter of course. They are far and few between in California waters, even aboard passage-making cruising yachts, probably because they are considered expensive luxuries in our generally moderate weather conditions. A good four-person raft costs between $1,500 and $6,000, which is a sizeable piece of change by any standards. The cheapest are the so-called platform type, which are inflatable discs that keep you out of the water, even if you get wet. Platforms are for inshore use, when you expect to be rescued within a short time. Coastal liferafts are built for situations where rescue is likely within 24 to 48 hours.

They are covered inflatables which offer some thermal protection. You can buy a more elaborate offshore design, but the coastal type is fine for California waters, where search and rescue facilities are within range and local ship traffic relatively dense. A nylon bag is adequate if you plan to stow your liferaft below, but a fiberglass canister is essential for outside mounting in the hot sun and spray. Whatever the design, size, and make, liferafts require annual servicing, which cost about $25 per person capacity. Most good designs are guaranteed for 12 years or so if you have them serviced annually at an authorized center. The service center inflates and repacks the raft, and checks the emergency gear packed aboard, progressively replacing each item in the package as the years pass.

For peace of mind, a well-maintained liferaft is the best insurance. Cruising sailors benefit from the vast experience obtained with merchant ship emergencies and government testing under controlled conditions. You may flinch at the initial expense, but even in our waters there may come a moment when your survival depends on pulling a liferaft release line. Though the survival kit provided with the raft will probably suffice for coastal passages, you may want to add a waterproof abandon ship bag packed with essential items, stowed within close reach of the helm.

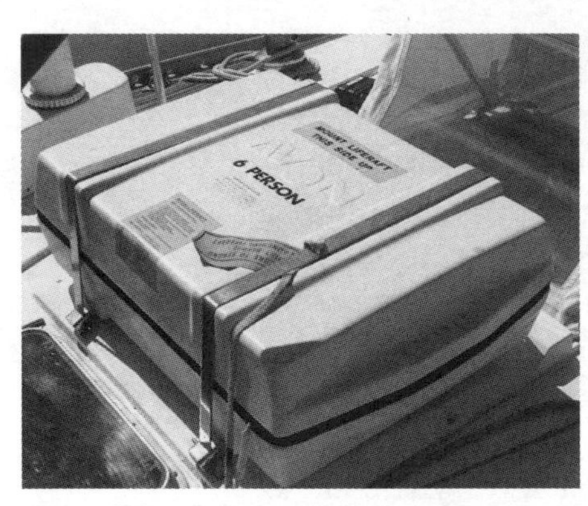

Avon liferaft in canister Brian Fagan

Some companies will rent you a liferaft for a few weeks or months, a useful option for people embarking on a long summer or once-in-a-lifetime cruise.

Ground Tackle

Despite the increasing restrictions on anchoring in mainland harbors, we are fortunate in being able to use our ground tackle more frequently than many other sailors. Lying in a quiet, rock-girt cove with the full moon overhead and cliffs high above, listening to swells beating on the ashore, sea lions barking far off is one of the pleasures of California cruising. The endless maze of bureaucratic regulation has not extended to most of the Channel Islands anchorages, nor are they congested with moorings. You can anchor along the mainland, too, behind convenient headlands like Pfeiffer along the Big Sur coast, or in the quiet beauty of San Simeon Bay while 30 knots of northwesterly blows close offshore. But to anchor in such places requires a sound knowledge of the art of anchoring, and first rate ground tackle adequate for the job.

Fierce arguments over anchors erupt wherever sailors gather. Each design has its passionate advocates, who swear by its outstanding qualities. All we can do is navigate through a confusion of conflicting opinions and lay out some general guidelines.

When equipping your boat for California cruising, you must assume you will use two anchors with some regularity, especially in crowded coves where dozens of yachts anchor in close proximity, their bows turned toward wind and swell. You should also assume that you will encounter different sea bottoms, most commonly sand and mud, rock, and grass-covered clay, so you need to carry more than one design of anchor aboard.

Here are some general guidelines for power and sailing yachts between 25- and 60 feet overall:

- **Your main (sometimes called bower) anchor** should be of adequate weight for the length and displacement of your yacht (see Table S.1). Opinions differ sharply as to the ideal design for California waters, but most owners ship out with a Bruce, CQR, or Danforth. All have their sterling qualities. For example, the CQR is a highly versatile anchor, which is tenacious in sand and clay, but said to be less effective on rocky bottoms (although I have had good luck with it). Many people prefer the Danforth on kelp-infested bottoms, while others swear by the Bruce, originally designed for oil barges and rigs. An increasing number of skippers are turning to Simpson-Lawrence's

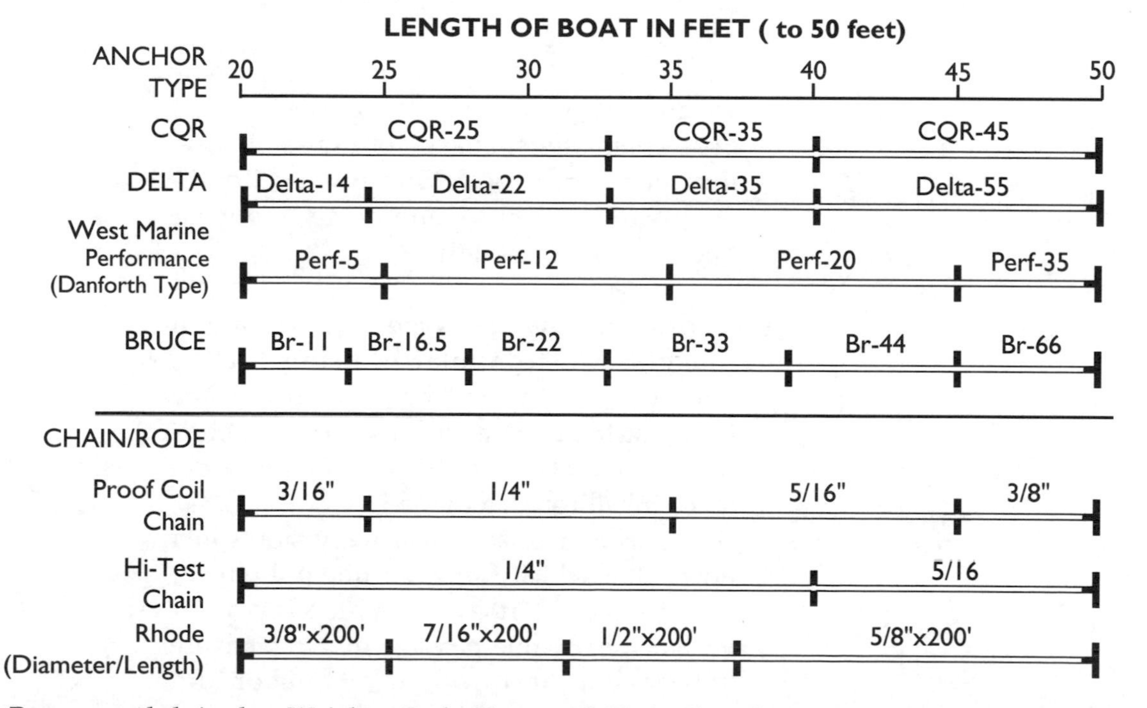

Recommended Anchor Weights, Rode Sizes, and Chain Sizes for Yachts Between 30 and 50 Feet Overall. (courtesy West Marine)

Delta anchor, which has no moving parts and superior setting qualities relative to its light weight.

A final thought: your anchor is only as good as the rest of your ground tackle.

Your kedge (or stern) anchor should be of a different design to your main one, simply to give you versatility of choice under varying sea bottom conditions. Most people purchase kedges which are about two-thirds the weight of their main anchors, on the argument they will carry less load. I must confess a preference for a kedge about the same weight, but this is not really necessary in coastal situations.

Anchor rodes should be a combination of chain and rode, with a length of chain in the order of 35 feet being adequate for most yachts. Nylon rodes are best. A main rode length of about 200 feet is adequate for California coastal waters, with about 150 feet for the kedge line.

While many serious cruising people swear by all-chain rodes, the technology of nylon rodes is now such that the lighter weight and greater versatility of rope outweighs any advantages the greater weight of all-chain offers. I have, for example, used my anchor rode as a long towing line in open waters, when none of my mooring lines were long enough.

Anchor and rode stowage requires careful thought. Most popular cruising yachts, whether sail or power, have an anchor line locker at the bow, either a sealed compartment accessible from the forecabin or a bin accessible through a hinged lid on deck.

The main anchor usually stows in a bow roller which forms an integral part of the stemhead fitting. If you keep your anchor there while passage making, ensure you have a pin through the anchor and some means of securing the shank and exposed chain on deck. You should also plug up your hawse pipe. If you do not keep your anchor on a bow roller, you should install sturdy chocks and lines on the foredeck.

Double bow rollers are essential for California waters, for anchoring to two anchors, and for Bahamian moors.

photos by Brian Fagan

Windlass. Anchor windlasses are probably unnecessary for yachts under 30 feet, although many owners now fit them, either on the foredeck or hidden away in the anchor locker. Fortunately, I have always had a ready supply of energetic young people, who love pulling up anchors, although I cannot imagine why. Electric winches such as the Lofrans or Maxwell are compact, powerful, and reliable, but be sure they can accommodate both rode and chain. Simpson-Lawrence makes an excellent line of manual winches, which can be strongly recommended, especially for yachts under 35 feet.

Useful accessories include a **trip line** and **buoy** for marking the position of the anchor and tripping it in an emergency. A bleach bottle with the yacht's name painted on it is more than adequate for the job. Carry chafing gear such as industrial hose pipe, rags, or leather, for use in rough weather. Even the most carefully designed and sympathetic fairleads can chafe a nylon rode when the yacht is swinging wildly to gusts.

Some owners carry anchor weights and handy billies to lessen snubbing, but I frankly think they are unnecessary in our waters.

You should **keep your anchor shackles greased,** and check the pins are wired in place before setting out on even a weekend cruise. Once you have had the pleasing sensation of dragging at 0300 because a shackle pin came loose on the bottom, you never forget this item on your checklist.

Anchor gear at bow

Mooring Lines

We used to call them "warps" in my youth, a term which seems to have gone into disuse. In these marina-bound days, we tend to take our mooring lines for granted, tailoring them to the exact configuration of our slips. Then you go on a cruise and find they are too short, or simply too idiosyncratic, for any other berth. In addition to your regular mooring lines, I suggest you carry at least two, preferably four, 50-foot 1/2- to 3/4-inch lines not only for securing in strange harbors, but to serve as spring lines, or simply for towing, rigging jury rigs, or even for games on the beach. Rope is relatively cheap, and comes in handy if you have to move your boat when the engine fails, or someone near you runs into trouble.

A useful hint I learned the hard way: put sailmakers' whippings on the ends, not end-splices. Then you can thread the line through small fairleads without having to wrestle with a bulky splice at the end. All mooring lines should be carefully whipped at each end, for fused strands invariably come apart at the wrong moment. The braided versus stranded rope controversy is a matter of personal preference. All modern ropes are highly chafe resistant and will last a long time with careful use and chafe guards.

Incidently, take the trouble to install cleats and fairleads amidships for spring lines. Far too few production yachts are so equipped, which makes using springs a veritable cat's cradle.

Good fenders are essential, especially in commercial ports and under circumstances where you raft up against other people. Most owners seem to prefer the white, tubular type, which, after all, look very nice. You can even buy color coordinated fenders and covers these days.

I prefer the massive, orange balloons used by fishermen. They act like cushions, last for ever (my present one, picked up in the middle of the Atlantic, is at least 13 years old), and protect you in any weather. Balloons require more space to stow, but their durable advantages more than outweigh this small inconvenience.

Brian Fagan

Brian Fagan

Dinghies

I love messing around in dinghies, paddling quietly through sleeping anchorages in the early morning watching sea lions play in the kelp, sunsets from water level. The proper dinghy makes all the difference to a successful cruise, especially if you have children. But selecting a dinghy requires as much care as your ground tackle and safety gear.

Most smaller yachts, and many larger ones for that matter, prefer inflatables. A sound inflatable is ideal for California conditions, where you tend to land on rocks as often as sandy beaches. Until recently, the very best inflatables were made by Avon and Zodiac, both European companies. Hard core sailing people tended to choose Avons, while power boaters and those who preferred to use an outboard selected a Zodiac. Both have their strong points, are well built and safe even in rough water. But they are imported products and expensive propositions, especially since second-hand inflatables rarely appear on the market. By all means try shopping around for a domestic design, but be sure that whatever dinghy you purchase is strongly constructed with well taped and bonded seams and adequate buoyancy. You must be able to row the dinghy against quite strong winds and lumpy waves even if you normally use an outboard. The towing attachment should be strong, the oars and rowlocks of sound design (test on the water before buying), and the repair kit and potential for service superior. Sometimes you see people paddling around in small yellow raft-like dinghies designed for beach use. Such toys have no place on a cruising yacht of any size. The heavens help you if an offshore wind blow you out to sea. Quite simply, you will not be able to row home.

Versatile and durable, inflatable dinghies are ideal for California waters.

Until recently, most people rowed their inflatables. Today, rigid bottomed inflatable sport boats are becoming

Brian Fagan

the rage, some of them as small as 9 feet overall. Instead of rowing, even diehard sailors use outboards. A motorized dinghy does enable one to cover quite long distances in short order, a consideration at places like the Isthmus on Catalina Island, where both moorings and public anchoring areas are some distance from shore. But the outboard requires care and attention, as well as a stowage bracket and place to stow flammable gasoline under way. Then there is the chore of lowering and hoisting a clumsy motor into the dinghy, quite apart from the risk of dropping it overboard when installing it. On the whole, I prefer to use oars and leave the outboard back home. Quite apart from anything else, the constant noise of outboards disturbs one's peace and quiet at anchor.

Brian Fagan

If you plan to use an outboard, purchase an inflatable with removable floorboards or a hard bottom. The manufacturer or your dealer will advise you on the correct horsepower of outboard for the dinghy of your choice.

A word of warning: Always remove your outboard from the dinghy and bring the inflatable aboard when cruising in open water. Inflatables have a tendency to flip over in heavy air and can even take off and fly aboard in a boisterous following wind, tickling the helm's ear as they nuzzle over the stern. Emptying a swamped inflatable in a bumpy sea is no joke, so best bring them aboard and partially deflate them.

Many owners of larger power and sailing yachts prefer a fiberglass or wooden dinghy to stow aboard. I love such craft, especially if they have a small sail, so you can enjoy quiet creeks and beaches inaccessible for larger craft. However, you must bring them aboard in even moderate seas, for they can be a real menace when filled with water. You then have to heave-to or stop and bail them out alongside, which is hazardous in rough water to say the least.

You can easily hoist a 8- to 9-foot dinghy on board using your main or spinnaker halyard and a short sling attached to two eyes installed in the tender at bow and stern. Some larger sailing yachts and power boats have stern davits, which work well, but tend to restrict visibility aft. The derricks installed on some trawler yachts allow you to winch even a tender as heavy as a Boston Whaler out of the water. If you do plan to use a hard dinghy, put considerable thought not only into hoisting and lowering her, but to how you will stow her on deck. Many larger sailing yachts carry their dinghies bottom up over the cabin house, which means they are out of the way on passage, yet easily accessible in harbor.

There are many good mass produced hard dinghy designs in the 8- to 10-foot range to choose from, but you should avoid small racing craft like Sabots or flimsy river boats. Neither is designed to take the heavy knocks of passage-making and anchoring.Your dinghy must be stoutly built, have adequate built-in buoyancy, be able to hold several adults, and be capable of being used to row out anchors and for other laborious chores. Equip it with Coast Guard mandated gear and ensure the tender itself meets USCG specifications. A properly designed dinghy is like a member of the family, which you can sail, row, and just enjoy to your heart's content.

Electronics

I learned my sailing in the 1950s where electronics were virtually unknown aboard small yachts. Over the years, I have grown to appreciate them for their convenience, but have never completely trusted them—which is just as well, because I have been plagued with unreliable instrumentation. The good news is that today's devices are compact and highly reliable compared with those of yesteryear. A judicious investment in electronics is a wise move **once other essentials like a reliable engine, adequate safety gear, and a good dinghy** are in place. Always consider electronics a luxury not an essential, for all their ability to fix your position to within feet, to prevent you going aground, or to tell you when a ship is bearing down on you sight unseen.

Choosing electronics is a matter of personal preference. Many skippers go far beyond the basics and equip their boats with navigational and radio gear which would not be out of place on a commercial vessel. I have a bias toward the simple, so content myself with listing a basic inventory, which will more than suffice for California passage making:

- **Speedometer and Log.** These are essential for maintaining Dead Reckoning plots, to say nothing of efficient sailing. If you have a built-in autopilot, GPS, or Loran, you might consider acquiring instruments which interface with them.

- **Apparent Wind Direction and Speed Indicator.** Most larger sailing yachts seem to fit these as a matter of routine, even if they do not race. Personally, I prefer a Windex indicator at the masthead, which never has fits of the vapors, but electronics are certainly a convenience at night.

- **VHF Radio.** An essential and relatively cheap piece of equipment which should be aboard every cruising boat.

- **Autopilot.** Essential in our waters, where you may spend long hours under power.

- **Global Positioning System (GPS).** GPS is the navigational system of the future, allowing yourself to fix your position within 300 feet at the moment, within 30 feet in a few years. You can build GPS into your boat and use it with electronic charts, an expensive, but wonderful option which will be near-universal in a generation or so. I prefer one of the compact portable GPS packages for coastal cruising. They are wonderful for peace of mind and a bargain at well under $1,000.

- **Loran C** is found on many boats, but is rapidly becoming obsolete with the advent of GPS.

- **Radar** is much more affordable and compact than a few years ago. Every year, smaller and smaller boats fit it, but I see no justification for such elaboration unless you plan frequent passages in foggy or congested waters.

Other equipment

When I sold my boat recently, I removed no less than five wheelbarrow loads of equipment from her, everything from voltmeters to pillows, and that in spite of my insistence that sailing be simple. Most of us cruising people are pack rats by inclination, so accept the fact your yacht will be congested with all manner of gear, most of it surplus to requirements. But here are some essentials, which should always be on board:

- **A strong boarding ladder** is an essential. If possible, invest in one that hinges down over the stern. You then have a permanent ladder for use in emergencies. Many mass-produced yachts now come with this feature as standard.

- **A comprehensive tool kit** and an **adequate spares inventory.** Your tool kit should include wrenches to fit every nut on the boat, including the stuffing box. Any good primer on cruising will provide you with a check list. Commonly used spares are engine belts, fuses, water pump impellers, motor oil and fuel and oil filters, shackles, winch parts, spare turnbuckles and rope, batteries, fuses for key electrical equipment, repair manuals, fiberglass repair kits, stove parts, batteries, and extra winch handles. Again, be guided by your own experience and that of others. It is pointless, for example, for a sailing yacht to carry a new starter motor in our well traveled waters when you can always sail to a nearby port within a couple of days. Make sure you carry plenty of spare halyards, as well as a reserve of fresh water and fuel.

- Your **galley equipment** will need little modification for offshore passages in California. I use lots of bag and seals to carry large, precooked casseroles aboard. A supply of large plastic garbage bags makes life easier, for no responsible skipper allows garbage to be dumped over the side.

- **A cockpit awning** makes sense on hot summer days. Bimini covers are probably unnecessary in our relatively cool climate, although many power boats carry them, especially in hot Sacramento Delta waters.

Brian Fagan

- **Self steering vanes** are becoming more commonplace on coastal cruising boats, but I would be inclined not to invest in one. Most of your sailing takes place in ship- and fishing boat-infested waters, where a good lookout is vital. In any case, few of your passages will last longer than 4 or 5 days. The money invested in a vane is better spent on a liferaft or some other essential. If you do decide to fit one, be sure to talk to people who own them first, preferably someone with a yacht like yours.
  Your gear inventory can expand to include every form of luxury, from refrigerators to flopper-stoppers. My counsel is to keep it simple, and enjoy sailing rather than maintenance.

Bureaucracy

Considering the number of pleasure craft in California waters, the bureaucratic requirements are surprisingly simple. Whenever on passage, you should carry:

- **Registration or documentation papers,** with correct stickers displayed at the bow, if applicable.
- **Insurance policy,** with extended coverage for passage away from home waters if applicable.
- **Radio license** for each VHF or other radio equipment aboard, also a Radio Log, which should be completed whenever calls are made.
- If you are cruising the Channel Islands, you will need a **Landing Permit** (see Chapter 12).
- **Evidence of Coast Guard inspections,** if any. These documents will save you the inconvenience of another safety inspection if you have been boarded within recent weeks.
- Some form of **personal identification** such as a driver's license.

Personal Gear

Everyone's preferences are different and range from the utterly casual (mainly in balmy Southern California) to the highly

Brian Fagan

Tools of the trade you always need—

organized and coordinated. Here are some general observations, aimed at passage making rather than harbor hopping.

Clothing

California is a cruising ground of layers, layers of clothing which are added and shed as weather conditions while on passage. The concept of layered clothing has been around for a long time, but only in recent years has it become a near-obsession with manufacturers. And rightly so, for we twentieth-century sailors have finally learned something the Inuit of the Arctic were aware of thousands of years ago: Windproof, well tailored layers of protective gear are highly effective in environments where temperatures change dramatically and wind chills are a factor. Layers are especially important in our waters, where days of warm sunshine and moderate breezes can lull you into a false sense of security, into believing shorts or jeans and a T-shirt and the occasional sweater are all you need at sea. Wrong! Even a 15-knot afternoon westerly with short wind waves can kick up deluges of spray and chill you dramatically in a few minutes. And if you are passage making north of Point Conception, even in summer, you need not only warm layers but good-quality foul weather gear.

Here's a minimal list, starting from the skin outward, for any serious cruising sailor, whether under sail or power (I assume that people with pilot houses do go on deck in rough weather sometimes!):

Inner layer: form-fitting long-underwear style layer, which wicks off moisture. Manufacturers like Musto and Patagonia make such garments, which are wonderfully warm and lightweight, as the innermost component in their layered systems.

Middle layer: thermal jacket and long pants with a polar fleece or equivalent lining and a windproof outer surface. This layer is for everyday use, and should be spray proof for those days when some water flies around, but not enough for discomfort.

Outer Layer: foul weather gear, long pants with high bib and suspenders, and jacket with hood. This outfit can be two-piece, although some sailors prefer one-piece overalls. Personally, I find one-piece garments the very devil to put on at night in rough seas, but this is mere bias...

When buying foul weather gear for serious passage making, even in summer, you should assume you are going to be wet for several hours on end. This means your garments should not only be waterproof but waterproof over a long period of time, as well as gortex-lined to minimize condensation. In other words, cheap foul weather gear is a false economy, especially if you are sailing in Central California waters. Only the most hardy of ocean racing and offshore cruising sailors will need deep-water waterproofs, such as those sold by Musto, Henri-Lloyd, and other leading manufacturers, but a set of moderate weight (sometimes called "coastal," or "passage-making") is probably ideal. If you plan never to leave Southern California, you could do nicely with a light weight set designed for warmer climates, provided you buy good quality garments. Beware of cheap plastic jackets and pants, which are little better than garbage bags taped together to resemble waterproofs. Do not compromise on foul weather gear. Buy the best.

Many better quality foul weather jackets come with built-in flotation and safety harness. These add to the bulk of the garment, and are a matter of personal preference. Since much of the time we sail in good weather, you may be better off having a separate harness and personal buoyancy system.

Acquiring layered clothing requires a substantial financial investment, but the outlay is well worth it for the serious cruising sailor, whatever your vessel. Quite apart from anything else, it saves you time and space when packing. Today's efficient, well insulated layered garments save you carrying large numbers of bulky sweaters.

Boots, Shoes

Anyone sailing regularly in rough waters needs seaboots. There are many excellent lightweight designs on the market, such as the widely used Romika brand. These combine excellent gripping qualities with good support at the ankle and high enough uppers to form a waterproof seal with your foul weather pants.

Boots are essential for sailing north of Point Conception, and I find them ideal for winter sailing in the Santa Barbara Channel. Many people ship out with good deck shoes instead. Such shoes have witnessed a technological revolution in recent years. The best designs are as durable ashore as they are tenacious on a slippery deck. All the major manufacturers make excellent shoes, with either synthetic or leather uppers. I prefer to keep away from leather, which dries slower and offers less ventilation, but this is a matter of personal taste. Velcro attachments make for convenience when you are in a hurry or at night.

Sandals are the latest footwear to go "hi-tech." They make good sense in warmer weather. You can buy them with deckshoe bottoms, making sandals ideal summer wear both ashore and afloat, but be sure you buy a pair which have the correct bottoms, or you will slide all over the place.

Bare feet and flip-flops have no place on deck while on passage. Both can cause you to slip on slick decks, or when the loose sole catches on a footrail or cleat. Best wear sandals, which offer a good grip and are as cool.

What you wear inside your shoes or boots is as important as the shoe itself. The special sea boot socks made by several manufacturers can be strongly recommended both for their insulation and drying qualities. While wool is cozy, the synthetic socks are far more comfortable when wet.

Brian Fagan

Other garments and personal gear

Having said all this about layered clothing, you can, of course, rely on cheaper, less specialized garments. Jeans, T-shirts, and sweaters are standard fare at sea, as are shorts. The important thing is to have adequate waterproof protection to hand, also a polar-fleece type jacket to keep out cool winds. A woollen hat is a great comfort on night watches, even in summer, as are gloves. The sailor's old adage of one more sweater than you may need applies, too.

Many skippers provide safety harnesses for everyone aboard, but some people prefer to carry their own. I keep my harness in my sailing holdall, so it goes with me wherever I sail, adjusted correctly for immediate use. The same applies to personal buoyancy aids. Experienced sailors often use their own lifejackets, equipped with lights, the equipment, once again, being fitted and tailor-made to their own needs. One option is a CO_2-inflated life-jacket, which you wear on your safety harness in a small holster. These work beautifully, provided you maintain them regularly, but they do not meet USCG standards.

Sunglasses are essential in our waters, and you should invest in a pair which give you adequate UV protection. Cheap, off the rack, drug store sunglasses are not recommended for people spending long hours on the water. While on the subject of sun protection, a broad-brimmed sun hat is essential, one with a stout lace to secure it under your chin. The Canadian-made Tilley sun hat sets the standard in durable headgear and should be part of every sailor's gear. A high number sunscreen is vital, even on bright days in mid-winter. And remember that even grey days can produce sunburn.

Seasickness patches or pills are a matter of personal preference and a doctor's proscription. In this day and age, it is just plain dumb to go to sea without taking the appropriate medication, unless, of course, you are one of those rare, and unlucky, people, who suffer from chronic seasickness. I have a serious problem, but a box of patches keeps me functioning even in very rough weather. The only side effect is a dry mouth, but this is preferable to vomiting. Oddly enough, the worst times are in flat, oily calms early in the morning, when cooking breakfast.

Brian Fagan

A sharp knife with marlin spike and shackle opener is an essential for all crew members. The best set-ups come in sheaths, worn on a belt or lanyard around the waist. **Never wear your knife around your neck.** It could catch on a rail or the rigging and strangle you.

You will endear yourself to your fellow crew-members, if you arrive with your personal possessions in a soft holdall. There are many excellent designs on the market, which double comfortably as airline bags.

Finally, when you have provisioned your boat and stowed everything aboard, take a few minutes to check each member of the crew knows exactly where every major piece of gear is located. Then you can rest assured the emergency tiller can be located in a few seconds when your wheel cable snaps in the middle of the fairway at Marina del Rey during Sunday afternoon rush hour. And I know people who have had that chilling experience!

Brian Fagan

CHAPTER 6

Hazards and Seamanship

> *And now let me say that should you spy my vessel on the water, do not expect her to be handled by a faultless seaman. I've misjudged every situation in this book at least twice and probably will again.*
>
> Roger Taylor
> *The Elements of Seamanship.*

We enjoy a cruising ground of great contrasts. The sailor can spend weeks on end sailing between remote anchorages and along rugged, rock-girt coasts without seeing an automobile or a high rise building. He or she can harbor hop and dine most nights in a different yacht club. Our waters cater to every taste. For the most part, California offers good, relatively predictable weather. Tides are moderate and currents not a major passage-making consideration, with the notable exception of the Golden Gate. The coastline is steep-to, with few outlying shoals and navigational hazards. But for all these advantages, cruising California takes prudence and forethought. Some of the most congested coastal waters in the world define California's 600-mile coastline. About 7,000 commercial ships of all kinds pass under the Golden Gate Bridge each year. Thousands more merchant vessels sail in and out of San Pedro and San Diego, fanning out in every direction—south to the Panama Canal, north or northwestward to Japan, Seattle, and points north, or across the Pacific to Hawaii and far beyond. All these movements are quite separate from those of fishing boats and smaller vessels like oil rig service boats. Commercial shipping is but one of the maritime hazards, for oil exploration, frequent fogs, and unpredictable swells from far offshore are among the hazards one can encounter off our coasts. This chapter explores some of these coastal hazards, discusses some basic points about seamanship which are important when cruising California waters.

Hazards

Shipping

A tanker or a container ship makes an impressive sight steaming along our coasts. The swells that cause you to roll continually in moderate beam seas barely affect the inexorable progress of the merchant vessel. Strong northwesterlies swirl aside in a cloud of smoke drifting far down to leeward of the vanishing ship. The same juggernauts when viewed from close quarters are far from majestic. In fact they have danger signals written all over them. The yachts run down by large ships increase in number every year, and the lives lost because someone did not keep a good lookout escalate. Shipping perils for California sailors grow increasingly serious because modern electronics allow ships to proceed at full speed in poor visibility and there are many more small craft crossing shipping lanes.

Commercial maritime traffic, especially near major ports like San Francisco or San Pedro, is heavy year-round. Fortunately, most shipping follows well traveled coastal routes, which pass either fairly close inshore, within 5 miles or so off Point Sur and Point Conception, or at least 50 miles offshore, outside exclusion zones. Most states have established exclusion zones within the past ten years to keep large supertankers and other vessels with hazardous cargos well offshore. This 50-mile exclusion zone may well be expanded to 100 miles off California within the next few years. So a tanker leaving the Golden Gate will sail 50 miles west away from the land, then turn north or south into a 8- to 10-mile wide corridor offshore.

Pat Leddy

Unless you are sailing to Hawaii or elsewhere in the South Pacific, the large ships which impact the heavily traveled offshore lane will only affect you in the approaches to major ports. Our concerns are primarily coastal shipping, which takes the most direct inshore route from origin to destination. Inevitably, most vessels keep to the shortest route, unless weather forces them to change course, a strategy dictated very often by the shipping line's use of commercial vessel routing services for passage planning. Commercial shipping generates predictable hazards. The chances are if you see one ship heading south off Point Sur, then you will encounter others, because commercial vessels tend to follow the most economical and direct route. Sailing 50 miles offshore, just outside the coastal exclusion zone far off the Golden Gate, you can literally draw a line in the ocean marking the edge of the shipping lane. At one moment, you may have ten ships in sight. An hour later, you will be alone. All

Lesley Newhart

Above all, give way to large ships in restricted waters where they have no space to get out of your way.

of which brings us to another fundamental point: Most shipping follows well-trodden routes. This makes navigation a little easier, provided you always keep a weather eye open for vessels heading inshore or on a less direct course. Ships and commercial vessels create a major hazard, even away from choke points like the mouth of the Golden Gate or the Santa Barbara Channel. You have only one defense. Keep a constant 360 degree lookout whenever at sea. And don't forget to look behind you. Ships travel silently and can creep up on you without auditory warning.

The hazard increases dramatically when you approach the Golden Gate, the Santa Barbara Channel, and the Catalina Channel. They support so much heavy traffic that shipping is routed through well defined shipping lanes, marked on the charts with purple slashes. Precisely defined traffic zones separate north/south or inbound/outbound shipping into controlled lanes. These are the marine equivalent of the center divider on a freeway. In the approaches to the Golden Gate, the Santa Barbara Channel, and off Los Angeles commercial harbors, ships subject to traffic control are controlled by land-based operators using radio and radar. Vessels effectively operate like aircraft.

The best protection against ships is to avoid them. Alter your course rather than insisting on your rights. If the larger vessel does change direction, maintain your course and speed. Make sure you signal your intentions clearly, using the prescribed horn signals. Hoist a large radar reflector in reduced weather and make sure you are thoroughly familiar with the International Rules for the

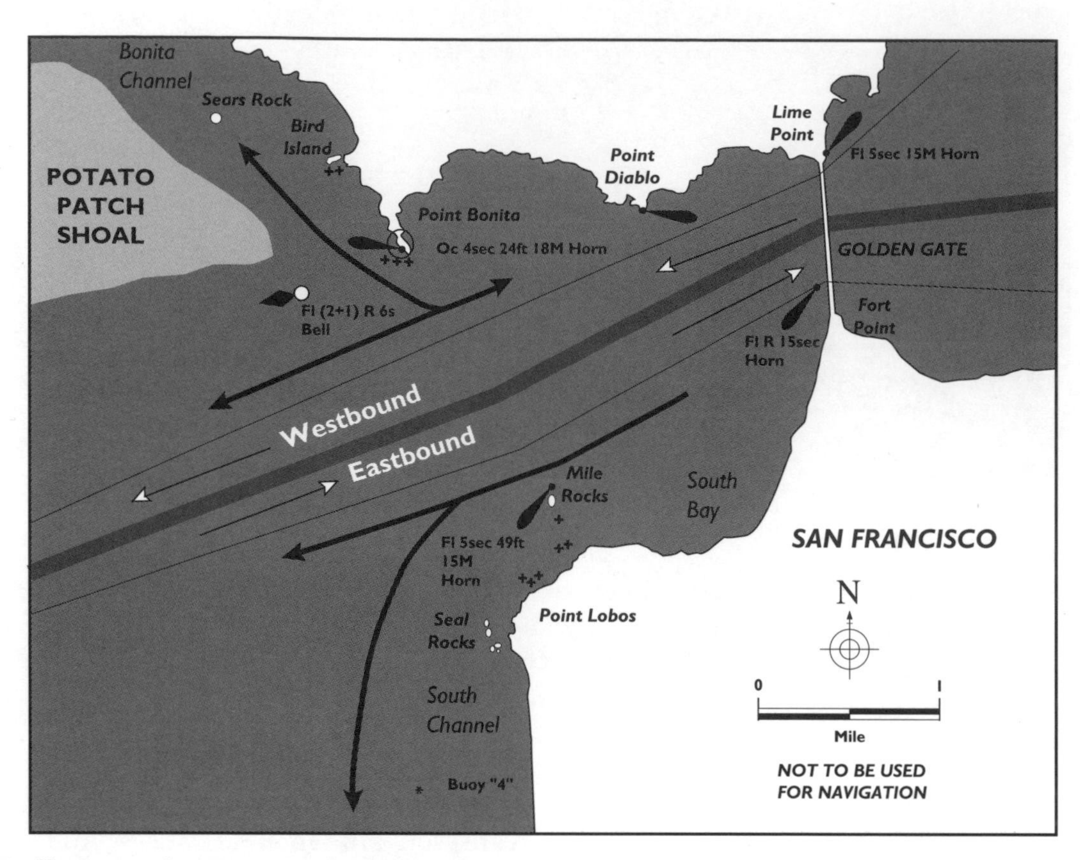

Traffic Separation Zones at the Golden Gate.

Prevention of Collision at Sea.

The Rules of the Road are specific about the responsibility of small craft in narrow channels and other congested waters. Remember that you are the equivalent of a light pick-up going up against an eighteen-wheeler. The congestion problem of large ships and small craft is particularly acute in the Golden Gate, where several nasty accidents have occurred because yachts have forgotten the rules of the road, or simply think they can nimbly leap out of the way. Some racing skippers, who want to win at all costs, are notorious for their so-called daring in ducking under the bows of merchant ships to gain a few yards. Their well-meaning friends applaud their macho attitude. A wise sailor knows: No race is worth lives.

In areas with well defined shipping lanes and separation zones, your responsibilities are even more specific. If you must cross such lanes, do so by the quickest route, or at right angles, giving way to any ships converging on you. If you are running in the same direction as a traffic lane, lay off a course that keeps you well outside the shipping line. On no account sail between the lanes, especially off the entrance to the Golden Gate. Follow the rule: Stay inshore, clear of the main shipping channel.

When on passage, brief your crew about the dangers of commercial ships and fishing boats, insist on a 24-hour and 360-degree lookout. Teach your crew to identify the angle of ships' lights, and how to take bearings to establish collision courses. Insist that they call the skipper if they have the slightest doubt about an approaching vessel. Display the correct navigation lights at night: Red to port, green to starboard, a white stern light, and a white all-round masthead light if under power. Never engage a wind vane or autopilot and forget to keep a lookout. Above all, obey two basic rules:

If in doubt, keep out of the way.

Peter Howorth

Search the horizon through 360 degrees at least every 5 minutes.

In some ways, commercial fishing boats are an even greater hazard than merchant vessels. At certain times of the year you can encounter large fishing fleets lying to their nets or trolling long lines. Your best strategy will be to stay well clear, and to alter course in good time.

Jim Aeby

Remember you are the one who can maneuver easily, while they cannot.

At night, fishing boats often display their legal lights for the type of fishing in progress, along with a welter of spotlights and illuminations. You can identify them from a long way off. But their lights make it difficult to decide which side to pass because the directional light clusters designed to give this information are lost among brighter spotlights. Familiarize yourself with major fishing seasons, such as salmon or swordfish months. Plan to avoid the coasts off Pacifica, Monterey, Santa Barbara, and much of Southern California during these congested seasons. Day fishing boats usually anchor in or near the kelp, or can be seen close to artificial fishing reefs. ChartGuide and other well known navigational portfolios often mark good fishing areas, so you can shape your course away from them.

Most commercial fishing people appreciate it when you alter course. Incidently, the same folk can give you valuable advice on little known anchorages that can provide welcome shelter on windy days, especially north of Point Conception. This book owes a great deal to the insights, friendship, and advice of commercial fishing people. They know the water above and below surface in ways we small boat sailors never will.

Military Activities

Whether we like it or not, some of this nation's most important defense facilities are concentrated in our cruising areas. Two relatively far offshore islands in Southern California, San Nicolas and San Clemente, are off limits to the public. The most obtrusive military areas are the vast segments of the Pacific Missile Range that radiate out to sea from Vandenburg Air Force Base off Points Arguello and Conception. Further down the coast lies Point Mugu facing San Nicolas Island. These defense bases cover the firing tracks of missiles and satellite rockets launched from the mainland. You must time your passage to cross the Pacific Missile Range when it is not in use. Otherwise, you will be chased by patrol boats and authoritative aircraft with loud hailers. No way can you continue until firing is over. You can contact the Duty Range Officers by calling "Plead Control" on Channel 16 (see Chapters 10 and 13). If you time your transits for holidays and weekends, then you have a good chance of a clear passage. Often at night, the firing ranges are inactive.

Oil Exploration

Whatever your views on big oil, you must contend with a boom in oil exploration and drilling in our waters. Most oil activity is presently concentrated off Points Arguello and Point Conception. The waters of the Santa Barbara Channel are dotted with enormous oil drilling platforms, surrounded with unlighted mooring buoys. Considerable small boat traffic runs between the rigs and the mainland. For months on end, temporary drilling platforms may be anchored offshore, engaged in exploratory drilling. The positions of fixed platforms are marked on government charts. You should consult Local Notices to Mariners for information on new rigs. Oil drilling gives us one welcome navigational bonus. The platforms make excellent landmarks in thick weather, especially since they sound 2-second horn blasts every 20 seconds. The oil rigs, marked with their individual names, are well lit with quick flashing lights at each platform corner. If you are tempted to have a close look at an oil rig, then stay at least 300 feet away from the platform to avoid trailing lines and gantries. Keep well clear of drilling ships anchored in open water. Their anchoring systems can extend up to 5000 feet from the vessel. Marked by orange and white vertically striped buoys, they are equipped with lights that flash 4 seconds.

Lesley Newhart

Oil facilities, like commercial shipping, are something to be avoided.

Artificial oil islands can be seen just south of Rincon Point near Carpinteria and in Long Beach harbor. Well lit, they should be

Lesley Newhart

treated like oil platforms: keep clear.

A great deal of complex oceanographic research gets conducted in California waters. Occasionally you may sight a large drogue or temporary buoys that are not marked on your charts. They may be military markers, or research stations. These short-term markers are identified in Local Notices, but few small boat sailors track these publications on a regular basis. Unlit white tanker moorings may be seen close inshore, off oil storage facilities. In a way, all these temporary markers are a hazard, in the sense they can confuse your navigation. The best advice is to rely on permanent navigational marks recorded on up-to-date charts.

An increasing hazard, against which you can do little to protect yourself, is unmarked floating objects. An astonishing amount of flotsam can be seen in California waters: logs from the Pacific Northwest, crates, telegraph poles, oil drums, even semi-submerged containers washed overboard in a distant Pacific storm. Most floating debris can be relatively innocuous. Though readily spotted by day, they represent a formidable hazard at night, when the first warning you may have is the crash as you hit a large log at full speed. Your only defense is to keep a sharp lookout, and to be mentally prepared for the possibility of an accidental holing. The remote danger of such a collision is the overriding reason why all passage-making yachts should carry a liferaft. Be encouraged, however: our moderate weather means that far fewer large objects are washed overboard or float away. You are more likely to hit a whale than a submerged log.

Peter Howorth

Seas and Swells

"We were in 20-foot swells..." "It was really rough. The waves were at least 10-feet high..." How often have you heard people describe their tribulations in rough weather. The swells always seem to get larger by the minute, for the motion rather than the wind tends to scare people into exaggeration. Yes, you can encounter large swells off the California coast, but they rarely exceed 8 feet in summer. Occasionally in winter, 20-foot swells off Point Arena and Point Conception have been known to occur. Five-foot swells can generate extremely unpleasant motion, especially if wind waves are setting across the prevailing swell, as often happens when a southeaster blows in winter.

The term "sea" refers to water disturbances caused by wind velocities both in our cruising area and further away. Swells develop when these disturbances move out downwind from their place of origin, often for hundreds, even thousands, of miles. The heights of seas and swells are measured as the vertical distance between wave crests and troughs in feet. Thus, an eight-foot wave measures eight feet from trough to crest. The waves may have a period of 20 seconds, the time it takes successive wave crests to move past the observer. Obviously, the height and interval of waves are of vital importance to small boat owners. Swells persist after the gale has passed overhead, and are often a greater danger to a vessel than the winds that generate them.

Swells formed far offshore sometimes batter the California coast, expending their final energy on beaches and cliffs. Islands and headlands can bend the direction of swells to conform to the shape of the coastline. As the swell approaches eastward toward shore, it may be affected by rapid shallowing, which tends to heighten the waves. In the Santa Barbara Channel, for example, sometimes tropical cyclones or intense winter storms far offshore bring heavy swells to the California coast even when calm conditions prevail inshore. You should exercise extreme care when passage-making under such conditions, for a small inboard engine is practically powerless against such swell conditions.

Jeff Barnhart

Afternoon wind waves, a common phenomenon in both summer and winter, can be particularly troublesome when coasting northward along the Big Sur or Santa Cruz coast. Because the afternoon northwesterlies kick up sharp whitecaps in a few short minutes, wind waves can impose a one- or two-foot wave on top of a four-foot swell in an hour or so. When the afternoon breeze funnels through narrow gaps in the mainland, or they blow against an ebbing tide, as they can do in the Golden Gate, the wind-against-tide effect raises very nasty, steep-sided seas, which can be dangerous for the inexperienced."Windy Lane," the famous alley where stronger wind cascades from Point Conception along the northern shores of the Channel Islands, can generate nasty wind waves. Be prepared to reef, and to steer off downwind for safety and comfort, if possible. If possible, keep hatches well battened down.

The celebrated Potatopatch on San Francisco bar is notorious for its turbulent, breaking waves. When wind sets against the tide sluicing out of the Golden Gate, you know you have dallied in the Potatopatch too long and you promise yourself you'll never do so again. Keep clear of this hazardous place, even in calm weather.

Currents

Generally speaking, currents are insignificant to California passage making. Locally, however, they can achieve one or two knots, and acquire more importance, especially in light weather and for racing sailors. We note such occurrences in the sailing directions.

> A current runs S parallel to the California coast out for about 300 miles for most of the year. The velocity rarely exceeds 0.2 knots, but is influenced by prevailing winds. Strong N winds tend to increase it, S winds to diminish it.
>
> The Davidson Inshore Current, named after George himself, flows weakly N along the coast between San Diego and Point Conception from July through February, and between Point Conception and Cape Flattery, Washington from November through February. The Davidson rarely exceeds one knot.

Neither of these currents are of real interest to the small boat sailor, but government tidal atlases provide general information. Both the military and the oil companies have supported long-term research into local and coastal currents and tidal streams, but, much of the resulting information is not in the public domain.

Tides are relatively minor players in California cruising. Tides move to center stage in San Francisco Bay, so I discuss them in more detail in Chapter 8.

There is no need to purchase government tide tables each year. Many marine stores hand out free tables. Electronic afficionados can buy world-wide computer programs, which provide tidal predictions for any cruising ground on earth.

Fog

Fog and low clouds, a common phenomenon in California waters, so much so, I tend to take them for granted. On many days, the inversion layer is such that the grey cloud base hovers about 500 to 800 feet above the sea surface. Visibility will be a half mile or more, safe enough for passage-making, provided you maintain a careful lookout and lay a safe course to your destination. Such fog periods last ten days, giving you enough time to make the passage from Southern California to the Bay area under power and in comfort. Low ceilings of 500 to 800 feet are prime conditions for a northbound voyage. You can sight land about a mile off. When a perceptible darkening of the fog betrays the presence of cliffs, or a white flash of surf breaking on rocks penetrates through the grey, you'll begin to discern yellow, sandy beaches at some distance. Always be sure to hoist a radar reflector and keep a close watch out for fishing boats and shipping. Radar, GPS, and Loran have made life much easier in foggy conditions, but you should always sound the correct fog signals and check your electronic fixes where and whenever possible.

Patrick Short

Thick fog banks, though rare, constitute a real hazard. They tend to be thickest in the early morning hour, will hang close offshore on summers' days. One moment you sail in brilliant conditions, the next you may be unable to see the bow from the bridge or cockpit. With no visibility, you better anchor in shallow water and wait for the fog to clear. At all costs, keep out of shipping lanes and do not attempt to make landfall on a strange coast. You will literally be ashore before you sight even the highest cliff. The golden rule of thick fog is to stay in port until it clears. If you are caught out at sea, sound fog signals, listen for approaching ships, and try to keep clear of traffic lanes.

Seamanship

Anchoring

Anchoring is an art, not a science. The best way to learn anchoring is to sail on other peoples' boats and to participate, observe, and learn. Then ship out in your own boat as skipper and practice and practice again. Find a convenient bay a morning's sail away and spend the afternoon setting and dropping anchor, developing procedures which are as foolproof and easy to understand as you can make them. By the end of the day, I wager you'll be tired, but you and your crew will have the hang of the basics. I went out with a novice crew last year for a day's anchoring off Goleta pier. We set the anchor again and again, approaching different spots, dropping the hook in a precise location, then paying out exactly the right amount of scope to let the anchor to set, the chain to lie along the bottom. We raised anchor under power, under sail alone, bringing the line up-and-down, then breaking out the anchor with a tack to port or starboard. The day was a marvelous lesson not only in the procedures of anchoring, but in the art of judgment and the basic physics of setting an anchor on the bottom. Anchoring is a matter of acquiring the confidence to judge when your anchor is properly set. With practice, you will have learned from observation and trial and error how to anchor safely in the company of other yachts.

Here's a set of principles, which provide a framework for safe and comfortable anchoring:

- **Carry the correct ground tackle** for the job (See Chapter 5). In California waters, this means two anchors, sufficient line for both of them to be used in at least 60 feet of water. The anchors and lines must have adequate fairleads, winches, and cleats.

- In **choosing a clear anchor spot,** cultivate the art of observing telltale signs to determine the best shelter such as dark gusts on the water. Clear away your gear and have the anchor over the bow at the waterline before you make your final pass. In other words, take your time, don't rush it!

- **Anchor with ample scope** (6:1 line, 3:1 chain), even if just stopping for lunch. Make sure your anchor is well dug in before laying out full scope.

- **Anchor well clear** of your neighbors. If they are lying to two anchors, do the same, so that you don't swing into them.

Allow for sufficient depth for the prevailing tidal range, especially when anchoring in shallow water. "Sufficient depth" in most California anchorages is 25 to 30 feet for an average sized yacht. Pay special care when anchored close to sandy beaches which shelve gradually, for example, a common phenomenon at the western end of the Santa Barbara Channel.

In most open roadsteads, such as Pfeiffer on the Big Sur coast, or Cojo Anchorage in the lee of Point Conception, you'll lie to one anchor, swinging in a broad radius with the wind. You might want to lay a second anchor to keep you head to surge, should there be a slight swell running into the anchorage. In more congested quarters, for example in Channel Islands coves, everyone tends to lie to bow and stern anchors, with the bow headed into the direction of the surge. Lying to two anchors is fine if the weather remains moderate. However, if you are subjected to strong winds on your beam, your two anchors

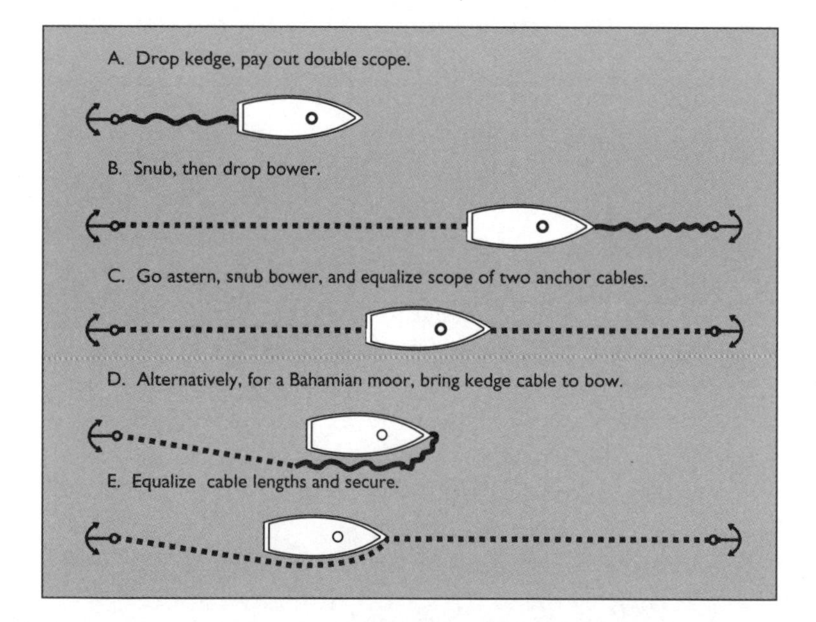

Laying a stern anchor underway (A through C) is easier than putting the bow anchor out first. The Bahamian moor begins the same way (A and B), but the kedge line is then taken to the bow (D) before the rode lengths are equalized.

may cause dragging. Double anchors allow boats to share restricted spaces. Lying in more-or-less parallel lines, spaced short distances apart, accommodates large numbers of boats. Since Southern California weather conditions are normally favorable during the summer months, this strategy works well, if everyone anchors properly and no one fouls their neighbors' anchors.

Some anchorages like Drake's Bay under the lee of Point Reyes, or Cuyler Harbor on San Miguel Island, have well deserved reputations for strong winds. Many yachts will stay put in winds of over 50 knots, lying to two anchors, each laid at 45 degrees to the bow with ample scope.

Congestion is a fact of life in California waters. Anchorages at the Channel Islands resemble marinas especially in high summer and at long weekends. I must confess my immediate reaction to the congestion is to look for another place to anchor, even if it is slightly more exposed than the more favored spot. I try to anchor outside the other boats, in deeper water, in as sheltered a position as possible. If you have to anchor among the crowd, be sure to make several passes through the anchorage, identify a clear spot, then find out where the neighbors' anchors lie. Anchor with sedulous care, dropping the bow anchor first, then backing down as you lay the kedge with the dinghy. In that way, you'll be able to place the boat exactly where you want her, with due attention to your neighbor's lines.

Courtesy

Whether anchoring or already in place, even if someone anchors right on top of you, insist on your rights, but with courtesy. Ask people to reanchor if you have to, but do it with a smile. I've learned you gain nothing by raising your voice, by demanding your rights in a threatening way. If your neighbors are discourteous, simply move elsewhere. And, when you are anchored, remember turn off your generators early and resist the temptation to party loudly. After all, we do go to sea for peace and quiet!

Heavy Weather

Compared with, say, the English Channel or Maine, our waters are blessed with week after week of good passagemaking weather. However, you are almost certain to encounter some rough conditions at some moment in your cruising career, if nothing more than a boisterous Santa Ana or a tussle with strong winds funneling through the Golden Gate. While you can sail for years south of Point Conception and never encounter a summer wind over 25 knots, you can run into nasty conditions north of the Santa Barbara Channel in any month of the year. We are lucky in that extreme storms almost never reach our coasts, but winds of 30 to 40 knots are not uncommon, and even higher velocities occur locally in winter. Very often, the seas are more of a limiting factor than winds. Whatever your cruising plans, you must assume for planning purposes you will encounter strong winds and steep seas. Be prepared: Equip your boat with sound gear, and be practiced in heavy weather seamanship. Rehearse reefing under way on calm days, make sail changes when you have all the time in the world to work out a routine, learn how to walk around on a heeling deck with sure feet. Such basic skills, once acquired, will not fail you on rough days.

Some general pointers:

- Sailing yachts, whatever their size, should have simple slab reefing. This enables you to reduce sail rapidly when encountering strong winds. Time after time, I have had to reef hastily in the Golden Gate or in Windy Lane. I have blessed the efficiencies of modern slab reefing setups. A fully battened mainsail makes reefing much easier, because the sail does not flap when you release the mainsheet.

- If you have a roller-furling jib, try it out partially unrolled in moderate weather and mark the positions for your sheet fairleads for the best leads. Mark your sail at each reef position, too. Your sail will set so much better and you will minimize leach flap. I strongly recommend a removable inner forestay for a small jib, which brings the rig inboard in rough weather and reduces the chance of a jammed roller furler in high seas.

- Always follow the wise old sailor's advice: Reef early and reef well. Only rarely will your speed drop and steering will be much less work.

- If you are passage-making to windward, you will soon find yourself making little or no progress, especially if the wind rises above 25 knots. Even in lesser headwinds, the ride soon becomes uncomfortable, even when reefed down. Consider either heaving-to (see below), or, even better, reaching or running to the nearest convenient and safe anchorage. Almost invariably, the wind will drop at sundown and you will be able to make progress to windward after dark. Yes, I know this sounds cowardly, but I go to sea for pleasure, not to prove my nautical virility. Some years ago, I tried to round Point Conception on a calm summer's morning. By 1100, the northwesterly was blowing 30 knots on the bow, increasing steadily, and my stomach was rebelling. We turned round, ran for Cojo Anchorage, lay in the lee of the Point until 2100. The wind dropped, we had a fine dinner, then motored all night to Morro Bay. Next morning, the unrelenting headwind returned, but we had reached our destination.

- If caught out in a full gale, stay out in open water, lie-to under bare poles or hove-to rather than running for shelter. You are much safer in deep water where seas run more regularly and winds are steadier.

- When the wind pipes up, insist everyone wear safety harnesses on deck. By the same token, don foul weather gear as soon as spray comes aboard. Keep your crew warm and dry.

- If there is a chance of bad weather, monitor weather forecasts with care over a period of at least 12 hours. Never set off on a long passage in the face of a poor weather forecast. Best wait until the system has passed, which means: Never leave long passages to the closing days of your vacation.

I have heard more definitions of gale-force winds at the bar than there are notches on the Beaufort wind scale. In truth, the definition of a gale varies with the experience of the owner and crew, and with the size and seaworthiness of the vessel. I once watched the Cunard Line's flagship, the QE2, steam effortlessly at cruising speed into a force 8 mid-Atlantic gale. The 10-foot swells were barely an inconvenience, the sense of power extraordinary. In the same conditions, I would have been hove-to under drastically reduced sail in a 40-footer.

Heaving-to

Surprisingly few cruising people know how to heave their boats to, so they make no forward progress through the water and lie comfortably athwart wind and sea. A north-south passage to or from the Bay area involves long hours on deck, with sketchy meals indeed if any sea is running. By heaving-to for a couple of hours, you can cook and enjoy a sit-down meal, then wash it up, while losing little ground to leeward. This modest investment in comfort will pay rich dividends in crew morale.

Heaving-to is simplicity itself:

- Search the horizon for any signs of approaching ships and ensure you have adequate searoom to leeward to keep you clear of the land.
- Lay the ship through the wind on to the opposite tack, but leave the jib sheeted in where it is.
- As you pass through the wind, the jib will go aback, while the filling mainsail holds her in place.
- Stabilize the boat with the helm, then lash the wheel or rudder down to leeward, holding the vessel on course. With a little adjustment of the helm, she will lie quietly just off the wind, easing over the swells, while drifting slightly to leeward.
- Go about your business, rejoicing in the peace and quiet, making sure you maintain a careful lookout.
- A word to the wise: **Do not heave-to in shipping lanes, where fishing boats are working, or off busy harbor entrances.**

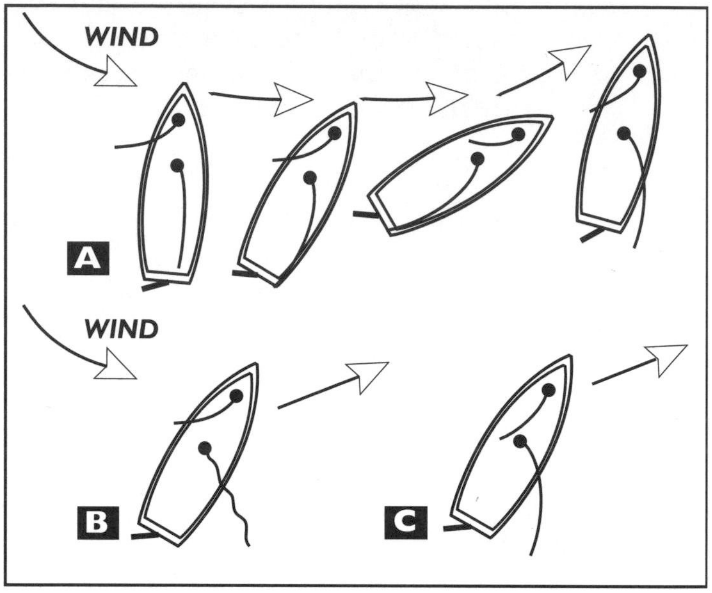

Heaving-to.
Vessel A is hove-to with the jib aback and the helm down. Some designs will vacillate in this mode. Vessel B is lying with main flapping and stays quiet. Vessel C is also lying quietly because both jib and main are sheeted less hard, the jib only just amidships.

In these days of jiffy reefing systems, few people heave-to to reef down or increase sail, but it takes a few seconds to do so, making everything safer on deck.

Night Passages

Night sailing in our congested waters requires displaying the proper lights at all times, and having a working familiarity not only with standard ships' light displays, but with those of trawlers, tugs with tows, and other esoteric vessels. You should exercise special care in crossing shipping lanes at night, especially when in the vicinity of the Golden Gate or busy harbors like San Diego or San Pedro, where a blaze of shore lights or busy small boat traffic may obscure you among a blizzard of radar blips on a big-ship bridge,

During the summer, the prevailing winds die down at sunset, leaving you with many hours of calm or near-calm conditions. Most night passages involve long hours of motoring under autopilot, making watchkeeping at best a monotonous pastime, especially when your eyelids are heavy. Stress on your crew the importance of stretching regularly, of maintaining a 360-degree lookout and checking the compass course. Instances of yachts running ashore when left to their own devices under autopilot are legion. Please do not join this lubberly crowd! At least once an hour, clip on and take a walk around the deck checking for loose gear. In foggy conditions, warn everyone to keep an eye out for dense fog banks and deteriorating visibility.

Setting watches is essential at night, even if you do not maintain them during the day. I recommend starting night watches immediately after dinner, rotating them each night, so that everyone has a turn at the graveyard hours. Most skippers use three- to four- hour watches. Normally, one experienced watchkeeper is sufficient in calm and moderate weather, especially if the autopilot is in use, but two-person watches with frequent changes of helmsperson are essential in gale conditions. Do not hesitate to call the entire crew on deck if a major sail change or reefing are necessary.

The skipper should also be a watchkeeper, although I never completely relax when off watch, especially if the crew on deck have not sailed with me before. **Impress on everyone that if in doubt they should call you without hesitation. This is particularly important when the watch suspects it is on collision course with a ship. Better to be called unnecessarily than at the last minute, in a panic situation.**

In these days of GPS and Loran, night navigation is fairly simple. However, monitor your passing landmarks, such as major lighthouses and navigation buoys.

Brief your watchkeepers about lights which may be sighted or disappear astern during their watches.

- Give them information on light characteristics, so they can check them on deck.

- Teach them a simple way of timing seconds without a stop-watch. If nothing else, the exercise will help pass the time.

If a change of course is required when abeam of a light, or the sighting is of critical importance, insist that you be called on deck. And at night, always maintain a dead reckoning plot on the chart, in case your GPS malfunctions at the wrong moment. A Davis Light and Buoy Card, readily available in marine stores, is a useful compass accessory for night passages.

Just occasionally, you may pick up a slight land breeze at night, which enables you to slip to windward close inshore, your sails just filling to a warm air smelling of dust and chaparral. If luck will have it, you can enjoy such a wind on a full moon night. The effect is truly magical. I once sailed along the remote Santa Barbara Channel coast from Gaviota toward Point Conception on such a late summer's night. I'll never forget it: Sitting out on the sea as it shone a brilliant silver from the full moon, the dark tendrils of the kelp bed just offshore stood out black in the still water. In the complete silence, with no lights ashore, I listened to the light gurgle at the bow as the boat slightly heeled, watching the sails gleaming white in the moonlight. And for a moment I felt at one with the sea.

Lesley Newhart

CHAPTER 7

Passage Making Strategies

Passages along the California coast fall into two broad categories, non-stop voyages with the intention of covering as much mileage as possible in the shortest possible time, and more leisurely cruises from port to port. Most people traversing the coast prefer to take their time, to explore different harbors along the way. Whatever your plans, the most successful passage-making in California depends on careful planning beforehand. If you are one of those sailors who leaves the Golden Gate and turns left at the proverbial lights outside hoping for the best, then stop reading now! This chapter discusses some of the strategies you, as a more careful skipper, can adopt to reach your destination in safety and comfort without battling head winds and steep seas or running ashore on Point Conception in zero visibility.

> *A Coast Pilot a few years old is a valuable volume to have aboard. And since its price is about that of a mediocre meal and bottle of wine, I think it is a good bargain well worth it for every small-boat navigator.*
>
> Leonard Eyges
> *The Practical Pilot*

Resources

Planning your voyage requires the correct charts and sailing directions for the task. You need not carry a vast library of navigational publications in our waters, such as you need in, say, Maine, or Scandinavia with their many islands and intricate channels. But you need the basics:

Charts

The accompanying text figure shows the main NOAA chart coverage for passages through Central and Southern California. You can buy these individually, which will cost you a bundle, or purchase bound sets published by Bay and Delta Yachtsman (Northern California), Chart-Kit (Southern California), and ChartGuide (Southern California and some points north, also Catalina Island). All three sets are reduced copies of NOAA charts, which technically should not be used for navigation. In practice, many people use them for harbor and close-in pilotage, but I would recommend using a full-size chart for all long distance passage making and dead reckoning, and in situations where you are plotting bearings. Each folio set comes with additional information, gleaned from a variety of sources. ChartGuide is especially comprehensive, providing

NAUTICAL CHART DIRECTORY

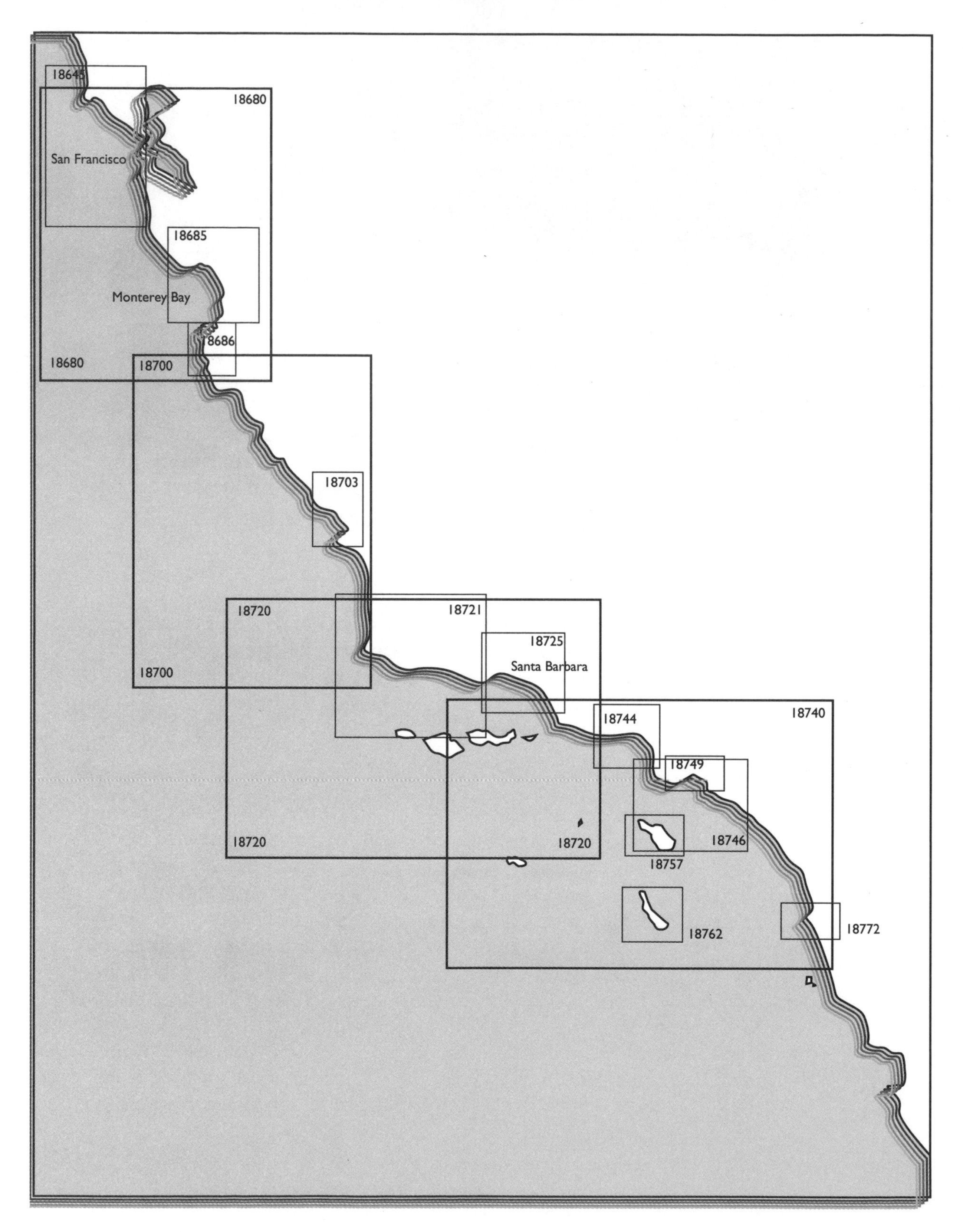

potted information on fishing reefs, facilities ashore, and other matters, laid out in panels on the charts or in the margins. (For further information, see Resources section at the end of the book.)

Whether you choose a portfolio or buy charts for your specific needs, keep them up-to-date, either by having them corrected, or by getting on the mailing list for Local Notices to Mariners, which contain a mine of information. Many Notices concern changes in regulations, temporary oil drilling activity, and other esoterica of relevance to big ships. But it is worth wading through the detail for the occasional priceless nugget of information.

Some people xerox NOAA charts at full size, indeed some stores offer this service. Whatever you do, make sure you have comprehensive coverage covering not only your line of passage, but alternative ports. I have never forgotten the experience of making landfall on the British Virgin Islands after a trans-Atlantic crossing with the aid of a sketch map in a charter company advertisement in a national sailing magazine! We were bound for the Bahamas and ran low on diesel fuel, necessitating a change of course off the margins of our passage charts. Never again!

Sailing Directions

This book, and the companion volume, *Cruising Guide to Southern California's Offshore Islands* (Caractacus Corporation, Santa Barbara, 1992) cover the basics for small boat navigators, and, of course, I recommend you carry them aboard!

Kimball Livingston's *Sailing the Bay* (Chronicle Books, San Francisco, 1981) is a minor classic, which is, alas, out of print, but a wonderfully evocative, and sensible, account of San Francisco Bay sailing. Haunt second hand book stores for a copy!

Charlie's Charts of the U.S. Pacific Coast (Seattle,WA to San Diego, CA) by Charles and Margo Wood (Charlie's Charts, Surrey, B.C., Canada, 1995) is designed primarily for yachts taking passage along the entire coast from Seattle to San Diego. The focus is on major ports and anchorages. Excellent maps and plans, plenty of commonsense information.

United States Coast Pilot 7 (Pacific Coast: California, Oregon, Washington, and Hawaii) (NOAA, 28th edition, 1993) is a veritable Bible of navigational information and bureaucratic regulations for the West Coast. Buy a copy for reference and for leisurely browsing, but do not try and use it while on passage. The information is too dense and requires careful matching with the relevant charts.

All sailing directions must be used in conjunction with charts. They are useless without.

Other Publications

If you have up-to-date charts, you have no need of light or radiobeacon lists when sailing our waters. The government produces tide tables annually, also current charts and the annual *Nautical Almanac,* the latter essential for celestial navigators. A current chart is essential, especially for the Golden Gate, but many marine stores hand out pocket-sized tide tables, which save you the expense of buying the government computations. Alternatively, you can purchase a tidal calendar for your waters, readily available at outlets like West Marine.

That's it, unless you want a videotape of the Channel Islands or the San Francisco Bay area, or feel you want to ship out with Richard Henry Dana, some wildlife books, or shoreside guides which inventory attractions ashore. The selection of land guides is so enormous and growing so rapidly, that recommendations here would be out of date before they appeared in print. Any good local bookstore will satisfy your needs.

General Strategies

Unless you are bound from the mainland to the Channel Islands or Catalina, almost all longer passages in our waters are to windward or to leeward. Whatever your destination, your advance planning, based on a set of fundamental principles, ensures a comfortable passage:

- Lay off courses to carry you clear of all navigational hazards. For instance, there's a nasty rock 220 yards off Point Conception, which has claimed many a victim trying to take a short cut in its day. To carry you past the point, keep at least 0.75 mile off the land, even more in rough weather.

- Maximize the prevailing weather conditions for the season of the year, using the various hours of day and night with proportional care between calm and windy hours.

- A good cruise plan reflects the objectives of your passage, also the realities of weather conditions and time available. For example, a harbor-hopping passage from Monterey to San Simeon Bay in summer needs careful timing to take advantage of afternoon winds, the reality of an unlighted anchorage at your destination, and off-lying rocks at Piedras Blancas just before your destination. The solution: time your passage so you arrive at San Simeon in late afternoon, in good visibility.

- Whatever your plans, be flexible enough to allow for sudden, and, if necessary, drastic changes in the case of bad weather, an emergency, or simply a desire to do something different. Plan to have charts of all alternative ports and anchorages aboard.

- Wise plans reflect the age and expertise of your crew. A crew of young, prehensile sailors can undertake a non-stop, offshore passage from San Pedro to San Francisco in a 35-footer with impunity. An elderly couple or a family with small children will have quite different plans.

These principles, though obvious, are often overlooked. I'm always surprised when I meet exhausted crews who have taken on too much and tired themselves out in the early days of a cruise. People who venture unprepared out of San Francisco Bay or north of Point Conception in entirely unsuitable weather conditions overtax their endurance levels.

The decision to start or not is left to individual skippers. Britain's Royal Ocean Racing Club starts every ocean race on schedule whatever the weather conditions. You can be sure those skippers have thought out their race strategies and alternatives very carefully if they do decide

Graham Pomeroy

to start in the face of a 40-knot gale. Every cruising sailor, whether in a trailer yacht or a plush megayacht, faces the same decision-making process every time he or she puts to sea. The decision to leave or not to leave is the question. With careful passage planning, answers become easier to make. Again, I reiterate: if in doubt, stay in port until you are absolutely comfortable about leaving. And, if you do set out and find conditions unbearably uncomfortable or deteriorating after 10 or even 20 miles, please turn back without hesitation. Better safe than sorry. And I wager as you snuggle down in your comfortable bunk as the northwesterly hums in the rigging, you'll thank your lucky stars you were wise, not foolish.

Remember, only the foolish go to sea to prove they are tough. The best sailors are quiet, low-key cowards, who will do anything they can to avoid bad weather or strong headwinds. They know the inevitability of meeting both one day and so never leave port unless well prepared for unexpected weather conditions.

Passage-making northbound: Windward passages

Whether we like it or not, we spend an inordinate amount of time voyaging to windward in California. The prevailing N to NW winds follow the shoreline and often blow with considerable violence. Without careful timing, a windward passage from Southern California to the San Francisco Bay area and perhaps points beyond can turn into a brain-numbing nightmare of headwinds and pounding waves.

Strategies for non-stop passages to windward

Relatively few people elect to sail non-stop from a southern port to the San Francisco Bay area unless they are in a medium- to larger-sized powerboat or are on a delivery trip. Even then, it may pay you to stop at strategic points such as Morro Bay, San Simeon, or Santa Cruz Harbor to await favorable conditions.

Sailing non-stop is a rarity in this day and age of efficient, lightweight diesels. The few skippers I know who have made this demanding passage have headed resolutely far offshore on the starboard tack, taking the fluctuations in prevailing winds as they come. By the time they are 50 or more miles offshore, they will encounter the sometimes more dependable NW winds which blow away from the coast. There is a danger, however, you will run out of wind far offshore, and you may encounter large swells that will inhibit rapid progress. A passage from, say, Santa Barbara or Channel Islands Harbor will take you offshore hard on the wind and well clear of Point Conception. You can plan on four or five days on this windward course before tacking inshore. The timing of the inshore tack requires nice judgment and depends on the course you make good to windward under prevailing conditions. This is where GPS is invaluable, for you can track your progress to the mile, then predict with reasonable confidence where your landfall will be. Make progressively shorter tacks as you near the San Francisco Bay area. This passage option is only for larger, well found yachts with experienced crews. Do not attempt this passage in mid-winter. Nor can it be recommended for single-handed sailors.

I have met only one skipper who enjoyed this passage. He was in a well-founded 40-footer, had a tough young crew who thrived on hard thrashes to windward, and steady winds of 15 to 20 knots most of the way. "The moonlight nights were magnificent 50 miles offshore, once we cleared the main shipping lanes." Even so, they encountered hours of calm, bumpy conditions when heading inshore. It took ten days before they sailed triumphantly through the Golden Gate. Richard Henry Dana made the passage several times. His fastest voyage was 20 days from Santa Barbara to San Francisco. His ship, the *Alert,* was under reefed topsails for a week and was blown a good way toward Hawaii.

Unless you are a true fanatic and just like windward passages, or you are racing, I strongly recommend you break up the passage and make progress northward close to the coast.

Lesley Newhart

According to George Vancouver, a skipper can sail long distances close inshore at night along the Central California coast, using the light NE land breeze to move you gently to windward. Such winds are erratic in their occurrence and they cannot be relied upon as part of a passage plan. However, you may encounter them when motoring at night, in which case—enjoy!

A few bold souls wait for winter southeasters, then ride the favorable wind far north of Point Conception. I have myself made the passage from Santa Barbara to the Golden Gate in a fast 40-footer in 34 hours, with a strong southeaster at our tail, but it was a gamble, for we knew well that the wind would switch on to our nose directly the system passed through. And so it did, just hours after we reached port. We made the passage because we had to. I would not recommend the strategy for most people, especially as southeasters turn the coast into a dangerous lee shore.

Powering non-stop is a viable option for both power and sailing yachts, especially those able to maintain cruising speeds of 10 knots or more, when the miles melt away. Northbound, the best course is the rhumb line, passing well clear of Point Conception and other headlands. If fuel economy is your goal, then consider taking four or five days and harbor hopping, to minimize head winds and seas.

Non-stop windward passages in Southern California are frustrating, often boring, especially if you are under sail. Under typical summer conditions, you will be lucky if you have six to eight hours of sailing breeze a day, from late morning to sunset. The rest of the time, you will be under power. Unless you prefer long hours becalmed in lumpy seas, or you have a specific destination about 8 hours ahead, I then recommend harbor hopping and motoring to windward in the calm hours. Once again, night-time land breezes can help you along, especially in late summer. Some bold souls ride northeasterly Santa Anas winds up the coast, but if you do so, have strong gear, be prepared for sudden gusts, and tuck in one or two reefs, especially when sailing near the mouths of canyons. The bonus is smooth water, especially inshore, but only experienced crews use these conditions, and even they hesitate. One of my most memorable passages off California was when we were caught on a lee shore at Santa Barbara Island. A Santa Ana came in unexpectedly. We clawed up the anchor, set a double-reefed main and storm jib, and enjoyed a magnificent sail northwestward past Anacapa Island and on into Santa Barbara. The Santa Ana dropped when we were two miles from port, just as the rising sun clothed the mountains in orange light. A memorable sail, for we had a stout ship. But it was rough!

Harbor-hopping northbound: Windward passages

If harbor hopping, the identical strategy applies both north and south of Point Conception: **Make progress to**

windward under power during the calm night and early morning hours. Stay in port and go for a walk ashore while the afternoon northerlies blow. If you are a purist who turns puce at the word engine, be my guest and sail from port to port. It will take you two to three times longer to reach your destination, and you will acquire a well earned reputation as a glutton for punishment. Personally, I thank the powers that be for a reliable diesel and scurry to windward whenever calm conditions permit. Then I can enjoy all the fast sailing I want on the leeward leg. Exactly the same strategy works best for a power boat, especially a trawler yacht, even if she has stabilizers, and you're in no hurry with only comfort in mind. As a matter of deliberate strategy, I always plan my windward legs in short, realistic bites, trying to time my arrival for mid-morning, leaving either after sunset or as early as 0400 if need be, so I don't have to fight headwinds. In terms of an overall cruising plan, this means that I harbor hop to windward, then sail longer passages downwind. Such a strategy works like a charm, especially if there are inexperienced sailors aboard.

It follows that the best conditions for passages to windward are during calmer periods, especially those when fog and low clouds mantle the coast. As we saw in Chapter 3, such cycles tend to last about 10 days, especially in early summer, and sometimes in fall. Very often, the afternoon winds and sea conditions are so light you can keep going day and night; a boon when making the long passage along the Big Sur coast, where about your only shelter is Pfeiffer anchorage. People often ask me what months are best for heading north to the San Francisco Bay area. I always tell them to look to June or September, though periods of calm conditions at night and foggy conditions in early morning can occur any time in summer and in winter. The chances of headwinds at night are somewhat higher in calm weather.

Slogging your way north in Southern California waters calls for long hours of hugging the mainland, motoring from port to port. Until you reach King Harbor or Marina del Rey, your options remain simple. On the next leg, shape a northbound course outside Anacapa Island during the night, arriving there in early morning. Just as you reach the Anacapa Passage by Santa Cruz Island, the afternoon westerly should fill in. Then take a long inshore tack under sail alone to Santa Barbara harbor. From there, it's a 40-mile passage from the city marina to

Cojo, an 8-hour journey that is best tackled by leaving at about 0400, then picking up the afternoon winds off Gaviota, as they sometimes allow you to lay a course for Cojo anchorage. If bound for San Francisco Bay, I would resist the temptation to visit the Channel Islands until your return passage. The slog to windward up Windy Lane can be very uncomfortable. After all, why motor, if you can sail?

Further northbound, the timing of your passage revolves around two key legs: the rounding of Point Conception and the long haul from Morro Bay or San Simeon to Monterey or Santa Cruz. Chapter 9 describes Point Conception waters more fully, and stresses that Cojo Anchorage in the lee of the point is the ideal jumping off point for rounding. Under prevailing summer conditions or in foggy weather, enjoy dinner, then up anchor and motor northward. By dawn you will be well clear of Conception and Arguello, rejoicing at your brilliant timing.

I would adopt much the same strategy when heading north along the Big Sur coast. You can shorten the journey considerably by spending a day at San Simeon Bay. A trip to the Castle and its ocean views will give you a foretaste of conditions further up the coast. When the wind drops, motor north all night, laying a course to keep you clear of all dangers. With a boat speed of 5 to 6 knots, you'll be well up to Point Sur, or even in Monterey Bay before the next day's afternoon winds set in. And if you cannot make it that far, you can dodge into Pfeiffer for a few hours, where there is reasonable shelter. A few bold skippers simply head inshore and find a temporary anchoring spot until the wind moderates. This may be a viable strategy in moderate weather, but is suicidal when any swell is running. Best leave such strategies to fishermen, who are used to operating close inshore.

You will sometimes receive help from a northbound current. Stay inside the 50-fathom line. You will avoid some of the large swells that run further offshore. Beware, however, of small fishing craft close inshore, and of thick fog banks. California's coast is to be taken lightly. Maintain an accurate DR at all times, even if you have GPS aboard. What if your favorite electronic device suddenly malfunctions?

You can make northbound passages comfortably in fall, winter, and spring, but you must monitor weather forecasts carefully. The calmest conditions of all sometimes occur in late fall, when pressure is high in the interior and Santa Anas are blowing in Southern California. If you encounter such weather, motor like hell for your destination. The landmarks will be clear, the sea negligible, and wind almost non-existent. I have only made the passage once under these conditions. We were in shorts and T-shirts much of the time. Do not attempt a northbound passage in unsettled weather. You are asking for all hell to break loose, and it will, on your very nose.

A typical itinerary northbound from the Santa Barbara Channel has several potential stopping places: Cojo Anchorage to Avila, Morro Bay, or San Simeon Bay, then to Monterey or Santa Cruz, on to Half Moon Bay, and finally the Golden Gate. With favorable conditions, the typical windward passage under power takes about five days from Point Conception.

If you are from Southern California, time your destination arrival for the late morning or early afternoon. You can then enjoy one of California's great cruising experiences: entering San Francisco Bay under the Golden Gate Bridge. Last time we did it, we passed under the bridge in a dense fog with a 20-knot wind behind us. Abruptly the fog lifted like a curtain. We screamed on towards Berkeley in bright, sparkling sunshine, feeling elated with satisfaction and sense of achievement.

Strategies for southbound passages

Theoretically at any rate, the wind is astern, so you just sit back and let her rip. If the northwesterlies are in form, the passage south from the Bay is definitely one of those times when the sailor has it over a powerboat skipper. I have vivid memories of surfing downwind past Point Sur, paralleling off to port the coastal mountains mantled in barreling clouds. The low rocks of Piedras Blancas came into sight at dusk. Our ship's main and jib were set wing and wing sailing downwind with the sea dead astern all afternoon. But the passage is more complicated than just laying off a course and heading along the coast non-stop, unless you are prepared to countenance long hours of motoring.

Just as when you head north, you must take advantage of the diurnal wind patterns when heading south. Unless you are racing non-stop from the Bay to Santa Barbara or Catalina Island, as people do, I recommend doing the trip in three or four relatively long legs. On the first day, I would leave the Bay at slack water, timing departure to use the first of the ebb and the midday wind to speed you rapidly on your way. Then spend the first night at Half Moon Bay, rising early the next morning

Point Sur Lighthouse.

Piedras Blancas Lighthouse.

for a full day's passage to Monterey Bay. Again, time your passage for maximum exposure to the afternoon winds. This time, use the winds rather than avoiding them. (Some people prefer to go all the way through to Santa Cruz in one day. It doesn't matter either way.) The leg from Monterey Bay down the Big Sur coast will involve a night at sea: Time your passage to take advantage of the winds and make mileage down the Big Sur coast in daylight. Such scheduling should have you off Morro Bay at dawn, a good choice in clear weather. In foggy conditions, I would leave Monterey Bay at night, and so allow yourself to enter port at your destination in the clear late afternoon hours. The fog can be very thick off Morro Bay.

Apart from the fact that Morro Bay is an attractive port, it is the ideal jumping off harbor for your memorable passage round Point Conception. Again, a successful passage is a matter of timing. Leave harbor comfortably after breakfast. As you clear the land, the wind will fill in astern, sucking you southward past Point Arguello and into the turmoil of Point Conception. If the wind shows signs of piping up, best put in a reef early in the game, as gusts can come in suddenly and lay you on your beam ends. With a stout breeze, you will have ample daylight in summer to tuck yourself into Cojo well in time for dinner. However, if night falls, do not attempt to find Cojo after dark. It is unlighted. Best stay in open water and reconcile yourself to a night at sea.

Unless conditions are quiet, resist the temptation of coming inshore north of Conception. Nasty swells can take the wind out of your sails and the terrain is brutal and unforgiving. I was once close inshore off Arguello on a calm winter's day in a fast powerboat, close to the unforgiving rocks. Suddenly, the skipper opened up to full throttle and spun the boat offshore. We climbed a huge, vertical-faced swell which swept inshore without warning. Had he not been watching offshore, we would have ended up capsized on the rocks. You can never relax in this vicinity.

Whatever the conditions, stay sufficiently offshore when sailing downwind to stay well clear of outlying dangers, especially of Point Arguello and its missile gantries, but well inside the commercial shipping lanes that pass about 10 to 20 miles offshore. The entire coast is lit by well spaced major lights, so navigation should not be a problem.

Once south of Point Conception, the weather conditions moderate dramatically, to the point sometimes that you may find yourself becalmed, sails aback, almost without warning. If you sail past Conception in the middle of the day, you will normally have sufficient westerly to carry you a considerable distance toward your next destination. Options include Cuyler Harbor on San Miguel Island, the anchorages along the north coast of Santa Cruz Island, even Santa Barbara harbor, although it lies 40 miles to leeward.

But a word of warning: On no account try to make a landfall on the extreme western end of San Miguel Island, especially in reduced visibility. The area is a morass of unlit rocks, uncharted currents, and submerged reefs and outcrops. Stay inshore of the island, identify Harris Point midway along the north coast, then steer inshore.

As you sail eastward in the Santa Barbara Channel, winds lighten and seas moderate, but the same strategy for passage making to leeward applies. Make good use of the afternoon winds.

If you do plan to sail non-stop from the Golden Gate to the Santa Barbara Channel or ports beyond, then what course should you take? Usually, when bound for Catalina or San Diego, I am faced with several decisions to make: Whether to pass outside the Channel Islands, or pass through the Santa Barbara Channel? And if bound for Santa Barbara or Ventura, whether to head inshore at Point Conception, or shape a different course, planning to spend the night at Secate, Refugio, or some other leeward anchorage? As always, skippers contradict one another, but here are some points worth considering to help you decide your course:

- To Point Conception, the rhumb line course appears to be most commonly used, aiming to pass between 2 and 5 miles off the point.

- Nearly everyone I have talked to complained of progressively lightening winds outside the Channel Islands, with a high probability of nighttime calms in the entrance to the San Pedro Channel, especially in summer. Most skippers seem to elect to ride "Windy Lane" down the inshore coasts of the Channel Islands, then head outside Anacapa Island, and from there stay some distance offshore into San Pedro Bay or head for Catalina Island.

Those who hug the mainland south of Anacapa Island will most likely, but not invariably, enjoy the sailor's kiss of death: flat calm at night.

If you decide to head into Santa Barbara from Point Conception in late morning, stay well offshore, on the edges of Windy Lane, then shape a course toward the mainland once Santa Cruz Island is well abeam. You will then reach fast toward the coast. Should the wind drop come evening, you may be lucky enough to pick up the light SE breeze that sometimes wafts in at about sunset. Never, never head inshore and follow the coastline east of Point Conception. The scenery is spectacular, but the wind drops early in evening, and you will just sit there.

The strategy to leeward involves judicious harbor hopping and making your priority the proper use of the afternoon winds. After all, you either have had, or will have, more than enough of your faithful engine bound to windward.

Once in the Los Angeles area, plan rhumb line courses to your destination. If bound for San Diego, stay offshore and clear of the commercial shipping bound for San Pedro and Long Beach. Again, keep your stops to a minimum and plan to get south as fast as possible.

A pleasant way to reach Enseñada in early May is to stop at Newport Beach and join hundreds of other crews on the annual Newport to Enseñada Race. All you need is a PHRF handicap, provided you enter in advance. The race is not only fun, but a magnificent spectacle. Entrants run the full gamut from ultra-dedicated racing crews to club racers, and dozens of yachts that go along for the spectacle and the partying in Enseñada. It is an unforgettable experience to drift southward surrounded by hundreds of red and green lights. The Enseñada Race is the ultimate cruise in company, especially with gourmet cuisine, even for the diehard cruising family. Again, opinions vary as to whether you stay out or work your way inshore. A course which takes the middle ground, some distance offshore, but not out of touch of land, seems the most conservative and reliable strategy.

The problem with the Enseñada Race is that you have to slog your way home. Unless you are lucky enough to encounter a rare southeaster, as happens on occasion, otherwise you have a long beat or a prolonged motor sail back to San Diego in front of you.

We southern sailors enjoy one advantage. At least we get our windward work over at the beginning of the cruise, so, as you reach your destination, you can sit back, relax, and know the worst is over. (Perhaps I should mention that I have classic sailor's luck. The wind invariably dies or blows in the opposite direction to my destination. Of course, every time I want to sail south past Point Conception, it's flat calm... and blowing from NW at 40 knots when I am bound north!)

Passages across the wind: Mainland to offshore islands

Sooner or later, most California sailors visit the offshore islands of Southern California. Invariably, they reach them after an open-water passage from the mainland of the Santa Barbara Channel or the Los Angeles area. A passage from, say, Newport Beach to Catalina Island, or from Santa Barbara to Santa Cruz Island, will bring you hard on the wind for the first few hours, then allow you to ease your sails onto a close reach for the last few miles. If you enjoy motoring, plan to leave early in the morning so you are anchored at the islands before the afternoon winds fill in. Those who prefer to sail usually leave about 1100, pick up the strengthening westerlies, and arrive in the late afternoon after 3 to 6 hours sailing. The return passage is normally a comfortable reach. If you depart about noon, the prevailing winds should carry you home in comfortable style.

The major complication of a passage to the northern Channel Islands is the famous Windy Lane, the zone of strong winds that blow down the islands' inshore side. It may be blowing 30 knots close to Santa Cruz Island when it is calm at Channel Islands harbor or Ventura. If you are even slightly doubtful about the island winds, try calling a yacht anchored there, or check National Weather Service weather. A sure sign of windy conditions offshore: tumbling clouds on the peaks of the islands, especially at the W end of Santa Cruz Island, or a layer of thick, almost pearly haze at water level on clear days. Be particularly careful on foggy days: the winds can be ferociously strong even when visibility is restricted.

Santa Barbara Island, San Nicolas, and the western offshore islands of Santa Rosa and San Miguel require careful passage-planning. The best way to reach Santa Barbara Island is from Catalina Harbor or Santa Cruz

Island, a 40-mile passage over open water. Check the Pacific Missile Range first, and choose settled conditions (Chapter 11). Santa Rosa and San Miguel are notorious for strong winds. The best way to reach them is by motoring to windward along the mainland, then crossing from Goleta, Refugio, or Cojo. Be sure to set an accurate course as a strong westerly set can sometimes be encountered in mid-Channel, taking you far off course.

Bound from San Diego to Avalon on Catalina Island, you are best advised to make an overnight passage from Point Loma to the island under power. You will arrive at Avalon for breakfast. The alternative is to hug the coast and call in at Oceanside and Newport first. This seems a waste of time when you can enjoy these marinas on a downwind cruise home.

You will find more information on island crossings in Chapters 11 and 12.

With careful planning of your longer passages, you can enjoy California's gorgeous coastline to the full. Throw tightly drawn cruising schedules out of the cockpit, stock up with food and good wine, and enjoy the sensuous experience of making landfall in the bosom of a fair wind.

Lesley Newhart

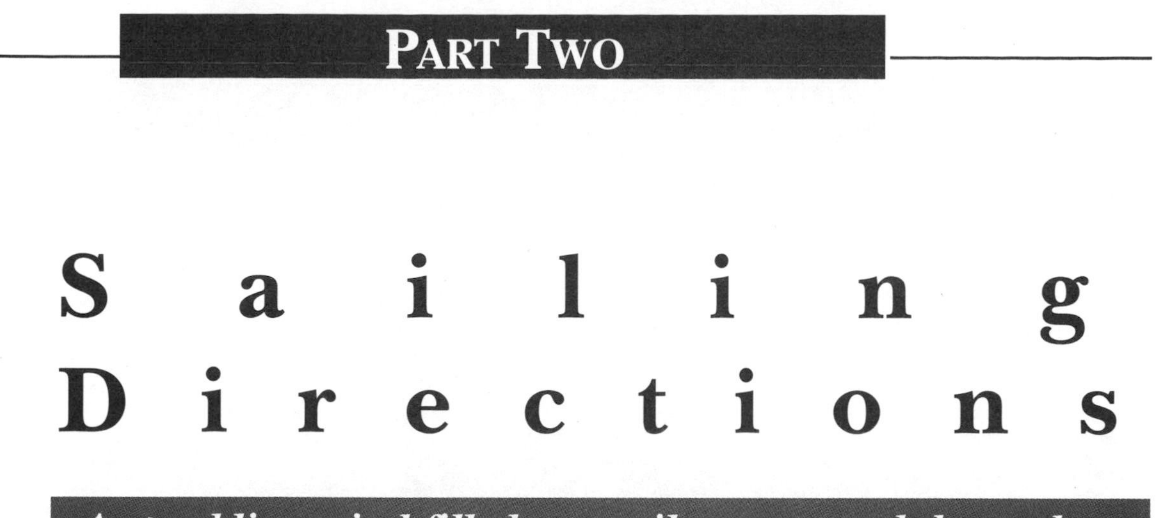

A sparkling wind filled our sails as we sped down the coast from San Francisco...Measuring our runs in days instead of hours we were content to let the roaring bow wave and the curving mast seduce our senses into thinking that time was relative, and at dawn on our first day out the Big Sur country looked strangely mysterious, for the tops of the highest mountains, hard and brown like a distant ridge in the Sahara desert, stood out above a veil of mist as though it were a mirage a hundred miles away.

Peter Pye
The Sea is for Sailing (1957).

San Francisco to Point Conception

Courtesy of the Bancroft Library, University of California, Berkeley.

Birds Eye View of San Francisco Bay, 1873.

CHAPTER 8

San Francisco Bay and Adjacent Waters

San Francisco Bay delivers summer wind, plenty of it. You can practically guarantee a dusting every afternoon from May to September. I have known people to make their way up-coast simply to spend a few days enjoying reliable wind, the chance to reef down and to drive their boats hard. A trip to San Francisco Bay is a sailing pilgrimage for people accustomed to wearing shorts at sea and foul weather gear about twice a year. The Bay is a sailor's paradise: Vital, invigorating, and a modern-day Wild West. A paradise, that is, for well prepared skippers who have studied weather conditions, tides, and selected their entrance route carefully.

> ***Four hundred twenty square miles on the surface, two trillion gallons in the volume. Give or take a bunch, that is the San Francisco Bay...Sea meets continent. Sea weather meets land weather, and the San Francisco Bay becomes the front line. It is a fine place to sail a boat, and a demanding one.***
>
> Kimball Livingston
> *Sailing the Bay*, 1981

The early Spaniards called the San Francisco Bay the "Mediterranean Sea." You can spend weeks exploring its well-charted and sheltered waters, or enjoy the myriad channels of the San Joaquin and Sacramento Rivers of the Delta region. This *Cruising Guide* gets you through the Golden Gate, tells you something of weather and tidal conditions in the Bay, and describes some of the marinas within easy reach of its entrance.

SAN FRANCISCO BAY WEATHER

San Francisco Bay, a meteorological world unto its own, where conditions change rapidly and are often unlike those outside the Golden Gate. Mark Twain was not taken with Bay weather. He wrote: "Even the kindly climate is sometimes pleasanter when read about than personally experienced, for a lovely cloudless day wears out its welcome by and by." Unlike sailors, he complained of the summer winds, and thought of falling on his knees and begging for rain, calling the winters something between spring and summer. Twain is right on one point. San Francisco Bay weather is unique. But anyone sailing regularly in these fascinating waters soon develops their own weather portents and local lore.

The Sea Breeze

For days on end, the onshore wind blows through the Golden Gate and through gaps in the coastal mountains. The Pacific High pushes air toward the coast. Meanwhile, the interior heats up, causing lower pressure over the land. The sea breeze persists over the bay between March and October, and especially during the summer months, when it is as regular as a trade wind. These conditions cause a strong and weak sea breeze. Intense heating of the land causes the natural inland flow of the winds to increase through the day. The onshore winds decrease when the land cools in the evening and overnight. A layer of grey stratus cloud persists all day, keeping the sea breeze low. The extent the sea breeze penetrates inland depends on the thickness of the marine layer, where fog and stratus cloud may form. The marine layer is usually about 1300 feet thick and will persist unless the land heats up to destroy the inversion (See Chapter 3). Thus, the thicker the marine layer, the further inland the sea breeze will travel. When the marine layer is only about 800 feet thick or less, fog and stratus clouds will not extend into the bay much further than the Golden Gate. A thick layer causes fog and stratus to mantle the entire Bay, and sometimes cover the skies as far inland as Sacramento.

The summer sea breeze can achieve considerable velocities, especially through the Golden Gate, where 30-knot winds are commonplace, flowing inland as far as the San Mateo Bridge and into San Pablo Bay as the day wears on. Typically, more sheltered locales like Sausalito enjoy less wind. Mornings are quiet, often flat calm. Then the sea breeze fills in about 1000, rising steadily to a peak around 1700, then decreasing gradually toward sunset. The sea breeze seems to blow in cycles of about a week to ten days, blowing over 30 knots for several days, then lessening for some time before the cycle begins again. A well-equipped sailing yacht will have no trouble handling the full brunt of the afternoon sea breeze, but the careful skipper will always be prepared for sudden, knockdown gusts, such as often occur in the vicinity of Angel Island and Davis Point. On many occasions, I have gone from full sail to two reefs and a storm jib and back again during a passage through the Bay. Sometimes the wind hits like a cannon, barreling through the Gate at whirlwind pace, ruffling the water dark blue as it comes. The first time I was caught in the westerly, I was sailing with full sail, boat on her beam ends, spray flying everywhere.

The next day, wiser for it, I watched for darkening ruffles at the Gate.

"Here we go," I cried, The water darkened to windward. We reached for our foul weather jackets, changed jibs and reefed down in record time. The boat heeled sharply, light on the helm. "Here we go," I cried as she forged ahead under perfect control, dancing toward the highrises of the city. I enjoyed a wonderful sail, spray flying, blue sky overhead, the yacht leaning to the gusts without complaint. The Bay was at its best.

The prevailing sea breeze tends to die down toward sunset, but sometimes persists through much of the night, in places averaging 3 to 10 knots or more. Land breezes are usually haphazard throughout the Bay, especially in the southern South Bay. Sailing after dark can be a quirky business, with winds whispering at you from many directions.

Local experts predict the strength of the afternoon sea breeze with some

Patrick Short

assurance, by observing pressure gradients, the position of the high, and the strength of the winds blowing offshore at Point Bonita and Pillar Point at the entrance to the Golden Gate. Light winds at those locations indicate the sea breeze will fill in later than usual, for the onshore flow will take time to overcome the gentle downslope winds of night hours. Only experience in all weathers can give you similar knowledge, although shipping out with an experienced racing skipper will be very educational. Because they know where the strongest winds and currents occur, they can predict wind shifts with uncanny skill.

San Francisco Fog

Last year, I bicycled over the Golden Gate Bridge on a foggy day. A stream of white fog was flowing through the Gate, just under the bridge. It was like cycling on a gray, billowy carpet. Minutes later, we were in bright sunshine, gazing backward at the fog cascading into the Bay and seeping over ridge tops. This sea fog, sometimes called advection fog, forms at sea, then flows into the Bay through convenient gaps. If it were not for the coastal ranges, San Francisco would be much foggier. On the day of my bicycle ride, the marine layer was relatively thin, but a few days later it thickened and the city saw no sunshine all day. According to the experts, advection fog hangs over the Golden Gate about 16% of the time during summer and fall.

The coastal fog bank off the California coast approaches or retreats from the shore as the Pacific High shifts position and the strength of the coastal current waxes and wanes. Warm Pacific winds are cooled by the cold water upwelling to the surface. They cool rapidly and rush through the convenient gap of the Golden Gate like a giant air conditioner, flowing fog over the Bay, and sometimes far inland. The variations in this natural air conditioner determine fog and wind conditions inside the Gate. Strong wind and an intense Pacific High cools the land so much over a period of days that the inversion collapses. The fog retreats, the wind drops, and the westerlies are light on the Bay. But, as the central valley heats, pressure falls inland so the inversion slowly reforms. The fog reappears and another cycle of strengthening winds begins. For days on end, too, the Pacific High weakens and wind circulations are slow offshore. Grey covers San Francisco day after day, as the wind and fog are never sufficient to cool the valley and cause marked cycles in the weather pattern.

By watching fog and wind patterns closely relative to local geography, you soon learn to predict weather trends with some accuracy. The secret is to sail Bay waters for several weeks, observing the weather closely and plotting the areas where winds blow strongest, and where tides can affect fog distributions. For example, a flood tide brings cool water from offshore into the Bay. Sometimes, the flood brings a dense blanket of white fog hugging the surface and reducing local visibility near the Golden Gate to almost zero. Foghorns blowing in the approaches give the only warning of a potential white out.

Radiation fogs occur in the Bay area in late fall through early spring. They occur when the surface of the land cools rapidly during clear, cold nights, especially during periods when high pressure settles over the Bay region and Central California. Then skies are clear, winds are light. When cool air flows lightly over the waters of the Bay, radiation fog may form, soon dispersing in the morning.

The sea breeze moderates as the Pacific High weakens in October and November. San Francisco sometimes broils under intense heat waves resulting from high pressure building over the interior. Then comes winter, with gentler breezes, except when storm systems pass between December and March. Usually winter winds in San Francisco Bay average about 8 knots, a far cry from the boisterous winds of summer. Spring and summer are the seasons to cruise the Bay, when you can enjoy her reliable winds to the full and rely on 20-30 knot breezes every day.

Tides and Currents

We Southern California sailors tend to be casual about tides and currents, until we meet the full force of the ebb and flood coursing through the Golden Gate. Then we take them seriously, as Bay sailors do.

Start with the NOAA tide tables and current charts, which are tidal predictions compiled from data from past observations, also many-dimensional calculations based on changes in the position of sun and moon. I have great respect for NOAA tables. They are remarkably accurate along the open coast, within half to three quarters of an hour or so, which is remarkable given the many variables which operate on local tidal streams. Their predictions are based on experience of local factors in the Bay area, with its complicated pressure and wind changes, and water discharging from at least sixteen rivers.

Patrick Short

Horseshoe Bay, Golden Gate.

When using tide tables, you will find two high and two low water times and level readings for each day. San Francisco Bay has semi-diurnal tides, with a mean tidal range of four feet at the Golden Gate. The equinoctial spring tide range is about nine feet. The falling (ebb) tide flows out of the Gate, the rising (flood) tide into the Bay. The young flood flows through the narrows, overcoming the weakening resistance of the ebb. Once inside the Gate, the rising tide moves more quickly in the South Bay, where high tide occurs earlier than in the North Bay. The tidal waters oscillate considerably within the Bay, flowing back and forward from the North Bay to the South Bay and back, since the times of high and low tide vary in each area. All this is very complicated for the visitor, and for the racing skipper, who starts with the official publications, then observes the local quirks of currents and tidal streams on the water.

The ebb and flood currents through the Golden Gate are of paramount importance to the visitor. The mean rise of the tide is about 5 feet at the entrance to San Francisco Bay. High and low tides occur about 1 1/2 hours later at the S end of the Bay, with a mean rise about 2.5 feet higher than in the Golden Gate. It takes about 8 hours for high water to pass from the Gate up the Delta to Sacramento on the Sacramento River, the mean rise being about 2.6 feet.

Entering the Golden Gate, the young flood tide crosses the Bar and converges toward the entrance. You will encounter it earlier off Points Bonita and Lobos than in the middle of the main ship channel. You may also be set slightly N and W by a coastal eddy current off the entrance, but this varies in intensity with the time of year. The ebb sets WSW along the S edge of the Potatopatch, through the main ship channel. Interestingly, it flows weakly through the Bonita Channel, the main small craft access route to the Gate from the north. You may experience a flood tide here while the ebb still flows strongly through the main ship channel.

The Golden Gate is 2 miles wide between Point Bonita and Point Lobos, a narrow, deep-water defile with strong tidal streams that sluice in and out of the entrance.

The strongest currents run on either side of the Golden Gate, close to Mile Rocks off Lime and Fort Points, the two termini of the bridge. Violent overfalls may be encountered in these areas, especially when a strong wind is blowing against the tide. Tidal streams change hourly, and can attain a strength of 6.5 knots under the bridge. The times of maximum ebb and flow can be obtained from the Tidal Current Atlas. This admirable publication provides a conversion table as well as hour-by-hour flow charts that enable you to predict the direction and strength of the tides for any hour of the day.

The flood tide sets straight into the Golden Gate, but you must guard against lateral sets and strong overfalls. The ebb sets out of the entrance at velocities up to 6.5 knots, flowing from inside the N side of the Bay toward Fort Point. On both ebb and flood, you will experience an eddy in the night between Fort Point and Point Lobos. Keep clear of Mile Rocks and at least 1/2 mile of Point Bonita, where heavy overfalls can be experienced on the ebb.

San Francisco Vessel Traffic Service

More than 9,000 large ships pass through the Golden Gate each year, navigating through narrow, tidal waters. The San Francisco Vessel Traffic Service (VTS) is the maritime equivalent of an airport traffic control organization, designed to prevent collisions and keep inbound and outbound ships well separated from one another. VTS controllers monitor all large ship movements in the Golden Gate area with VHF and radar. Each vessel over 300 tons checks in before arrival and departure, entering and leaving port under VTS control, with a pilot aboard. Small craft are exempt from VTS, but you can monitor traffic on VHF channels 13 and 16.

Three Traffic Separation Schemes, from north, south, and west, converge on Buoy SF (Fl. W 6 sec. 14 miles), 14 miles SW of Golden Gate Bridge, bringing ships into a 6-mile radius Precautionary Area surrounding the buoy. Here vessels pick up pilots and alter course preparatory to entering or leaving the Main Ship Channel or one of the three Separation Schemes.

Customs and Immigration

Most visitors will not need Immigration or Customs clearance, but here are the relevant telephone numbers for the Port of Entry San Francisco/Oakland:
Immigration: 415-876-2876 (day) and 415-495-6667 (outside business hours)

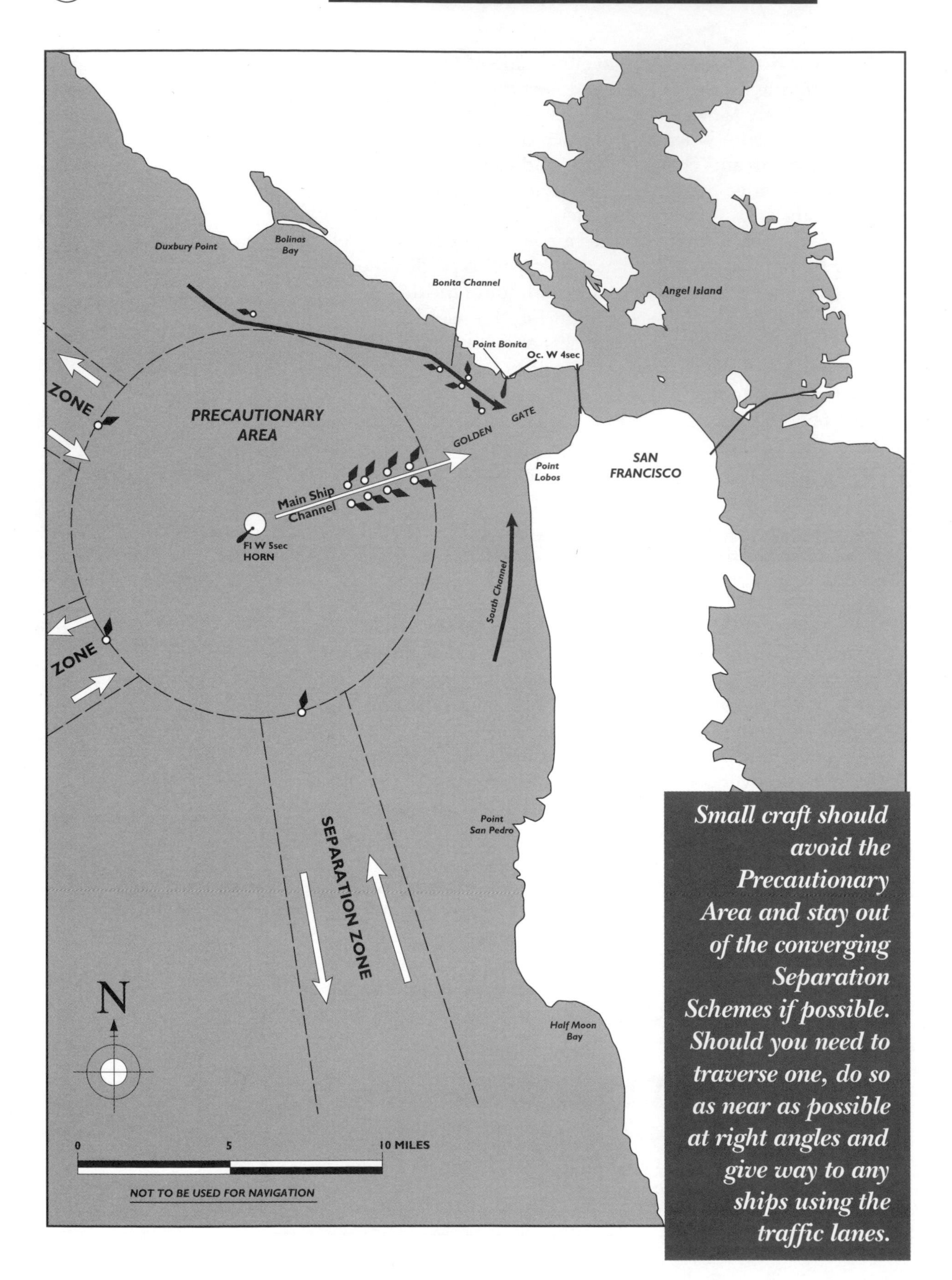

Small craft should avoid the Precautionary Area and stay out of the converging Separation Schemes if possible. Should you need to traverse one, do so as near as possible at right angles and give way to any ships using the traffic lanes.

Customs: 415-556-2844 (day) and 415-876-2812 (outside business hours)

Entering the Bay

General Considerations

The Golden Gate is definitely a place where you use the tides to your advantage. Use the Tidal Current Atlas to coincide your passage with a favorable tide, or with slack water, which normally occurs for a short period three hours after maximum flood and ebb.

Do not attempt passage when a strong wind is blowing against a full contrary tide.

The resulting steep seas and overfalls can be very dangerous.

Any approach to the Golden Gate involves crossing the San Francisco Bar, which extends in a broad arc some 5 miles offshore from the Golden Gate Bridge from 3 miles S of Point Lobos to about 1/2 mile off Point Bonita. The most dangerous part of the Bar is Four Fathom Bank, a notorious area of vicious overfalls and shallows, known generically as the Potatopatch, where water depths are little more than 23 feet. Avoid this nasty place at all costs. The safest route across the Bar is the Main Ship Channel, but even this can be hazardous to small craft in rough weather, especially when the wind blows against the ebb tide.

Do not attempt to enter the Golden Gate in strong winds and high seas unless you have long experience of local conditions. Better to wait for the weather to moderate.

If possible, time your entrance for slack water on a first time visit, even in moderate weather.

Approach Landmarks from Seaward (Charts 18680 and 18649)

The Golden Gate is readily identified from both north and south in clear weather by a series of useful approach landmarks. These include:

The Farallon Islands, 23 miles W of the Golden Gate, a group of rocky islets that extend NW for 7 miles. Southeast Farallon, the highest land mass, is 350 feet high.

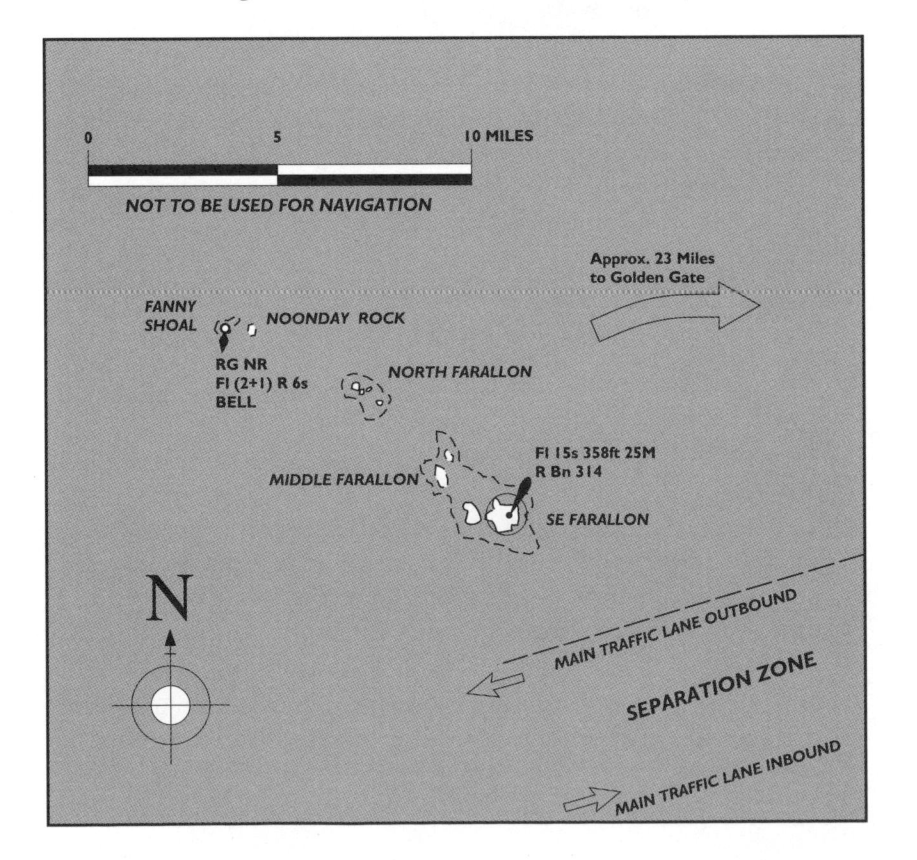

Farallon light (Fl. W 15 sec. 25 miles) is located here and is an invaluable guide at night. You can anchor in about 50 feet in Fisherman Bay just N of the light, but this is very much a fair weather berth. Keep well clear of the Fanny Shoal 9.8 miles NW of the light. Noonday Rock, the shallowest part of the shoal, has only 13 feet. A red and black whistle buoy "NR" (Qk. Fl.) lies 0.6 mile W of this danger.

Mount Tamalpais, 7 miles N of Point Bonita, the northern extremity of the entrance, can be seen from as far away as 60 miles. The three summits, the easternmost of which bears a lookout tower, are conspicuous. This densely vegetated mountain contrasts sharply with the surrounding countryside.

Point Bonita, a 100-foot high black cliff, surrounded by high slopes, the northern promontory of the Golden Gate. The white lighthouse (Oc. W 4 sec. 18 miles) can be seen from a considerable distance in clear weather. A 100-foot high black and white rock lies a third of a mile to seaward.

Point Lobos, the southern promontory at the Golden Gate, is a rocky point with a water tank on its summit. The houses of San Francisco and Pacifica cover the shoreline S from Point Lobos. The white hospital buildings high above the Golden Gate are also conspicuous E of the point.

Point San Pedro, 11 miles S of the Golden Gate, is easily recognizable either N- or S-bound. San Pedro is the termination of the Montara mountains inland.

The russet red piers of the Golden Gate Bridge can be discerned above the city as you approach from S, but the bridge as a whole is only visible if you approach from W.

San Francisco Approach Lighted Horn Buoy (SF) lies 9 miles WSW of the Golden Gate entrance. This huge red buoy is 42 feet high and is lit (Fl. W 6 sec. 14 miles).

The suburbs of San Francisco spill over the low hills and coastline between Point San Pedro and Point Lobos to the S of the Golden Gate and are a convenient landmark from some distance offshore, especially in clear weather.

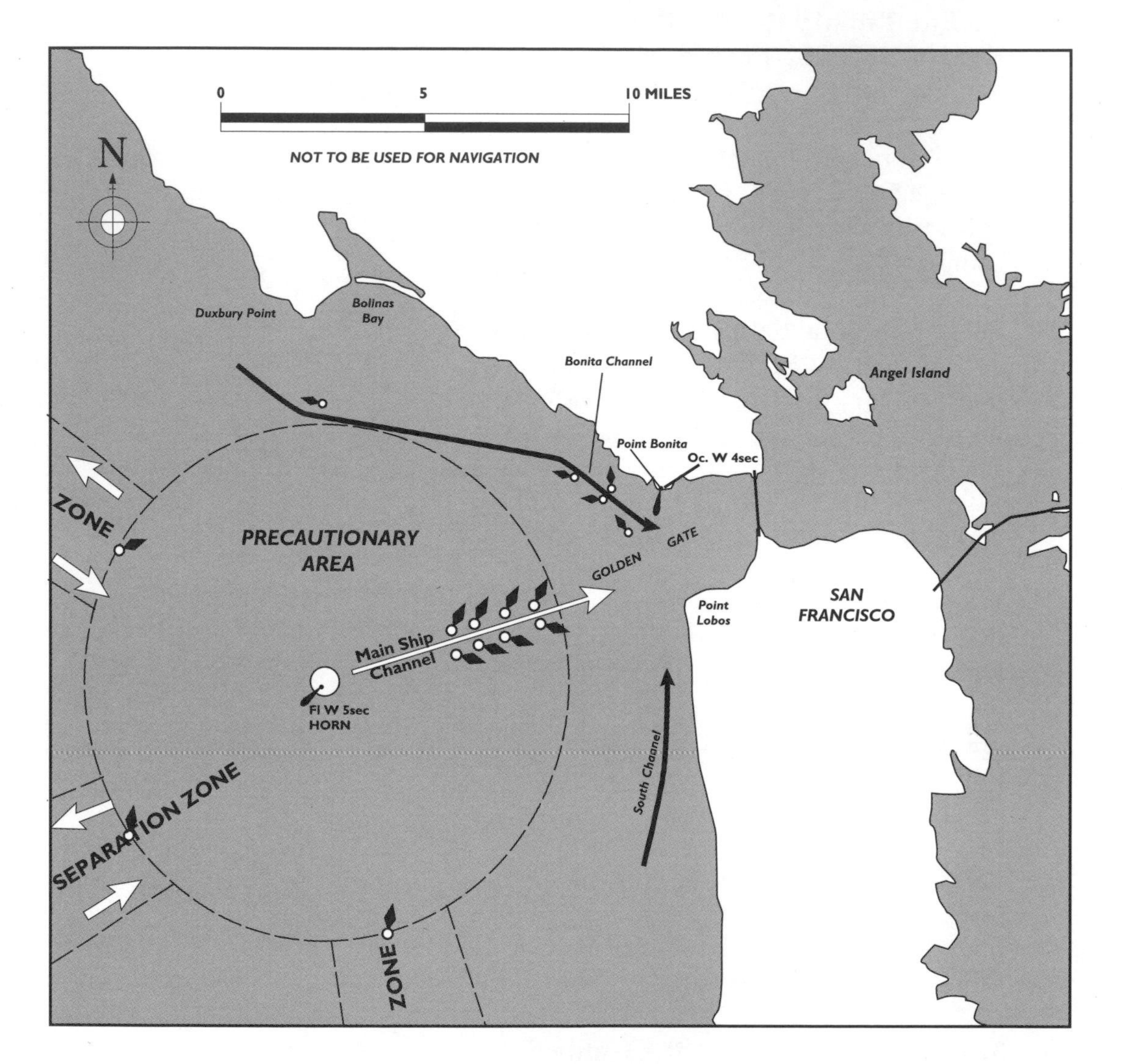

Approach from W: the Main Ship Channel

Most coasting yachts will approach the Golden Gate from N or S, using either the Bonita or the South Channels.

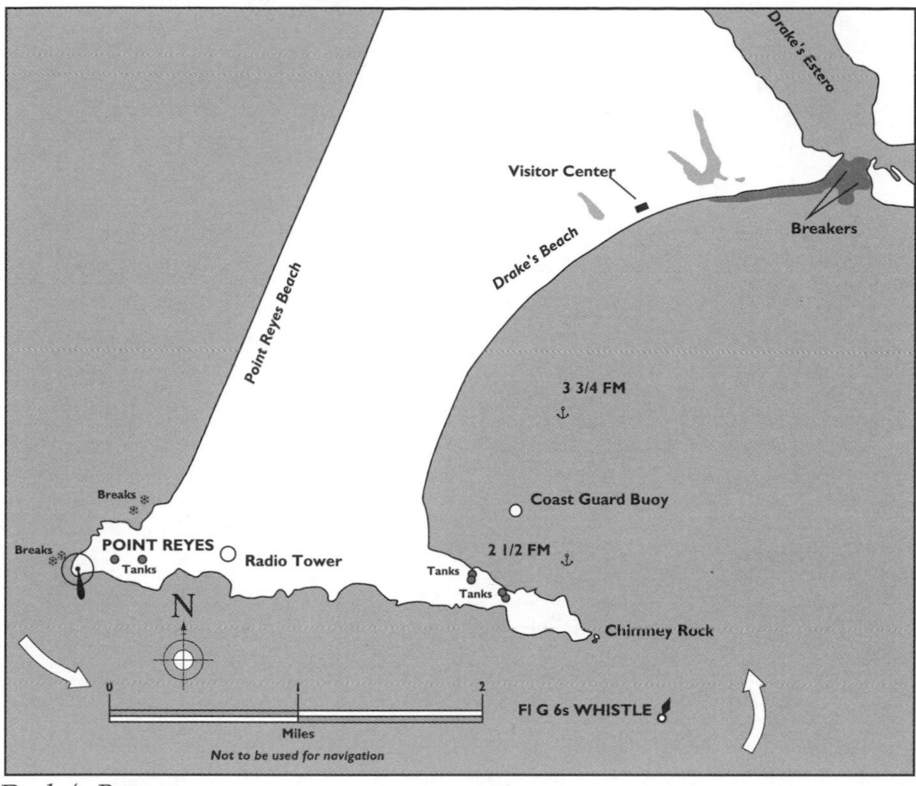

Drake's Bay

Approaching from W, identify San Franciso Approach Lighted Horn Buoy (SF), (Lat. 37 deg. 45 min. N, Long. 122 deg. 41 min. 50 sec. W) 14 miles SW of the Golden Gate Bridge. A 6-mile radius Precautionary Area surrounds Buoy SF, where three Traffic Separation Schemes converge. Keep outside the Precautionary Area and pass well inshore before picking up the buoyed Main Ship Channel.

You can use the Main Ship Channel (070 degrees toward Alcatraz light), provided you follow the traffic flow. Keep to the right of the channel, just outside the four pairs of marker buoys. This way, you'll be clear of large ships, yet in deep water. You must always give way to such vessels in the Main Ship Channel.

Once inside the four pairs of marker buoys, shape your course through Golden Gate Bridge, keeping well clear of shipping and of the strong eddies which swirl around the bridge foundations.

Approach from N: Drake's Bay and the Bonita Channel (Charts 18647 and 18649)

Small craft arriving at the Golden Gate from N usually use the Bonita Channel. This route is popular with local yachts spending a weekend at Drake's Bay. Many southbound yachts from the Pacific Northwest also stop over here.

Drake's Bay Anchorage (Chart 18647)

Drake's Bay is named after the rollicking Sir Francis, and has been an anchorage of refuge for sailing craft large and small for centuries. The bay provides excellent shelter in strong NW winds and prevailing summer weather, but is dangerous in SE gales. The Point Reyes State Recreational Area ashore offers magnificent walking and wild life observation.

Approach

The approach is straightforward, once the bold, rocky headland of Point Reyes and its lighthouse have been identified. Point Reyes light (Fl. W. 5 sec. 24 miles) (Lat. 37 deg. 7 min N, Long. 123 deg. 01 min W) stands 265 feet above the water atop a square building. The promontory makes an excellent radar target in thick weather.

The US Coast Pilot says of the Golden Gate tides: "The flood current sets straight in, with a slight tendency toward to N shore, with heavy overfalls both at Lime Point and Fort Point when strong. It causes an eddy in the bight between Point Lobos and Fort Point. The ebb current has been observed to have a velocity of more than 6.5 knots between Lime Point and Fort Point, and it sets from inside the bay on the N side toward the latter point. Like the flood current, it causes an eddy in the bight between Fort Point and Point Lobos, and a heavy rip and overfall reaching about 0.25 mile S from Point Bonita." The Pilot also warns of strong eddies near the bridge foundation piers.

Approaching from N, the point may appear as an island, on account of the low ground nearby. Stay well offshore, but clear of the shipping lanes, especially in foggy or windy conditions, to avoid two rocks 275 yards W of the light, with a least depth of 3 feet and marked by breakers in even moderate seas. High swells and strong winds are sometimes encountered in this vicinity.

Once Point Reyes is astern, follow the 3 mile-long peninsula E toward Drake's Bay, identified by its white cliffs, which run from SW about 6 miles in a NE curve, ending in sand dunes. Give the peninsula an offing of at least a mile, passing outside the lighted whistle buoy "1," 0.6 mile SE of Chimney Rock (Fl. G 6 sec.). From the whistle buoy, shape a course into the Bay itself.

Approaching from S, again identify Point Reyes and the white cliffs of Drake's Bay. Set a course to bring you inshore about 0.5 to 1.0 mile E of Chimney Rock.

Anchorage

Drake's Bay shelves gradually with a sandy bottom. Most small craft anchor in a depth of 18 to 25 feet off the beach, well outside the breaker line. Anchor according to prevailing wind and swell conditions, looking out for the telltale dark gust lines, which show the paths of wind funneling across the bay. If anchoring at night, look out for the numerous fishing boats which use the bay and the fish pier on the inner side of the peninsula.

Facilities

None, except for a snack bar and the Visitors' Center on the main beach.

Drake's Bay to the Golden Gate via the Bonita Channel (Charts 18647 and 18649)

From Drake's Bay shape a course past a coast of high cliffs and sandy beaches to pass 2.5 miles outside Duxbury Point and Duxbury Reef, giving both point and reef a wide berth. This course will take you outside whistle buoy "DR" (Fl. G 6 sec.), which marks the outer edge of the reef. Be extremely careful in this vicinity in rough weather. Strong currents can set you northward toward the rocks.

You can anchor, sheltered from prevailing NW winds, in Bolinas Bay, E of Duxbury Point in 24 to 36 feet, sand, but keep clear of Duxbury Reef. In quiet conditions, you can explore Bolinas Lagoon through a narrow channel drawing less than 3 feet. This is a good spot for kayaking.

Bound for the Bay, time your transit through the Bonita Channel and into the Golden Gate for the flood, which begins in the channel while the ebb is still flowing strongly in the Golden
Gate. With clever timing, you can carry the flood through the Bonita, then into the Golden Gate. Once "DR" is astern, alter course to the east, closing the rocky coast about 3 miles N of Point Bonita, the northern promontory of the Golden Gate. Identify the red channel buoys, which identify the offshore side of the Bonita Channel, and the green buoy "3," (Fl. G 4 sec.), which marks Sears Rock, Centissima Reef, and the inshore edge of the Bonita Channel. Exercise caution: At its narrowest point, Bonita Channel is only 0.2 mile wide.

Point Bonita is a sharp, black cliff, 300 foot high on its seaward face. Point Bonita light (Oc. 4 sec. 18 miles) lies 124 feet above the water on the S head of the point, the tower and radar antenna of the San Francisco Vessel Traffic Service being conspicuous on the N head. Keep at least 0.5 mile off the point, altering course to enter the Golden Gate when the Golden Gate Bridge opens up ahead. A bell buoy with red and green bands (Fl 2+1 R 6 sec.) marks the southern end of the Bonita Channel and the edge of the Potatopatch Shoal.

Once inside the entrance, proceed under the Golden Gate Bridge, keeping clear of the main shipping lanes. If you want to anchor in the entrance area, try Bonita Cove, close under Point Bonita, in about 36 feet. Here you are out of the strong currents, which run in this vicinity, but look out for unpredictable eddies.

Caution: Use extreme caution when departing the Golden Gate and using the Bonita Channel on the ebb. Strong tidal sets can push you toward the rocks off Point Bonita. Sets toward the Potatopatch are also reported.

Approach from S: South Channel (Chart 18649)

Most yachts approach the Golden Gate from S, coasting past the shore of South San Francisco inside the Traffic Separation Zone, but well clear of off lying coastal rocks. This approach is fine in calm and moderate weather, but should not be attempted in rough weather or when high swells are running.

Your approach begins N of Pillar Point, when you identify Point Montara, with its light 70 feet above the water (Fl. W 5 sec. 15 miles) (Lat. 37 deg. 32.2 min N, Long 122 deg 31.2 min W). Point San Pedro lies 2.5 miles N, a rocky promontory which is the seaward end of Montara Mountain, remarkable for a large, triple-sided rock with a white southern face projecting about 0.3 mile from the point.

Keep at least a mie offshore past Point San Pedro. A rocky area with breaking swells that extends a mile N of the point.

Courtesy of the Bancroft Library, University of California, Berkeley

Fort Point looking across to Marin skyline, 1870's.

Your next landmark is a conspicuous Municipal fishing pier about 2.5 miles NE of Point San Pedro. Follow the coast northward toward Point Lobos and the Golden Gate, staying about 0.7 mile offshore. Keep a sharp eye for day fishing boats, which operate close inshore in this area. This course will bring you into South Channel, an unmarked channel with least depth 15 feet, which runs parallel to the peninsula shore with a width of 0.7 mile. South Channel is dangerous if any sea is running. Under these circumstances, it is best to stay offshore 1.5 miles until you reach the main ship channel.

Maintain a course through the middle of South Channel, until Point Lobos is close ahead. A large water tank lies on its rocky summit. The Cliff House on the S side of the point and Seal Rocks close offshore are conspicuous. Give Seal Rocks a wide berth. Mile Rocks, 700 yards NW of the northern extremity of Point Lobos, are two 20-foot high

San Francisco's first hotels were abandoned sailing vessels beached at the waterfront during the California Goldrush.

A ceremony of Atlantic waters being poured into the Pacific symbolizing the fraternity between Boston and San Francisco.

California Historical Society

black rocks about 100 feet apart, marked by an orange and white horizontally banded tower on the outer **most rock (Fl. 5 sec. 15 miles). Do not attempt to pass between Mile Rocks and the shore.** Pass well outside Mile Rocks light and shape a course for Golden Gate Bridge ahead, keeping clear of the main shipping lanes.

The Golden Gate Bridge has a 4,028 feet channel span between the two 740-foot-high supporting towers. A fixed green light with three fixed white lights in a vertical line above it marks the center of the span.

The *US Coast Pilot* says of the Golden Gate tides: "The flood current sets straight in, with a slight tendency toward to N shore, with heavy overfalls both at Lime Point and Fort Point when strong. It causes an eddy in the bight between Point Lobos and Fort Point. The ebb current has been observed to have a velocity of more than 6.5 knots between Lime Point and Fort Point, and it sets from inside the bay on the N side to the latter point. Like the flood current, it causes an eddy in the bight between Fort Point and Point Lobos, and a heavy rip and overfall reaching about 0.25 mile S from Point Bonita." The *Pilot* also warns of strong eddies near the bridge foundations.

Entering the Golden Gate under sail ranks among the finest of California cruising experiences. The high, rugged cliffs, the strong winds and fast-flowing currents, eddies of white and grey fog rolling in and out of the entrance: All combine to give this short passage an atmosphere all its own. As you sail under the russet-red Golden Gate Bridge, you burst into another world of high skyscrapers and wooded hills, of rollicking winds and ever-changing tides. Find yourself a comfortable home base, grab the Tidal Current Tables, and enjoy sailing the Bay. It's an addiction all of its own. San Francisco Bay is the place where you can enjoy boats large and small, cruise at 30 knots in a fast motor yacht, plane frantically in a Laser dinghy, man the windward rail in a high-tech ocean racer. Enjoy the Bay in wind fair and foul, heavily reefed down, dodging rocks on a foggy day, rowing softly in a mahogany dinghy in the quiet of morning. All this is sailing the bay, so much so that Kimball Livingston wrote one of the immortal books of western sailing with this very title.

Ports and Anchorages in San Francisco Bay

The marinas and facilities available to San Francisco Bay visitors need a book of their own, as do the unique attractions of a leisurely cruise in the Sacramento Delta. When you first arrive in the Bay, you need a comfortable harbor close to the Golden

Gate and attractions ashore where you can rest, reprovision, sightsee, and, perhaps, to lick one's wounds.

North or South shore? It's a matter of personal preference. San Francisco has all the attractions of a major tourist city close at hand, but you will need to use buses, taxis, or a rental car for any serious provisioning or laundry. On the North shore, Sausalito, Emeryville, Berkeley, and the Oakland/Alameda area provide all the yacht repair and provisioning facilities you will need.

If you are staying in the Bay area for any length of time, it's worth renting a car, not only for shopping, but for excursions to the wine country, beaches, and other attractions.

San Francisco (Chart 18650)

While yachts are welcome in San Francisco marinas, berthing facilities tend to be crowded, with few transit slips available at short notice. Your options are:

Marina Yacht Harbor

Close to the Marina District and the Saint Francis Yacht Club, this modern facility is well protected from barreling summer winds. Once Fort Point is astern, identify the Palace of Fine Arts building on the starboard bow, then the Anita Rock buoy with its quick flashing light. The Marina breakwater (Qk Fl. R) and the white buildings of the Saint Francis Yacht Club lie close on the starboard bow. Visitor slips are available, but the length of stay is restricted. A supermarket and laundry facilities, also fuel, are within easy reach.
Aquatic Park, 0.5 mile E of Marina Yacht Harbor, offers limited anchorage behind a low breakwater, giving some shelter on a muddy bottom in about 9 to 12 feet. The historic ships lie alongside the eastern shore of the sheltered area. You cannot enter this anchorage under power, under sail alone. Look out for moorings and swimmers, who enter the water year-round. Aquatic Park is not a long-term anchorage, but has the advantage of being close to Fisherman's Wharf, the Maritime Museum, and the San Francisco State Historical Park. You can obtain supplies at Fisherman's Wharf. The anchorage is also close to the Powell Street cable car terminus.

Lock up your boat here if you leave her unattended.

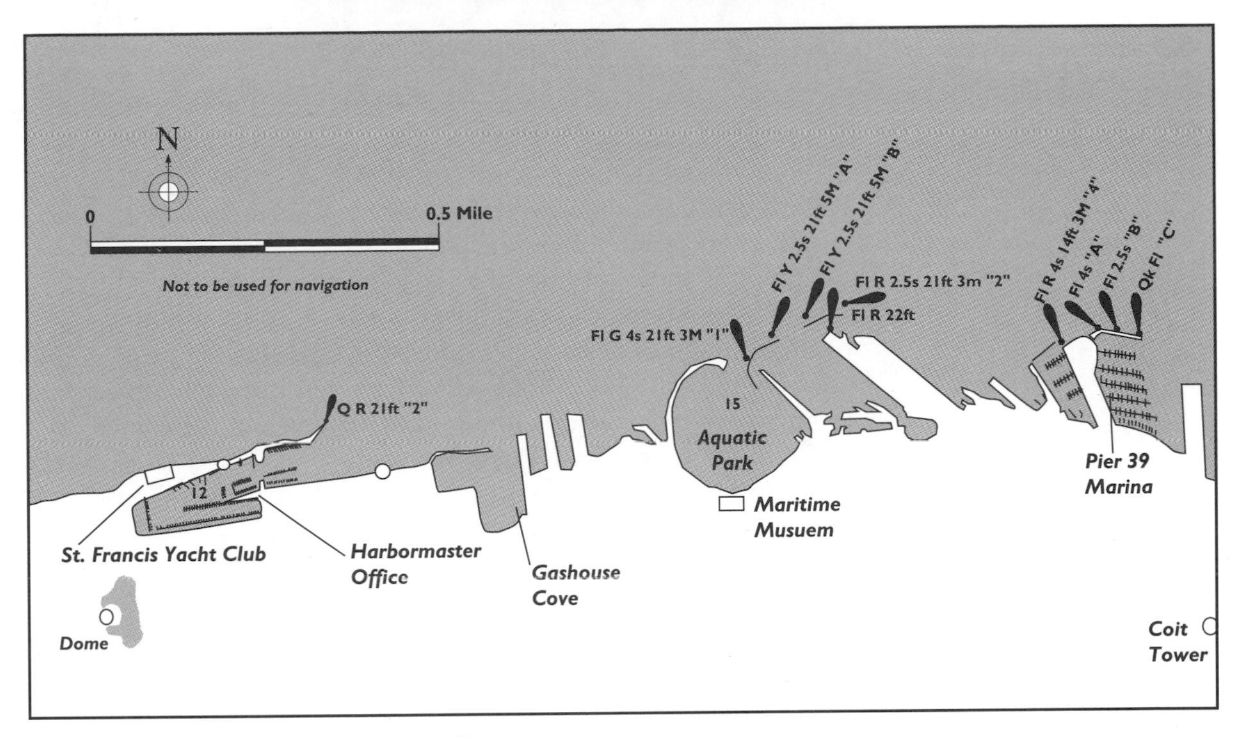

San Francisco Maritime Park and adjacent marinas.

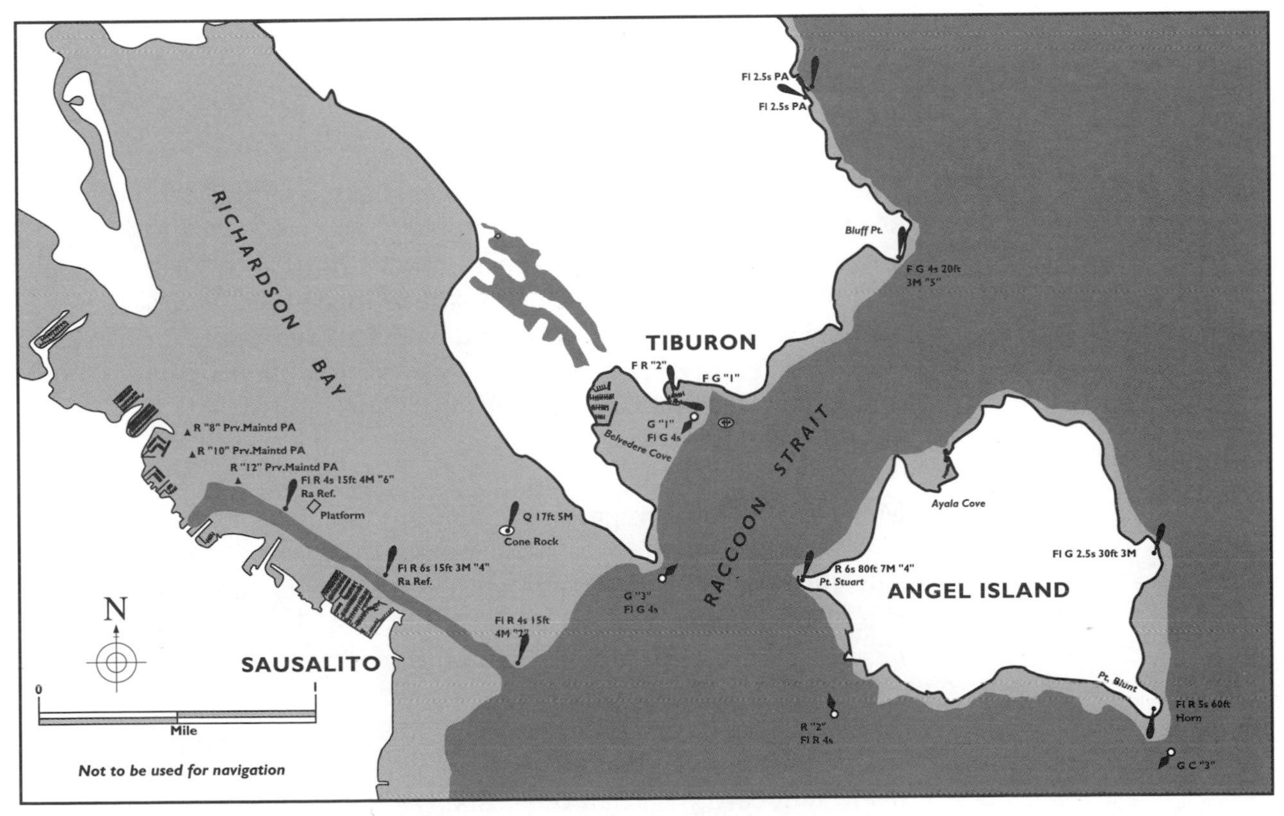

Sausalito and approaches.

Pier 39

This marina, famous for its resident sea lions, is close to the sometimes frenzied action of Pier 39 and Fisherman's Wharf, with their many shops and restaurants, but it's crowded and sometimes noisy. Bay Area sailors use it frequently, for there are many good restaurants nearby. The twin breakwaters of the yacht harbor lie E of the barrack-like buildings of Fort Mason, just beyond the shop-covered Pier 39. The last time I was there, visiting yachts had to make slip reservations in advance, or you can call VHF-16 for a slip assignment. Fuel, water, and some marine supplies can be obtained at Fisherman's Wharf.

Sausalito Chart (18653)

I strongly recommend Sausalito as a first stop in San Francisco Bay. The town lies in well sheltered Richardson Bay. It offers excellent facilities for all kinds of repairs, sheltered berths, plenty of fun ashore, and easy access to San Francisco itself. The marinas are also relatively close to the Golden Gate, but offer only a limited number of guest slips.

Approach

Once inside the Golden Gate Bridge, shape a course NE, keeping well clear of the land until the town of Sausalito and Richardson Bay open up to port. Identify the red channel buoys marking the outer side of the lighted access channel (Buoy "2" at the outer end is Fl. R. 4 sec) and proceed up the fairway, keeping a close eye for other boats leaving the crowded marinas to port. The channel has a least depth of 22 feet.

Marinas and Anchorage

Sausalito is a yachting town, with every facility imaginable. Visitors are welcome, with transient berths available in some marinas at relatively modest cost.

Schoonmaker Point Marina is easily identified on the port side, opposite the conspicuous platform outside the channel to starboard. This harbor is usually very crowded.

Clipper Yacht Harbor is the largest marina, housing 700 yachts in three basins. Follow the dredged channel closely, watching for traffic emerging from the crowded slip areas to port. Note that the channel passes behind the breakwater opposite Basins 3 and 4. Shoal ground surrounds the dredged areas. I have always found this a friendly marina with every facility and good restaurants to hand.

Kappas Marina lies further W, somewhat away from the bustle of downtown. I have not stopped here, but have heard good reports.

Anchorage may be obtained in the shallow southern portions of Richardson Bay, in an area bounded by Cone Rock light (Qk Fl. W 5 miles) to the NE and the dredged channel to the SW. Pay careful attention to the tidal range and to your depth sounder when anchoring in these shallow waters. The berth can be uncomfortable from passing wash.

Facilities

Sausalito offers easy provisioning, every kind of marine supplies, excellent boat yards, and The Armchair Sailor bookstore, where charts and all kinds of good reading can be obtained. Although touristy, Sausalito is a wonderful place to relax after an arduous coastal passage, and a perfect base for sailing the Bay.

On occasion, I have made my first call much further downwind, at Emeryville, Berkeley Harbor, and the marinas at Oakland and Alameida. They offer attractive alternatives and excellent facilities, but are somewhat further from San Francisco. The weather is warmer in the estuaries along the Oakland estuary. Here the winds are lighter, there are many guest slips, and numerous restaurants. On a first visit, I would be inclined to seek harbor closer to the Golden Gate, then moving on when you have familiarized yourself with local conditions. But: "You pays your money and takes your choice," as they say.

Anchorages

Bay area sailors use two anchorages inside San Francisco Bay, both of which are admirable for a first night in the area.

Ayala Cove (Chart 18649) is on the N side of Angel Island, within easy sailing distance of Golden Gate Bridge. Follow the N shore of Angel Island round from Point Stuart, staying about 0.5 mile off the island, but out of the rougher water in Raccoon Strait. Pay careful attention to the tidal streams, which flow fast and furious through the Strait, especially around Points Blunt and Knox. Ayala Cove will open up behind the spit of Point Ione. The tide can flow rapidly through Ayala Cove itself, especially on the spring ebb, when a 4-knot counter-current can cause havoc with moored boats and for people entering and leaving slips. Check the mooring buoys or pilings for current flow and adjust your course and speed accordingly. Be careful maneuvering at low tide, especially near the beach, launching ramp, or slips.

The 47 slips in Ayala Cove are almost always full in summer, available in 22, 30, and 40-foot sizes. You can pick up one of the 25 moorings in the bay, but you must use fore and aft lines to prevent unexpected swings with the tide change, either securing to two buoys and laying out a stern anchor.

The cove is part of Angel Island State Park. Angel Island was visited by native Americans at least 3,000 years ago, served as a Civil War garrison and immigration processing station, and was the site of a Nike missile base in the 1950s. The State Park maintains a museum and visitor's center in one of the restored government buildings at the head of the cove.

Ayala Cove can be crowded, and busy with traffic to the landing, so many Bay area sailors anchor off the E side of the island, or use the moorings by the East Garrison Ferry Landing. This is a quieter berth except for the wash from passing ships.

Jim Aeby

Clipper Cove (Chart 18650) is between Yerba Buena and Treasure Island, site of the Treasure Island Marina. Treasure Island lies about 2 miles E of Alcatraz Island with its prominent penitentiary buildings. Pass round the N end of Treasure Island at a distance of about 0.5 mile, following the island round until Clipper Cove and the marina open up to starboard. Anchorage may be obtained clear of other yachts in 15 to 20 feet (mud and sand). No facilities for visitors at the marina.

But whatever you do in San Francisco Bay, do not fail to sail the Bay, if nothing else just for the sheer joy of being alive!

CHAPTER 9

Golden Gate to San Simeon Bay

The first stage of a passage from the San Francisco Bay area to Southern California takes you out of the Golden Gate through the South Channel, close under Point Lobos, then along the rocky, and often windy coast to Monterey Bay.

After doubling Point Piños we bore up, set studding sails alow and aloft, and were walking off at the rate of eight or nine knots, promising to traverse in twenty-four hours the distance which we were nearly three weeks in traversing on the passage up . . .

Richard Henry Dana
Two Years Before the Mast, 1840.

Notes on Passage-making

You must time your departure from the Golden Gate for slack water. Leaving on the ebb often brings you into steep waves when it encounters the prevailing northwe-serlies. If you have a long passage ahead, you may prefer to depart under power, so you can make full use of the prevailing afternoon winds as you sail down the coast. But if time is not a consideration, then a beat out of the Golden Gate is an invigorating start to the passage, provided sea conditions in the entrance are favorable.

The coastal passage between the Golden Gate and Monterey Bay can be broken at Pillar Point Harbor (Half Moon Bay), which requires careful approach on account of the reefs near the entrance. Otherwise, few outlying dangers present a hazard on passage. At an average speed of five knots, you will need about 4 hours to sail from Point Lobos to Pillar Point Harbor at Half Moon Bay. It's about 9 1/2 hours from there to Santa Cruz Harbor at the same average speed.

This stretch of coast is well lighted and easily navigated even on the darkest night, using the major lights on Point Lobos, Pillar Point, and A§o Nuevo as signposts. Keep a sharp lookout for fishing boats and coastal shipping.

Point Lobos to Pillar Point Harbor (Chart 18680)

The South Channel passes close inshore of the San Francisco Bay bar. (The transit is described in Chapter 8.) Thereafter, keep about 0.75 miles off the low lying coast with its long, sandy beach, with the suburbs of South San Francisco and Pacifica to port. Identify 640-foot-high Point San Pedro and its conspicuous off-lying rocks, and shape a course to pass 1.5 miles offshore. Beyond Point San Pedro, the coast rises steep and rocky as far as 60-foot-high Point Montara (Lat. 37 deg 32.2 min N; Long. 122 deg. 31.2 min W), which exhibits a light (Fl. 5 sec. 15 miles). Identify red buoy

10A, which lies 1.5 miles off the point and pass outside, avoiding the reefs and other obstructions off the promontory. Montara Mountain, with its bare trees, makes a conspicuous landmark 2.5 miles inland. From N, the summit looks like a flat-topped mountain with four hillocks on the summit. The same hillocks look less prominent from S, where the mountain appears to be a long ridge. I have used Montara Mountain as an offshore landmark for the Golden Gate on several occasions.

Pillar Point, 18 miles S of the Golden Gate and 4 miles S of Montara Mountain, forms the southern end of a low ridge which extends S from Point Montara. The two white radar dish antennae and white building near the summit of the point can be identified from a long distance. They offer an excellent landmark north- and south-bound and make a convenient point of reference for the approach to Pillar Point Harbor. You can see their bright lights from miles away at night. Offlying rocks extend over 30 yards S of the point. Half Moon Bay lies between Pillar and Miramontes Points.

Point Pillar Harbor (Half Moon Bay) (Chart 18682)

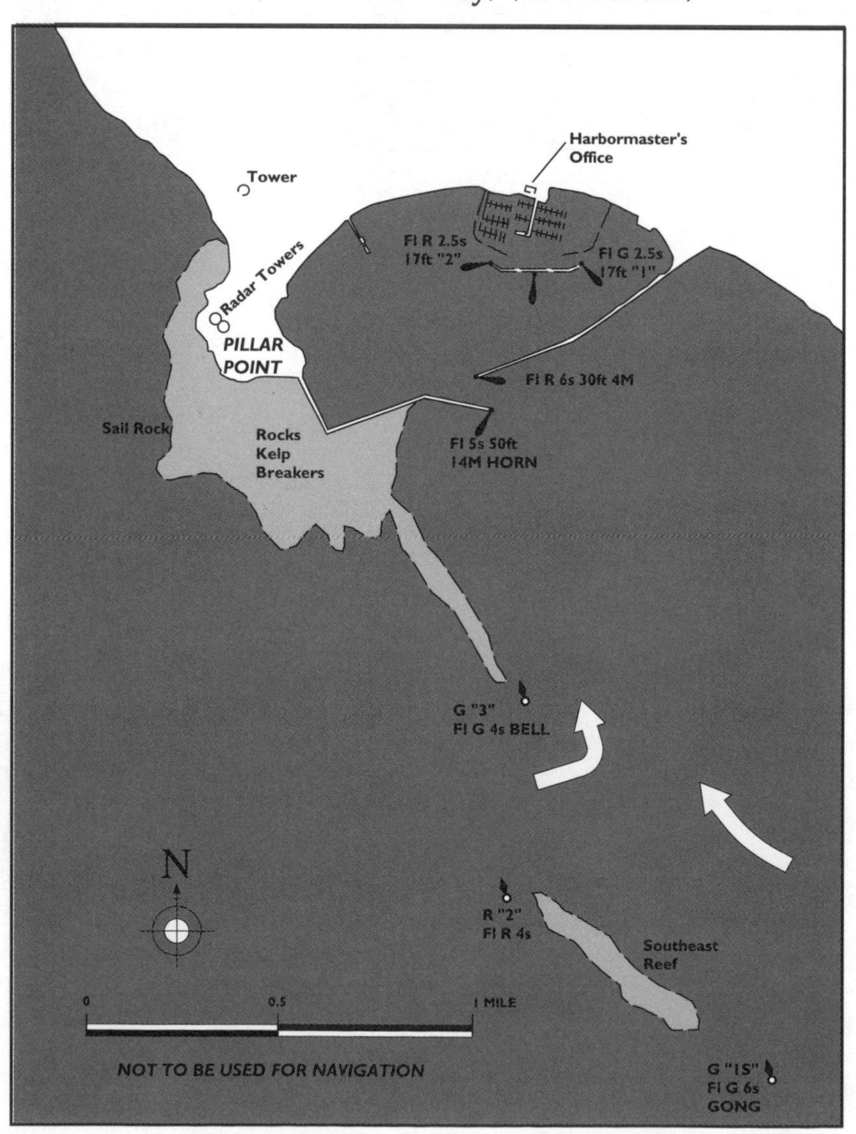

Pillar Point Harbor and approach

Pillar Point is a fishing and pleasure harbor, an easy day sail from the Golden Gate. The harbor, formed by two long stone breakwaters, is lit with two lights. You can see the light on the southern breakwater for 14 miles (Fl. W 5 sec.).

Approach

From N. The approach from N means a wide detour to avoid the ledges and rocks lying off Pillar Point. Pass outside buoy "1" (Fl. G 2.5 sec) SW of Pillar Point. Then shape your course for bell buoy "3" (Fl. G. 4 sec.). For extra safety, plan to turn inshore when the buoy is broad on the port bow. Once inshore of the buoy, steer for the entrance, which lies just W of N.

From S. Northbound, identify Pillar Point and its two radar antennas, then look for the two buoys which mark Southeast Reef. Southeast Reef extends over 2 miles SE of Pillar Point, has a least depth of 4 to 20 feet, with a pinnacle rock awash at the extreme SE end at low water springs. A gong buoy (Fl. G. 6 sec.) marks the S end of the reef. Leave this to port, pass outside buoy "3," then steer for the entrance breakwaters.

The approach to Pillar Point Harbor can be tricky in thick weather or at night, when the buoys are sometimes difficult to identify. The approach can be hazardous in strong SE winds.

The outer breakwaters angle out from Pillar Point and the mainland respectively, the entrance trending NW between the two lighted ends. The outer harbor is congested with moorings, while the marina lies behind three breakwaters at the NE corner.

Moorage

A marina protected by three breakwaters offers transient slips for yachts. The outer breakwater is marked by three lights (see chart 18682) with about 12 feet at the slips. Apply to the Marina Office by the pier for a space on an end tie or a mooring if one is available. But you can anchor in the outer harbor (12 to 20 feet mud and sand), where there is space for hundreds of boats. The anchorage offers complete shelter, even in NW winds up to 45 knots. However, you must be careful to anchor clear of the permanent moorings, which take up much of the space.

Facilities

Water and fuel can be obtained in the marina, while all provisions can be purchased within a short distance. Limited repair facilities.

Pillar Point Marina, No. 1 Johnson Pier: (415) 726-5727.
Harbormaster: (415) 726-5727.

Half Moon Bay to Santa Cruz Harbor (Chart 18680)

The 46-mile passage between Half Moon Bay and Santa Cruz takes a full day. The coastline consists of high, often yellow bluffs, a short coastal plain, and low, tree-covered mountains. The scenery can be particularly attractive in the spring and early summer, when the coastal hills are heavy with green vegetation.

Immediately S of Half Moon Bay, the shore line comprises low and flat tableland for about 9 miles, marked by deep gullies. This tableland culminates in a prominent, whitish cliff over 10 feet high. A pale yellow building with numerous antennae is a conspicuous landmark to the S. The cliffs now become more rugged as you approach Pescadero Point, the next headland along the coast. S of Pescadero, the reddish coastal cliffs form a near-straight line. Keep about 1.5 miles offshore here, well clear of the many offlying rocks.

By this time, 115-foot-high Pigeon Point lighthouse Lat. 37 deg 10.9 min N; Long. 122 deg. 23.6 min W) (Fl. 10 sec. 24 miles) will be clearly in sight, associated with white buildings with red roofs. The light is 20 miles S of Pillar Point and cannot be seen E of a line which joins the two points. Pigeon Point is named after a nineteenth-century clipper ship wrecked in this vicinity, a low promontory about 50 feet high, which forms a ridge inland, with offlying rocks.

Pigeon Point lighthouse and Point Año Nuevo both make unmistakable landmarks. Nuevo, with its conspicuous sand dunes is 5 miles to the S. The distinctive skeletal tower and associated white houses leave you in no doubt where you are. Pass at least 1.5 miles offshore, well outside the lighted buoy (Fl. R 6 sec.), which lies S of the tower. Temporary anchorage may be obtained immediately S of Año Nuevo, in a bight protected by the rocks and kelp extending SE from the point. Anchor in the smoothest water inshore, with the light bearing about 260 deg. M. You will find about 5 to 6 fathoms, sand. Año Nuevo anchorage is much used by fishing boats and provides a welcome respite when northbound against strong winds. A strong smell of bird droppings emanating from the rocks to windward can spoil your berth, however.

If you are southbound, then the final moment of decision will be Año Nuevo. A visit to Santa Cruz or Monterey will take you a considerable distance off the rhumb line course to points further S. If you decide to continue S, lay off a course of 142 degrees M, which will take you to a position about 3 miles outside Point Sur on the far side of Monterey Bay.

The 18-mile coastal passage to Santa Cruz Point is extremely pleasant with a commanding wind. Sail well inside the 20-fathom line, following the shoreline. However, there is often heavy kelp off the coast, so stay well off to avoid it. As it trends toward the SE, there are no significant offlying dangers. The rock formations and colorful cliffs show up well in the afternoon sun. The steel tower and buildings of the Davenport cement works which lie 9 miles S of Año Nuevo can be seen from a considerable distance.

Santa Cruz Point light (Fl. W 5 sec. 17 miles) is displayed from a 39-foot high white lantern house on a square brick tower and brick building near the S extremity of the point. Shape your course to pass outside the lighted black and white whistle buoy "SC" (Mo. (A) W) 1.1 miles SE of the light. Santa Cruz Harbor lies in the bight between Santa Cruz Point and its light and Soquel Point 2.5 miles E.

Monterey Bay

Monterey Bay forms a large bight, extending from Santa Cruz Point round to Point Pinos. Much of this large bight is backed by long sandy beaches and sand dunes, swept by strong summer NW winds. The so-called Monterey Wind Gap sucks onshore breezes and fog into the low terrain between the mountain barriers to N and S of the bay. Monterey Bay can be a very windy place, where fogs persist for days on end. At the same time, the prevailing NW-WNW swells off the coast change direction to W as they enter the bay. The long, curved beaches at back of the Bay make for a very nasty lee shore indeed, even in typical summer conditions. Most sailing yachts keep well offshore and sail direct between Santa Cruz and Monterey. Moss Landing does offer shelter, but the entrance is dead to leeward and should not be attempted in strong winds or at night without prior experience.

The 528-foot smoke stack at Moss Landing is visible from a long distance, providing a useful barometer as to wind conditions. On summer mornings, the smoke plume blows offshore nearer the surface, but onshore at higher elevations. By late morning, the smoke streams vertically, flowing inland as the afternoon wind strengthens.

Santa Cruz Harbor (Chart 18685)

Santa Cruz Harbor is a crowded, but delightful haven with a narrow, artificial entrance which can be dangerous in SE conditions. The weather is delightful here in summer, and the harbor has a very active sailing community.

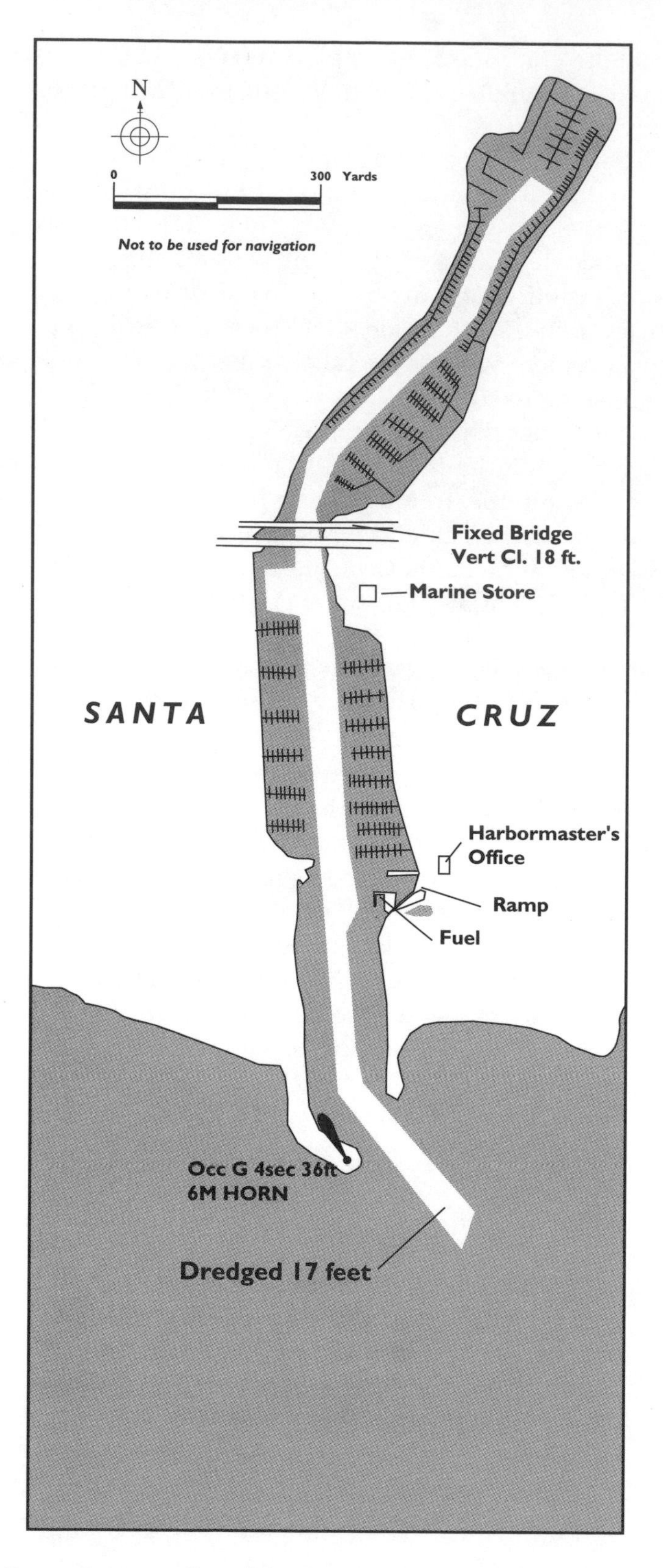

Santa Cruz small craft harbor

Approach

From N, identify Santa Cruz Point and buoy "SC." Santa Cruz municipal pier will come into view, extending 0.4 mile into the ocean, with 26 feet at its outer end. The harbor lies 0.8 mile E of the pier. Once the pier is abeam, look for the harbor breakwaters, also the roller coaster and casino, which are famous landmarks E of the town.

From S, identify Santa Cruz Point light and Soquel Point, then steer for the roller coaster, visible from some distance offshore.

Two breakwaters protect the harbor, the longer lying to the W, where a light is displayed (Oc. G. 4 sec. 6 miles). The narrow harbor entrance has about 20 feet in the seaward end of the channel. Constant dredging has made the channel safe in summer, but you must exercise caution in winter.

Do not attempt entrance in strong SE winds or when high ground swells are running, as extensive shoaling can develop.

If in doubt, contact the Port Director's office on VHF channels 9, 12, or 16. The harbor authorities will guide you through the entrance on request.

I would be careful about entering Santa Cruz Harbor at night without prior daytime experience, especially in foggy conditions.

A fixed bridge with 18-foot clearance separates the upper and lower harbor basins.

Anchorage and Berths

Anchorage may be obtained on either side of the municipal pier in 30 feet, sand, with good shelter in northerly conditions, especially closer inshore. However, a heavy ground swell can sweep in to the anchorage with strong NW winds. This berth is completely exposed to the S. Note there are restrictions on approaching the pier. Small buoys mark the swimming areas.

Guest slips are available in Santa Cruz Harbor on application to the Port Director's office at the SE corner of the harbor, or by calling Channel 16. The harbor is a very busy place, especially in high summer or during regattas. Berths are assigned on a first-come basis and you may be rafted up against other yachts.

Facilities

Fuel, water, and marine supplies are available at the harbor, while full provisioning is within easy distance.

Port Director, 135 Fifth Avenue: (408) 475-6161.

Santa Cruz Harbor to Moss Landing (Chart 18685)

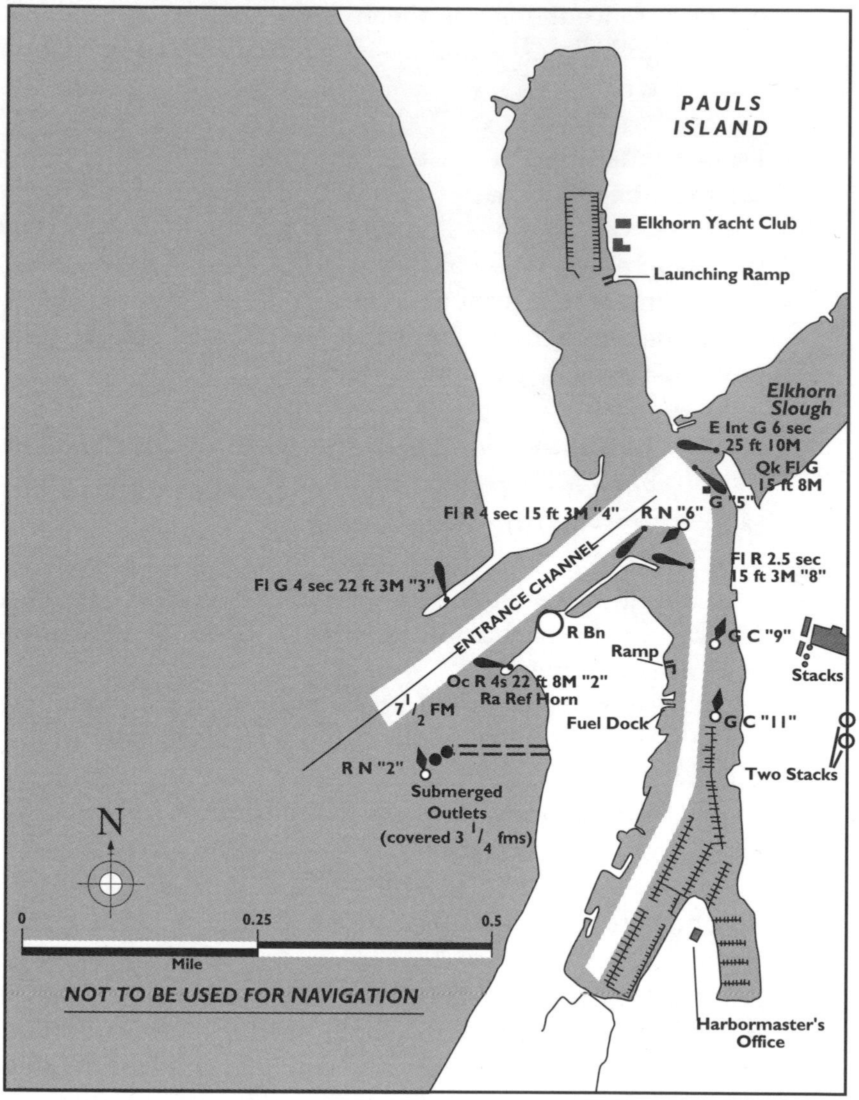

Moss Landing Harbor

You will have deep water close inshore all the way from Point Soquel to Moss Landing, with 60 feet 0.75 mile off-shore. Nevertheless, exercise caution along this coast. Fog can be very thick in the summer months, especially in the early morning hours. Heavy swells can be experienced along the shoreline, making it hard to claw to windward. A Naval Operating Area lies NW of Moss Landing. Regulations can be found in the Coast Pilot.

Moss Landing

Moss Landing is a small fishing harbor, overshadowed by a vast Pacific Gas and Electric generating plant.

Approach

From both N and S, Moss Landing is easy to identify from the 528-foot-high twin smokestacks of the enormous power plant which operates behind the harbor. For working purposes, the smokestacks can be used to identify the general position of the harbor entrance until you are close enough inshore to identify the stone breakwaters and approach buoy. Two conspicuous radio masts mark Palm Beach, 4 miles N of Moss Landing.

Under strong NW conditions, approach the entrance from upwind to counteract any leeward set below the harbor entrance.

A mooring and fueling facility for deep draft vessels exists 0.8 mile NW of the harbor entrance, its limits marked by white buoys. A buoy in the center of the demarcated area marks the fuel pipe line. Keep well clear of this vicinity.

Entrance by day or night is straightforward except in strong onshore winds. Seas can be very confused in the approach, especially in SE conditions, or after a local wind shift. Exercise extreme caution under these circumstances. Identify the red and white approach buoy (Mo (A) W.) and keep to seaward of it until the northern stone breakwater (Fl. G. 4 sec. 3 miles) is clearly in sight. The S side of the entrance has a shorter breakwater (Oc. R. 4 sec. 8 miles). A private buoy 250 yards SW of the south jetty light marks an area of violent water discharge from the power plant. Keep clear of this danger.

The entrance channel carries about 15 feet, with the center line marked by leading marks on a line of 052 deg. T at the back of the turning basin. These marks are lighted and visible from about 8 miles out (see chart 18685). The concrete bridge carrying highway 1 across Elkhorn Slough is conspicuous from seaward.

When traversing the entrance channel, keep to the N side in strong NW winds, if traffic permits, to avoid any possible leeward set.

Once in the turning basin, visitors should turn to starboard and follow the Inner Channel into the marina area. A shallower channel to port with about 8.5 feet and marked with private buoys leads to the Elkhorn Yacht Club and a small boat launch ramp. Do not attempt this by night without local knowledge and sound carefully by day. There is a 5 mph speed limit in the harbor.

Facilities

Visitors' berths are assigned by the Harbor Office at the head of the Inner Channel, on the port side. You can visit in person, or call on VHF Channel 16. Berths must be vacated by 9am on the day of departure and all visitors are warned they may have to locate on a day-by-day basis. Moss Landing has an excellent fuel dock, where water can be obtained. Provisions can be obtained near the harbor, showers are available, and you can pump out your holding tank at a facility in front of the Harbor Office. Marine mechanics, who service the many fishing boats in the harbor, are also available.

Elkhorn Yacht Club is very friendly and welcomes visitors to its two guest slips. Sea otters often play around the boats, while pelicans and sea lions sun themselves on the nearby sand spit.

A dinghy excursion into Elkhorn Slough Ecological Reserve can be recommended, but check local restrictions and regulations first.

Harbor Office, 7881 Sandholt Road: (408) 633-2461.

Moss Landing to Point Piños (Chart 18685)

Sand dunes and yellow beaches mark the featureless, low lying coast between Moss Landing and Monterey Harbor. Keep outside the 10-fathom line when making passage close inshore. The 18-foot line is about 150 yards offshore, so you have little warning of shallow water when sailing here at night.

The coastline rises and becomes more rugged at Monterey and NW to Point Pi§os. George Davidson described it as "rugged, composed of granite, and covered with a heavy growth of fir." To which one now adds urban sprawl, for the coastline is heavily developed. Monterey is now a bustling tourist resort, fishing harbor, and foreign language center. Davidson records how small Portuguese whaling boats operated in Monterey Bay from May to November. Over 16,000 gallons of whale oil came from these hunting operations in one year alone.

Point Pi§os, which marks the S end of Monterey Bay, is low and rocky, with offlying rocks about 0.3 mile offshore. Point Pi§os light (Lat. 36 deg 38 min N; Long. 121 deg. 56 min W) (Oc. W 4 sec. 17 miles) is exhibited from a 43-foot white tower and is 89 feet above sea level. When rounding the point, pass outside the bell buoy (Fl. R. 6 sec.) 0.7 mile off the land.

Monterey Harbor

Monterey was a favorite port of call for early Spanish ships, and for nineteenth-century steamers, which anchored off the town sheltered by Point Pi§os. In foggy weather, an approaching mail ship would fire a gun when off the point, listening carefully for an answering report from the town, fumbling her way to anchor by monitoring the gunfire, a far cry from today's sophisticated navigational aids. Today, a busy fishing harbor offers shelter in any weather and can be approached in all but the strongest winds.

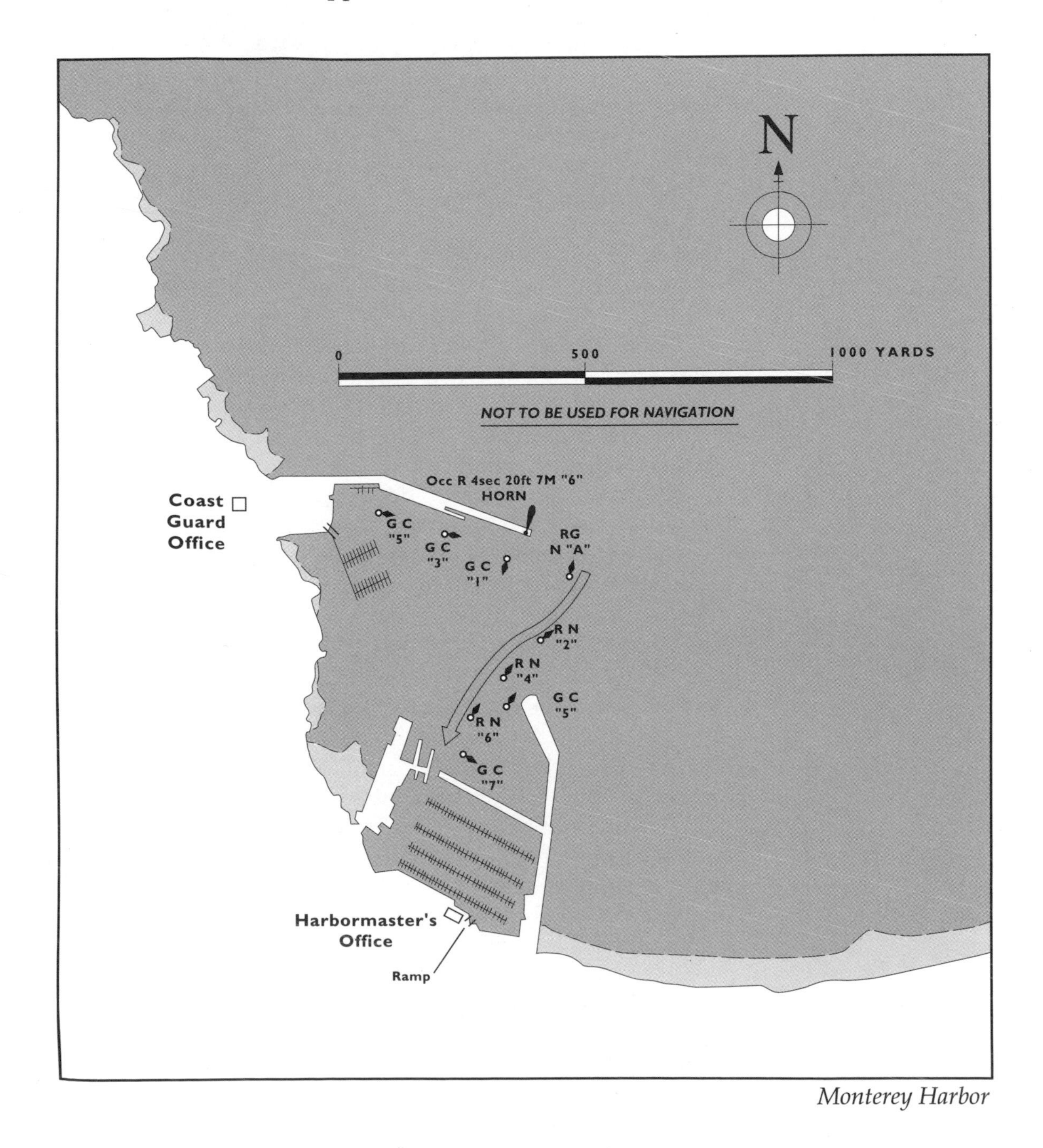

Monterey Harbor

Approach

From N. Most small craft will approach from Santa Cruz Harbor or points N. When offshore, identify Point Piños and the higher ground with buildings immediately W of Monterey. The harbor lies 3.0 miles SE of Point Pi§os. Nearing shore, identify the two radio towers close inshore at Marina, 6.5 miles NE of the harbor. Approaching land, you will pick up highrise hotel buildings, and the smoke stack and buildings of the Monterey Aquarium just SW of the harbor entrance.

Next pick up lighted bell buoy "4" 0.5 mile off Point Cabrillo. The long rock breakwater of Monterey Harbor (sometimes called Coast Guard Pier) lies 1.0 mile further SE. A light (Oc. R. 4 sec. 7 miles) is exhibited from at piling at the end of the breakwater, where a horn sounds in foggy conditions.

From S. Round Point Piños, passing outside the offlying bell buoy, then shape a course SE along the shore staying 0.75 mile off the land until buoy "4" is identified.

The harbor entrance lies between the main breakwater and Municipal Wharf Number 2, which forms the eastern boundary of the harbor. Enter midway between the pier and breakwater, keeping a careful eye for fishing boats and other local traffic.

A narrow entrance between Municipal Pier 1 (Fisherman's Wharf) and a sea wall extending out from Pier 2 leads to the inner harbor where the slips lie. Exercise caution when using this narrow defile.

Anchorage and Berths

Anchorage may be obtained S of the breakwater in 30 feet or so, sand and clay, but this is an uncomfortable berth. You can also anchor E of Municipal Pier 2 in similar holding ground, but watch your depth meter for shelving.

Visitors' slips lie on Pier H, inside the seawall. Call the Harbormaster on VHF Channel 16 before entering harbor. Some people prefer to take a transient slip in Breakwater Cove Marina closer to Fisherman's Wharf, but a reservation is advisable.

Laundry, fuel, water, and provisions are readily available, as are marine supplies and mechanical or yacht service. A small trolley comes into its own here, for town is a short walk from the harbor.

Harbormaster: (408) 646-3950
Breakwater Cove Marina, 32, Cannery Row: (408) 383-7857.

The Big Sur Coast (Charts 18686 and 18700)

Point Piños to Point Sur (Chart 18686)

The coastline between Point Piños and Pinnacle Point is densely populated and low lying, with patches of dense woods. Pacific Grove, the Pebble Beach Golf Course, and Carmel extend more-or-less continuously along the shore. The lights of Carmel and Pacific Grove can be seen from a long distance offshore on a clear night. Keep at least 1.0 mile offshore along this stretch of coast, to avoid offlying rocks.

Carmel Bay lies between steep and low lying Cypress Point, and Pinnacle Point 2.8 miles S. It forms an open bight, where heavy swells can roll in, especially in winter. Water depths are extreme here, owing to Carmel Canyon in the SE corner of the Bay, with 50 fathoms near the beach in places.

Brian Fagan

Carmel Anchorages

Anchorage may be obtained in northerly conditions in Pebble Beach Cove to the W and Stillwater Cove to the E, both on the N shore of Carmel Bay. Anchor in 9 to 30 feet, rock and gravel, avoiding kelp beds where possible. Both bays offer quiet berths in normal summer conditions, but do not enter them at night on a first visit, as caution is required in the approaches. According to several recent visitors, Stillwater Cove is now so choked with kelp that holding is affected. Also, morrings in the anchorage area leave little space for visitors to anchor.

Whaler's Cove, in the SE corner of Carmel Bay, offers shelter in S conditions, but is in the Point Lobos State Ecological Reserve. Anchor in 9 to 12 feet, gravel and rock, watching out for the subsurface outcrop (8 feet) near the center of the bay. **This cove can only be used as a refuge anchorage and not under normal circumstances.**

Point Sur looking from the NW. © Geri Conser 1994

Pinnacle Point is the outer point of Point Lobos, a jagged headland about 100-feet high. You will often see sea otters and sea lions here. Give the rocks at least a mile berth. 200-foot Whaler's Knoll is conspicuous 0.5 mile ese of the point and forms a convenient landmark for finding Whaler's Cove.

From Pinnacle Point, the coastline becomes bold and rocky, becoming increasingly steep as you approach Point Sur. Several headlands project from the shoreline, but pass at least a mile offshore and shape your course to pass clear of Point Sur. Ventura Rocks are two prominent rocks about 0.6 mile offshore, 2.2 miles N of Point Sur. The conical and northernmost rock makes an excellent landmark when sailing S, for it stands out against the sand bluff N of Point Sur. When traversing this stretch of coast, you will have highway 1 as your companion. The headlights of passing cars flash continually at night as they speed along the last length of relatively straight highway before Big Sur.

Point Sur stands out from the coast at a great distance, so intermediate landmarks become unimportant, except when close inshore. The Coast Pilot describes it admirably: "A black rocky butte 361 feet high with low sand dunes extending E from it for over 0.5 mile. From N or S it looks like an island and in clear weather is visible about 25 miles." 121 miles NW of Point Arguello and 96 miles SSE of the Golden Gate, Point Sur is a major landmark by any standards, with a lighthouse 250 foot above the water (Lat. 36 deg 184. min N; Long 121 deg 54.0 min W) (Fl. W 15 sec. 25 miles). Give Point Sur a wide berth, for winds can be strong and seas confused in this vicinity. Most yachts on passage pass about 2 miles offshore, sometimes further, shaping their course to pass within sighting distance of Point Piedras Blancas, 49 miles S, if bound for Morro Bay or San Simeon Bay.

Northbound, try and time your passage round Point Sur for the night or early morning hours, when winds are calm or of lower velocity. If necessary, take shelter in Pfeiffer Anchorage, a few miles S, until the wind drops down.

As you pass Point Sur, remember the Navy dirigible USS Macon, the largest humanly-made object ever to fly. The 785-foot-long airship was held aloft by 6.5 million cubic feet of helium gas. On February 12, 1935, she was gliding north 3 miles off Point Sur when a sudden gust shattered her upper fin. The Macon suffered structural failure, lost lift, and settled tail-first into the Pacific. In 1990, the wreck of the Macon was located by a Navy submersible in 1,450 feet of water. The corroded girders of the bow and forward lie on the bottom, also the control car, where chairs and chart tables can still be seen. Four "hook-on" Sparrowhawk F9C2 fighter planes went down with the **Macon.** Their silt-covered remains are in surprisingly good condition, although they would probably fall apart if an attempt was made to lift them.

General Remarks: Big Sur Coast

A passage along this stretch of coast ranks among the most spectacular for scenery anywhere in the world. The shoreline often swept by gale-force winds and high ocean swells, especially in winter time makes for dangerous offlying waters. You do not linger along the Big Sur coast, except on the calmest of days, when a small boat with a powerful engine can explore all manner of small coves and deep water nooks. Northbound vessels tend to keep close to the land, making landfall on major headlands along the way. This strategy allows you to take advantage of nearby refuge anchorages if the wind pipes up on the nose. Maintain an accurate Dead Reckoning Plot at night, to monitor your progress and to allow estimates of when Point Sur light will be sighted. Southbound sailing yachts usually find themselves with a dead run, often before a considerable swell. Many skippers stay well offshore and set a clear course, while others tack downwind, to minimize the danger of gibing, and to stay in touch with the land. A course about 5 miles offshore will often leave you with the tops of the mountains clear, while lower elevations remain in fog.

Timing a journey along the Big Sur Coast requires nice judgement.

Southbound, I always try to be well past Point Sur as the midday wind fills in from astern. You then enjoy a fast passage with spectacular scenery, reaching San Simeon Bay by sunset. If bound further afield, I stay well offshore, to avoid thick fog banks which can sometimes form off Piedras Blancas and Morro Bay. A typical afternoon in summer brings a healthy NW and surprisingly steep wind waves, so you enjoy a boisterous roller-coaster ride, often under reefed main and jib. Even if the wind is blowing, you can encounter areas of restricted visibility, so keep a sharp lookout for fishing boats, which operate in all weathers within the 5-mile zone.

Northbound, I try and leave San Simeon Bay as the afternoon wind dies down, so I am close to, if not beyond, Point Sur by morning. If you meet headwinds up the coast, you can duck into a refuge anchorage like Pfeiffer, or Carmel, then slip on round to Monterey or across Monterey Bay in the evening. A non-stop passage from the Piedras Blancas area to Santa Cruz and points beyond is entirely possible when a 10-day fog cycle hangs over the coast (I have timed my last three northbound passages for such conditions and had flat calm most of the way). For planning purposes, however, I would advise breaking up the trip into shorter segments in your mind, so you have alternatives available if you need them.

Point Sur to Pfeiffer Refuge Anchorage (Chart 18700)

Immediately S of Point Sur, keep at least 2 miles offshore, to avoid offlying rocks along much of the 6 miles of coastline between the point and Pfeiffer Point, the next major landmark. Pfeiffer Point is a bold headland at the seaward end of a 2,000-foot-high ridge 1.5 miles NE of the point, is light-colored when viewed from S. From N, the pointed summit stands out from a considerable distance. A conspicuous, 172-foot-high pinnacle rock marks Cooper Point, 1.5 miles NW of Pfeiffer. The first time I came south, this rock was a useful landmark for identifying Pfeiffer.

Many fishing boats use a refuge anchorage 0.9 mile ESE of Pfeiffer Point. This convenient bight offers considerable shelter in summer N and NW conditions, making it an ideal stopping point when seeking respite from strong headwinds. The approach is straightforward. Identify Pfeiffer Point, then shape a course to head inshore into the shelter of the land. Select an anchoring place in about 40 to 50 feet, sand, setting your anchor clear of the kelp beds. Although I have used this anchorage in quite strong winds, I would not recommend it in gale conditions. Access ashore is limited and there are effectively no facilities.

Pfeiffer Point to Lopez Point Refuge Anchorage

You now pass the most spectacular section of the Big Sur Coast, where high mountains rise precipitously from the shore. The coastline forms a series of shallow bights, offering no shelter to small craft. Only fishing boats move inshore along these 17.5 miles. The cuttings and bridges of Highway 1 are visible from seaward, as are the headlights of occasional cars at night.

Several mountain peaks form good landmarks, notably Junipero Serra Peak, 10 miles NE of Lopez Point, identified by the pine trees growing on and near its summit.

Point Lopez is a 100-foot-high tableland feature, marked by 51-foot-high Lopez Rock, which has a prominent cleft in the middle, lying 0.3 mile off. Give Lopez Point a berth of at least 0.75 mile, to avoid an offlying shoal SW of the promontory. Anchorage may be obtained in an open roadstead in the lee of Point Lopez. The best berths lie about a mile SE of the point inside the kelp bed in about 60 feet sand. (Depths are substantial all along the Big Sur Coast. Lay plenty of scope.) Keep an eye out for a rock (5 feet) in the kelp 0.5 mile SE of the point. I have never used this refuge anchorage, but it is said to offer some shelter in NW conditions.

Point Lopez to San Simeon Bay

From Point Lopez 9.5 miles to Cape San Martin, the coast continues rugged, forming an open bight. While most small craft will keep well offshore, a distance of 1.0 mile off will keep you clear of all dangers. Beware, in particular, of Tide Rock, 4 miles N of Cape San Martin. People who have passed it in calm weather say it leaves little disturbance on the surface in these conditions.

The three San Martin Rocks extending 0.5 mile offshore, readily identify Cape San Martin, a precipitous headland. The innermost rock is white, 144 feet high, and stands out from S. A cone rock and a triangular-shaped rock make up the other two. Willow Creek bridge, 0.3 mile N of the Cape, makes a prominent sight from offshore.

From Cape San Martin to Piedras Blancas covers a distance of 16 miles, with the topography changing dramatically at Ragged Point, the 10-mile mark. The rugged cliffs fall away, as the coastline becomes low bluffs and rolling, treeless hills. Few notable landmarks appear before Ragged Point. Easily recognized, it is the first point S of the deep San Carpoforo Valley. I always keep some distance off the coast here, for numerous kelp-fringed rocks extend offshore.

You can anchor SE of La Cruz Rock, 3 miles NNW of Piedras Blancas, a berth said to be safe in strong NW winds, but I have no first-hand experience of this spot.

Piedras Blancas is a low, rocky point, which projects out about 0.5 mile from the general coastline. Two large rocks lie about 500 yards offshore and about 0.8 mile E of the promontory. George Davidson said: "Nothing else like them is found on this part of the coast." He's right! Piedras Blancas light with its 74-foot white conical tower is 142 feet above sea level (Lat. 35 deg 39.9 min N; Long. 121 deg 17.1 min W) (Fl. 10 sec. 25 miles). It is visible from a long distance day and night (see page 143).

Most passage-making yachts pass at least a mile offshore, then head for San Simeon Bay or Morro Bay Harbor. But you can anchor under the lee of Piedras Blancas in about 25 feet, sand, with the lighthouse bearing about due W, distant about 0.2 mile. I have not used this anchorage myself, but people have told me it offers moderate shelter in NW winds.

A lowlying coast leads to tree-covered San Simeon Point, which projects SE. The dark trees, visible from a considerable distance, offer an excellent landmark for the anchorage tucked behind the point. At night, the lights of Hearst Castle can be seen 2.7 mile NE from far offshore.

San Simeon Bay (Chart 18700)

This pleasant cove makes an excellent stopping point both when waiting for suitable conditions to traverse the Big Sur Coast, and also for visiting Hearst Castle. San Simeon Point offers good shelter in NW conditions, although swells can sometimes come round into the anchorage. The cove becomes a suicidal lee shore in strong SE winds.

San Simeon Bay from WNW

Approach

From N, identify the dark patch of trees on San Simeon Point, then the bell buoy (Fl. W 6 sec.) 0.4 mile SE of the point. Pass outside the buoy, then shape a course for the middle of the cove, well clear of kelp and any moorings.

From S, the red-roofed buildings and pier may be more obvious than the dark trees of Point San Simeon. You will also see Hearst Castle and the new Visitor's Center inshore. Steer for the middle of the cove, leaving the bell buoy well to port.

Owing to extensive kelp and the lack of approach lights, arriviang and departing at night is not recommended.

Anchorage. In the center of the bay, in 30 feet, hard sand. Take careful account of the surge when settling on a berth. Extensive kelp grows outside the anchorage and sometimes inside it, so set your anchor accordingly.

Landing and Facilities

Land at one of the ladders on the pier, but look out for surge on windy days. Do not leave your dinghy at the pier, but beach her. This is a wet landing in any swell, so tend to land toward the W at the head of the bay, although this is no guarantee of a dry arrival.

San Simeon Bay is a State Park. There are restrooms and a small concession ashore. The main attraction is Hearst Castle. The modern Visitor's Center is a short walk ashore on the other side of Highway 1. Conducted tours of parts of the 168-room Castle run throughout the year. Shuttle buses leave from the Visitor's Center. For reservations and information, call 1-800-444-4445. Hearst Castle, a unique experience, should not be missed, even by the most ardent socialist.

From San Simeon Bay, you can enjoy an easy day's sail to Morro Bay, or embark on a more ambitious passage to Point Conception and Southern California.

Chapter 10

San Simeon Bay to Point Conception, including Cojo Anchorage

George Davidson surveyed Point Conception in 1853. He spent endless days on the windswept headland, remarking with some feeling that "once seen it will never be forgotten." By the same token, a rough weather passage around this headland makes a memorable experience. The sailing directions in this chapter describe the coastline between San Simeon Bay and this most famous of Pacific capes. Included are strategies for rounding Conception.

> *Point Concepcion is the most prominent and interesting feature between San Francisco and the peninsula of Lower California. It has very justly and appropriately been termed the "Cape Horn" and the "Hatteras" of the Pacific, on account of the heavy northwesterlies that are met here..."*
>
> George Davidson
> *Directory for the Pacific Coast,* 1858.

San Simeon Bay to Morro Bay Harbor (Charts 18700 and 18703)

San Simeon Bay, in many peoples' view, is a jumping-off point for a passage past Conception. A visit to Morro Bay can be strongly recommended, especially for those in need of fuel or provisions.

From San Simeon, the coast runs nearly straight in a SE direction 14 miles to Point Estero. The mountains recede from the coast here, leaving rolling topography at a low elevation. Good cattle country. George Davidson observed how "wild oats growing here over six feet high-not one or two stalks, but in acres." Today, highway 1 the San Simeon motel sprawl run behind the cliff, where thick groves of pine trees are scattered on higher ground. Cambria village lies about a mile inland 6.5 miles S of San Simeon, with some of the houses being visible from offshore. You cannot anchor or land at Cambria, beyond which the cliffs become higher. Maintain a course to pass at least a mile offshore, keeping an eye out for water breaking over submerged Von Helm Rock (8 feet), 7.2 miles NW of Point Estero and nearly a mile offshore.

Point Estero marks the N extremity of Estero Bay (Chart 18703), which curves E for 5 miles, then S for 11 miles to Point Buchan. The northern shores of Estero Bay are often heavily infested with kelp, with some off lying rocks. The Estero area is notorious for its fogs, which persist for days on end in summer. Low bluffs, cliffs, and sandy beaches extend from Point Estero to Morro Rock, which lies 6 miles N of Point Buchan.

Cayucos pier lies in the NE part of Estero Bay, 4.5 miles N of Morro Rock. There is 12 feet at the outer end. Anchorage may be obtained over a sandy bottom in 50 to 60 feet with the white concrete tank on a hill W of Cayucos bearing about 010 degrees M. I have never used this anchorage, but it is said to offer only limited shelter in N and NW conditions.

Morro Rock not only marks the entrance to Morro Bay Harbor, but is the most prominent natural landmark in Estero Bay. Named by the Spaniards El Moro, the cone-shaped rock stands out from the lowlying coastline and can be seen from miles away.

Keep clear of the tanker mooring area, marked by white buoys, for 3 miles N of Morro Rock. You will sometimes see quite large tankers loading crude close inshore from these moorings.

Morro Bay Harbor (Chart 18703)

Morro Bay, one of my favorites, perhaps because I have used it so many times. This busy fishing port has escaped much of the ruthless gentrification which has descended on so many of California's harbors.

Approach and Entrance

From N: Morro Rock and the three 450-foot powerplant stacks 0.5 mile E of the rock clearly visible from a long distance, provide all the landmarks you need to find the harbor on a clear day. In foggy conditions, Estero Point, Morro Rock, and Point Buchan make excellent radar targets. As you approach the Rock, stay well offshore until you sight the approach buoy (Mo (A) W), and the stone breakwater extending 600 yards S of the rock. This breakwater is lit (Fl. 5 sec. 36 feet 13 miles), with a fog horn. You can then shape a course for the entrance, which lies between this breakwater and other built out 600 yards from the sand dunes protecting Morro Bay.

From S: Once again, Morro Rock and the powerplant offer excellent landmarks. Stay well offshore and sight the two breakwaters, which are inconspicuous against the land, especially on foggy days.

The Morro Bay Harbor entrance, notorious for rogue waves, strong currents, and shoaling, especially in rough weather, can be dangerous. The harbor bar can also be hazardous, with breaking waves at low water, especially during periods of strong W and SW winds, or when the entrance has not been dredged for a while. If you have the slightest doubts about the entrance, call the local Coast Guard office or Harbormaster on VHF Channel 16. It's a good idea to approach the entrance from SW, looking out for strong currents, especially during the flood. Keep to the W side of the entrance, as the worst shoaling is on the E side. The buoyed channel is shifted according to shoaling conditions, and you must keep within its boundaries.

Once inside the breakwaters, follow the buoyed channel round into the harbor area protected by the sand dunes and mud flats that form Morro Bay itself. Look out for strong flood streams, which may set you toward the city dock.

Anchorage and Berths

Most visitors who are yacht club members avail themselves of the Morro Yacht Club's hospitality. The club maintains a dock and a row of moorings opposite the clubhouse, which lies about 0.5 mile up-harbor from the Coast Guard pier. The club harbormaster monitors Channel 16 from 1630 to 1800 most days, especially in summer. I have always found this a very friendly club.

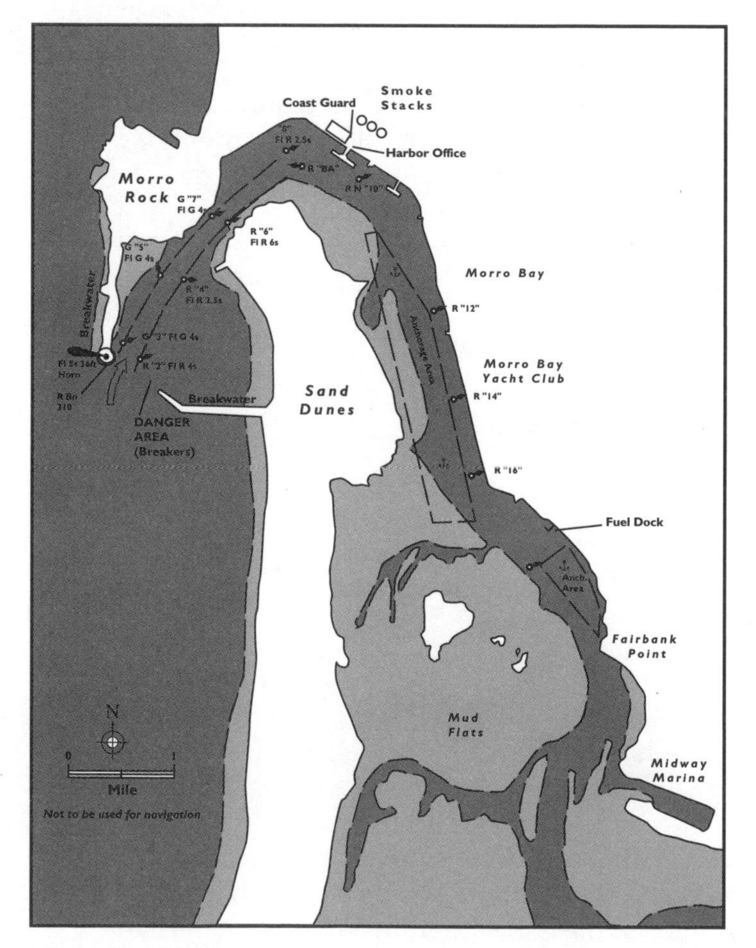

Morro Bay Harbor

You can tie up to a floating dock near channel buoy 12 for a maximum of 30 days, or anchor outside the harbor channel opposite the same marker. The tide runs strongly in the anchorage, so use plenty of scope or consider a Bahamian moor, with anchors set in direction of ebb and flood.

The Morro Bay State Park at White Point maintains a small marina, but there are no visitors' facilities. There is a launching ramp S of Morro Bay Yacht Club.

Facilities

Morro Bay is a tourist town with excellent sea food restaurants. All provisions are available in town, while fuel and water are obtainable at waterside. Diesel maintenance and other marine services are at the harbor.

Coast Guard cutter: (805) 722-1293

Harbormaster (at the foot of the city pier): (805) 722-6254

Morro Bay Harbor to Port San Luis

Diablo Nuclear Power Plant © Geri Conser 1994

Point Buchan forms a distinctive headland 6 miles S of Morro Bay. The cliff rises 40 feet high with a low tableland behind it. A whistle buoy (Fl. R 6 sec) lies 1 mile WSW of the point. Pass outside the buoy, even in calm weather.

The coast now trends SE for 9 miles, much of it cliffs between 40 and 60 feet high, with submerged rocks and ledges extending more than a mile offshore in places. Mount Buchan's rugged mass dominates this stretch of coast and can be seen from many miles away. On a clear day, Saddle Peak 4.1 miles NNW of San Luis Obispo light, is visible for over 40 miles. The two concrete domes and other large buildings of Diablo Canyon nuclear powerplant, 5.8 miles NW of Point San Luis light, are visible from well offshore. The 136-foot-high Lion Rock, with a leonine profile, lies 0.9 mile NW of the powerplant. You may encounter fishing boats working the artificial fish reef 3 miles WNW of Port San Luis light. Point San Luis marks the W side of Port San Luis. San Luis Obispo light (Lat. 35 deg. 09.6 min N; Long. 120 deg 45.6 min W) (Fl. W 5 sec. 116 feet 24 miles) on the point has a fog horn. Both this bold promontory, and Point Buchan, make good radar targets in bad weather.

Port San Luis (Chart 18704)

Port San Luis from SE © Geri Conser, 1994

Port San Luis serves as the harbor for the town of San Luis Obispo, 10 miles inland. Predominantly a commercial oil and fishing port, San Luis has little appeal for passage-making yachts with Morro Bay so close to hand, although it can be warmer and less foggy, and has more room for anchoring off. It offers good shelter in NW conditions, but can be very rough in SE gales.

Approach

From N and W, pass a mile offshore until the breakwater running SE from Whalers Island off Point San Luis is identified. You can pass inside Westdahl Rock buoy (Fl. G. 6 sec.), 1.3 miles SW of San Luis Obispo light, laying a course to go outside the whistle buoy "3" (Fl. G 4 sec.) at the end of the 2,400-foot-long breakwater.

From S, identify Point San Luis and the Whalers Island breakwater. The tank farm at the NE corner of the anchorage stands out against the land. Lay off a course to pass between Westdahl Rock and Souza Rock buoys, the latter lying 1.5 miles SE of the breakwater (Fl. (2+ 1) R 6 sec). This heading will bring you to a safe point E of the breakwater.

The bay is clear of dangers, except for Atlas and Lansing Rocks inside the breakwater. Steer between the two buoyed rocks toward Port San Luis pier.

The commercial oil port is on the N shore of the bay, its head surrounded by mooring buoys. Sometimes a tanker will be loading here. Keep clear of this pier and of the County Wharf special anchorage area below the village of Avila Beach and the tank farm at the NE corner of the bay.

Anchorage

Fishermen make heavy use of Port San Luis wharf. You can use the busy boat launching ramps lie N of the pier.

Anchorage may be obtained in an area inside a line between Fossil Point, below the tank farm, and the outer end of the main breakwater. You must, however, avoid the two special anchorage areas under Avila Beach and in the western part of the bay, shown on the chart. In practice, the harbormaster may tell you where you can anchor, but if not, keep clear of the moorings and tuck in as much as you can to avoid the surge which often rolls into the bay. The maximum tidal range is about 9 feet at equinoctial springs, so lay anchor accordingly. Alternatively, apply to the harbormaster for a visitor's mooring, which costs a modest sum. Every time I have tried to get one on a summer's weekend, they have been booked up, so try reserving one ahead of time.

Fuel, water, and limited repairs and marine supplies are available near the wharf, where there is a 60-ton mobile hoist. Provisions can be obtained within walking distance.

Port San Luis to Point Arguello (Charts 18700 and 18721)

The eastern shore of San Luis Obispo Bay, of which Port Luis is a part, is lowlying, a mixture of sand dunes and long, sandy beaches, ending in Point Sal. The houses and hotels of Pismo Beach and Shell Beach, famous for their clamming, string along the shoreline near Port Luis. Pismo Beach pier is 1,200 feet long, but should not be approached owing to submerged pilings and the ocean swell which can reach considerable heights close inshore. I always keep well offshore along the 14 miles of coastline down to Point Sal. There is nothing to attract the sailor, and, in most cases, small craft are on passage around Points Arguello and Conception.

"A peculiar and remarkable headland...Once seen it will never be forgotten."
George Davidson, *Directory for the Pacific Coast of the United States*, 1858.

Point Sal is a bold headland, remarkable for its patches of yellow sandstone, visible from some distance, especially in the oblique light of morning and evening. From NW, Sal looks like a conical hill, with two conical hills behind it, rising gradually to a ridge 3 miles E. From S, Point Sal tends to merge into the surrounding coast, but can be identified by 54-foot-high Lion Rock, 200 feet off its southern face. Stay at least a mile off Point Sal, for reefs and breakers extend 0.6 mile S and W.

George Davidson's sketch of Point Conception from NE, drawn in 1850.

Anchorage may be obtained under the lee of Point Sal in 30 to 50 feet, sand, but the berth can be uncomfortable, with relatively little protection from the swell the odd times I have put an anchor down there. The best anchorage is about 500 yards SE of Lion Rock, but look out for the shoal water on the SE corner of the area. Fishing boats are the common users of Point Sal anchorage. Coasters used to load hides and tallow here during the 19th century.

From Point Sal, the coast trends S for 19.5 miles in two shallow bights separated by Purisima Point, 10.6 miles N of Point Arguello. Although there is deep water inshore, there is little of interest along this lowlying coastline, except for the missile gantries of Vandenberg Air Force Base, which seem out of place in such a remote landscape. The Southern Pacific railroad runs close inshore. The yellow station house and a white water tower about 7 miles N of Point Arguello are prominent.

Rounding Point Arguello and Point Conception (Chart 18721)

We come now to the area known since the nineteenth century as the "Cape Horn of the Pacific." Points Arguello and Conception form a pair of formidable headlands, fog-ridden, extremely windy, and famous for their winter storms. The very names put fear into even the seasoned small boat sailor's heart. Every cruise up or down While caution and prudent seamanship are the order of the day, there is no reason why a well found vessel cannot navigate these stormy waters in complete safety. The secret lies in advance preparation.

The golden rule of rounding Point Conception is to time your passage for the right time of day and weather c Let's begin by describing the underlying causes of the high winds and

Point Conception looking from NW. Jim Aeby

rough seas off Point Conception. Then we'll discuss strategies for a southbound rounding, followed by the sailing directions for the coast between Points Arguello and Conception, also the approaches to Cojo Anchorage. We'll leave the strategies for a northbound passage until the end of the chapter, on the grounds that sailors headed north will be leaving from Cojo and following the coastal landmarks in reverse order.

The Point Conception Phenomenon

Why is Point Conception called the "Cape Horn of the Pacific?" Point Conception, like Cape Flattery, Washington, or Cabo San Lucas in Baja, create a bold edge to a major landmass, a promontory backed by mountains that function as a barrier against the prevailing winds. Its cliffs interrupt steady onshore winds that have suffered minimal friction loss over the ocean and long, regular Pacific swells that have been thousands of miles in the making. Thus, local weather conditions can differ drastically from those a few miles away. These unusual circumstances make the waters around the point notorious for their turbulence.

Daylight calms are unusual between Arguello and Conception. When offshore winds are relatively stable and cool, the point causes the air to lift some seven to nine times the height of the Cape to windward, leaving a fluky area immediately windward of the promontory. Both wind and sea conditions quiet down and conditions off Point Conception are peaceful. This stable weather condition usually occurs at night during periods of cooler, settled weather, when fog is present. Sometimes the calm conditions persist into the daylight hours and you can enjoy an idyllic passage around the Cape. Once I sailed close offshore on a calm evening when the wind was barely 10 knots and the entire landscape was bathed in pink, sunset light. I felt uneasy, for it was as if Conception was holding its breath, gaining strength for another day.

Point Conception rarely enjoys such stable conditions, for there are many factors that act together to make air flows more complex. If unstable offshore conditions, and frontal systems or pressure changes threaten far out in the Pacific, then there will be no lifting and the onshore winds will hit the Cape in full force. The air compresses, then squeezes past the point in a funnel effect that channels it through a small area at the land. This causes wind velocity to increase sharply. The As a general rule, coastal winds tend to lie down late at night or in the small hours, then pick up during the morning and strengthen during afternoon and evening. The diurnal cycle starts with offshore winds that blow at dawn and dusk when the land cools down. Then the onshore winds fill in and increase as the sun begins to heat the land. Warm air rises in a thermal effect, a sea breeze circulation now causes lower pressure at Point Conception, and the onshore wind accelerates to fill the gap. Offshore, the downflow of the sea breeze brings gustier, upper level air down to the surface. This mixture of sea breeze and upper level, higher speed air is then drawn into the airflow, funneling around

Point Conception. Under these unstable conditions, Point Conception winds can be 50% to 130% higher thanthe strong breeze well offshore. In other words, an 18 knot wind offshore can have a local velocity at Conception as high as 27-42 knots. Strong gusts, irregular swells, and wind waves accentuate heavy weather conditions off the point. Great swells refract off the cliffs and can hit you in several directions at once. The onshore wind will increase all day as the sea breeze effect gains strength and heating persists.

My first southbound passage around Conception was in a 32-foot, heavy displacement sloop. Four miles NW of the point we broached-to under a reefed main and small jib when a gust hit us at the same time as a confused swell on the quarter. The cockpit flooded. It took an hour to clear up the mess below. Had we not been wearing safety harnesses, someone would have gone overboard.

So exaggerated are local conditions that a giant wind shadow can extend up to 20 or 30 times the height of the point away from the land to leeward. You can be taken aback in a few seconds as you sail into the shadow, which can be felt up to a mile off of Point Conception.

Swell conditions off Conception are rougher than offshore. The headlands refract swells, already heightened by the increased wind speed. You will normally encounter the roughest water where the winds are strongest or immediately to leeward of the windiest area.

Fog is a major problem past Conception. You can count on between 12 and 20 foggy days a month at Arguello between June and October, days with visibility of less than 0.5 mile. The worst months are September and October. Foggy conditions are highly localized, so that Conception can be clear while Arguello is fogbound. Although wind conditions tend to be quieter on foggy days, this is not an invariable rule.

If you plan a cruise round Point Conception, be prepared for strong winds and steep seas, also unpredictable weather conditions. A high degree of Russian roulette comes into play. The last four times I have been up at the Point, it has been flat calm, yet I know others who have waited for days in Cojo Anchorage for that quiet night when they can motor north in comfort. Point Conception is always a gamble, but one where intelligent planning reduces the odds of a rough baptism.

Planning a Southbound Passage

Southbound's the easy way under sail, for chances are you'll have a strong northwesterly to speed you on your way. Most people set out on the downwind passage from San Simeon or Morro Bay. The most economical passage is from San Simeon, for you avoid the extra miles into Morro Bay. Timing is of the essence if you are bound for Cojo Anchorage in the lee of Point Conception, for the approaches to the cove are unlit and there are no lights ashore to help you find your way toward land. Plan the entire passage so that you arrive off Conception in full daylight. Such timing takes advantage of the afternoon northwesterly as you approach the Arguello-Conception area with time left to anchor safely. As you come abeam of Purisima Point far to port, the wind will increase, dramatically, sucking you downwind toward your destination. Reef down, watch for gusts, and enjoy the ride!

Timing this particular passage requires an early morning start and some hours of powering until the wind comes up, but the effort's worth it.

If you are bound non-stop for Santa Barbara, Channel Islands, or destinations beyond the Santa Barbara Channel, then timing considerations are of lesser importance. However, you will enjoy the passage more if you carry the full strength of the afternoon wind past Conception.

While under power, you will find the smoothest conditions for your passage during the calm night-time hours. Unless you have radar and GPS, the same cautions about Cojo Anchorage apply. Be sure to keep well off Conception to avoid the outlying rock.

When bound non-stop from Northern California past Conception, your best course lies about 5 to 7 miles offshore, where you will miss the worst of the confused seas off the point.This course will take you into the Santa Barbara Channel, while allowing you the benefit of the stronger winds which blow along the N shores of the Channel Islands. As you approach the mouth of the Channel, you will encounter shipping entering the Traffic Separation Lanes in these waters.

Before departing on a passage past Conception, check the Vandenberg Missile Range firing schedule on Channel 16 "Frontier Control," or by calling (800) 648-3019 for a recorded message on the status of the Range. If you can time your passage for a weekend or public holiday, you are practically guaranteed no missile activity.

Sailing Directions

Points Arguello and Conception lie in a magnificent natural setting. South of Purisima Point, the coast becomes rockier, with the railroad trestle over La Honda Canyon 2 miles N of Point Arguello being conspicuous. Give the shore a wide berth. Onshore currents frequent this vicinity, and swells close inshore can be extremely dangerous. The seaward end of the Santa Ynez mountains is near Arguello. The 2170-foot Tranquillon mountain can be seen behind the jagged, rocky promontory. Arguello is inconspicuous and rocky, projecting about 800 yards W of the coast as a whole. The small light structure exhibits a powerful flash (Lat. 34 deg 34.6 min N; Long. 120 deg 38.9 min W) (Fl. W 15 sec. 24 miles) from a height of 120 feet above water level. The point is unmistakable because of the huge missile gantries that rise like silent monoliths close inland. The railroad passes immediately inshore of the coastline.

Hondo, just north of Point Arguello, witnessd one of the worst disasters in U.S. Naval history in 1924. A crack flotilla of destroyers bound south past Point Conception at full speed and relying on Dead Reckoning plots in the days before radar, turned inshore too soon in a thick fog. Six of them ended up on the rocks, fortunately with relatively minor loss of life.

I once sailed close inshore at Arguello on a quiet summer's evening. The visibility was perfect, the wind a soft 10 knots. Even the swells were minimal, birds fishing from the weathered rocks close to the water's edge. The landscape resembled a moonscape of razor-sharp rocks, desolate grass, and the ever present sounds of the Pacific. The missile gantries towered high above us, silent and menacing in the soft light. Arguello was a surrealistic experience, and an awesome place even on a calm evening. This is no place to be caught on a lee shore. No sane sailor should approach this headland under anything but calm conditions.

S of Arguello, the coastline forms a 12 -mile bight of cliffs and sandy beaches. Keep well outside this large bay, where currents are irregular. The shallow water swells on this coast must be seen to believed. Temporary anchorage may be obtained inside the kelp off Jalama State Beach, but only in quiet conditions.

Point Conception is a bold headland with relatively low land behind it, so much so that you can confuse it for an island from offshore. The light (Lat. 34 deg 26.9 min; Long. 120 deg 28.2 min W) (Fl. W 30 sec. 26 miles) is displayed from a 52-foot high tower behind a house at the W end of the point, and is 133

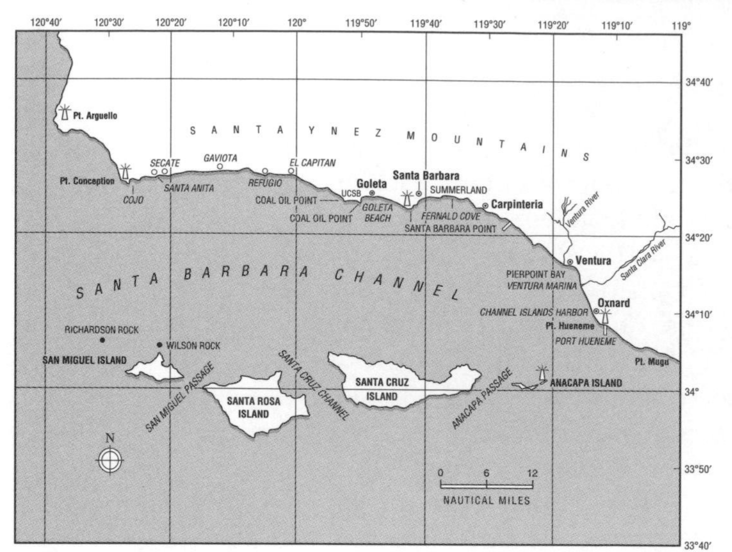

Santa Barbara Channel

feet above sea level. From S, the sloping geological strata and yellow cliff are very marked. The land trends sharply E at the point, as you enter the Santa Barbara Channel. If passing close inshore, give Point Conception a berth of at least a mile. A low, black rock lies 220 yards SW of the light, "upon which some of the California steamers have struck in very foggy weather," George Davidson tells us.

Chances are you'll sail past the point in fine style, perhaps well reefed down. As you admire the spectacular scenery, the wind suddenly drops to less than 10 knots, or dries up completely. This line is a testimony to the localized weather conditions in this area, for you have now entered Southern California waters, where benign weather conditions are a relaxing norm.

Jim Aeby

Cojo anchorage looking from SW.

Cojo Anchorage (Chart 18721)

Cojo Anchorage has been a popular resting spot ever since the days of the conquistadors. Named after a long forgotten Chumash Indian chief, Cojo was a major whaling cove in the early nineteenth century. Davidson considered this anchorage was preferable to that off Santa Barbara, where the artificial harbor was only built in 1927. He admired the sweet flavored beef, spoke of plentiful firewood, but complained of the "disagreeable" water. The large roadstead is well sheltered from prevailing N and NW winds. Cojo is extremely uncomfortable even in moderate S and SE winds. NW gales can be bumpy here.

Approach

From W: We cannot improve on George Davidson: "Gradually round the bluff one mile distant from the cape, giving it a berth of half a mile run on a NNE course for three quarters of a mile, when the valley will open up with a sandy beach off it." A high railroad embankment traverses the back of the anchorage immediately above the beach, disappearing behind a high cliff to the S. A conspicuous railroad culvert offers a good landmark for entering the cove. Stay well offshore to avoid heavy kelp growth.

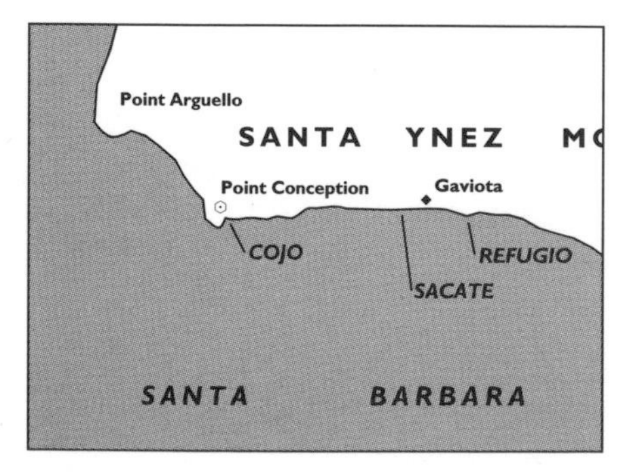

From E: Shape your course to make landfall about 1 mile E of Point Conception, then identify the railroad embankment behind the anchorage. Once again, the culvert is a good steering mark for the anchorage. Coasting along the shore inside the kelp from Gaviota, you can identify Cojo from the railroad embankment and low bluff just E of Conception.

Do not confuse Cojo with Little Cojo, 1.7 miles E of the anchorage Little Cojo is heavily kelp infested. The bottom is rocky.

Anchorage

Opposite the railroad culvert or under the cliff, clear of the kelp in 25 to 40 feet, hard sand. Keep away from the mooring buoys, which are used by oil tender boats. Such vessels come and go at all hours of the day and night.

Facilities

None.

Planning a Northbound Passage round Point Conception

None other than the great British circumnavigator Eric Hiscock waited for days at Cojo Anchorage to round Point Conception. He retreated in despair, remarking to a friend of mine that the California coast was a demanding cruising ground.

Like the keys to a southward passage, the keys to a northbound voyage use the same set of general weather conditions: Be sure to round the point during the calm night hours. Although there are no guarantees, the best months for rounding Conception are early summer or September and October, when fogs are commonplace and fog cycles can last ten days or more. Under these conditions, you may be able to motor north past the Point in the middle of the day, with a reasonable guarantee that the afternoon northwesterly will not be unduly strong.

Predicting weather conditions at the Cape is not easy, for area forecasts refer to areas north of Conception, or a broad corridor of the Pacific labeled as "from Point Conception to San Nicolas Island and outer coastal waters." While strong winds in this forecast may well mean heavy air at Conception, conditions are so localized that you may find a quite different situation at the cape when you finally reach Cojo Anchorage. If you are bound from Santa Barbara to Conception, you can sometimes predict wind and swell conditions at "Cape Horn" by studying the wave sets on Leadbetter Beach, immediately west of the harbor breakwater. Steady, quite high waves despite locally calm conditions may be a sign of high afternoon winds at the cape. It takes some days to get accustomed to the changing sets on the beach, but after a while, you can tell which sets mean wind at Conception. When foggy conditions have settled over the Santa Barbara Channel for a couple of days, you can be relatively confident that winds at Conception are calm, making these the best circumstances for motoring north.

Whatever wind strengths you expect at the cape, your best strategy northbound is to anchor in Cojo Anchorage and then wait for a period of calm winds, such as often prevail at night. It's always a mistake to generalize about the weather anywhere, let alone at Point Conception, but even strong afternoon winds tend to drop at nightfall on many days of the year. With patience, you'll have the calm conditions you need.

While some brave (or rash) souls make non-stop passages from Southern California past Conception, a first-time voyager should pause at Cojo, to enjoy the luxury of choosing the calmest hours for rounding the point. Many people adopt the strategy of leaving Santa Barbara in early morning. They arrive at Cojo anchorage after a passage of about 40 miles in the late afternoon. Once at Cojo, they enjoy a leisurely dinner and a short sleep. Then up anchor at midnight and round Conception about 1.5 miles offshore. Even if conditions are calm, you may experience some bumpy swells, but be closing Morro Bay or San Simeon by mid-morning. Be prepared, however, for a wait. You might be forced to remain in Cojo for several days before conditions are suitable, even at midnight. Both fog and wind should shape your decision. Do not hesitate to return if you find open water conditions unsuitable.

If circumstances dictate you not stop at Cojo, then time your arrival off Conception for the late evening, so you can motor northward during the calmest hours. To attempt the passage at midday is to invite discomfort and slow progress.

The non-stop passage from Conception to Morro Bay or San Simeon takes you through the oil fields of Point Arguello, where you can expect small boat traffic. The offshore oil rigs are brilliantly lit, but keep well clear and keep a lookout for unlit mooring buoys in their vicinity. You can fix your position electronically, or by regular bearings on Arguello and Conception lights. On a foggy day, your first landfall near Morro Bay will be somewhere close to Point Buchan, perhaps on the large conspicuous domes of the Diablo Canyon nuclear power plant. Bound for San Simeon, you may remain out of sight of land until somewhere around Cambria before the fog lifts. At that point, you should be able to see Hearst Castle and the white buildings at San Simeon Bay ahead.

Again, let's reiterate. With careful planning and a well found yacht, there is nothing to fear from Point Conception.

Part Three

Sailing Directions

The passage [from Santa Barbara] to Newport, California, is a distance of only a hundred and twenty miles, but it took us three days. The mist hung on, and for a day and a night we navigated by the sound of the traffic along the coast road, coming about, for the wind was ahead, when the roar grew too loud, and again when it had almost ceased..."

Peter Pye
The Sea is for Sailing (1957).

Santa Barbara Channel to Enseñada, Mexico

CHAPTER 11

Mainland Coast: Point Conception to Point Hueneme

The wind line at Point Conception draws a symbol of a very different, less boisterous world in Southern California. The sun seems hotter, the sea warmer directly after you leave Conception's waters. You are also entering the Santa Barbara Channel, one of the finest cruising grounds along the West Coast, perhaps in North America.

I have described the many anchorages and harbors of the Santa Barbara Channel in *Cruising Guide to Southern California's Channel Islands* (Caractacus Corporation,1992). Anyone planning to linger in the Channel or at the islands might want to refer to the book for more detailed sailing directions. In the following pages, I confine myself to general passage-making strategies, and to descriptions of major ports and convenient, popular island anchorages.

The surface of the sea, which was perfectly smooth and tranquil, was covered with a thick slimy substance, which, when separated or disturbed by any little agitation, became very luminous, whilst the light breeze that came principally from the shore, brought with it a very strong smell of burning tar, or of some such resinous substance. The next morning... the sea had the appearance of dissolved tar floating upon its surface, which covered the ocean in all directions.

George Vancouver,
on a natural oil seep near Goleta,
1798.

Passage-Making Strategies

The strategies for longer passages in the Santa Barbara Channel vary considerably depending on your destination. South-bound, you have the advantage of prevailing winds behind you, while a journey northward flies in the face of afternoon westerlies. Channel crossings to and from the Channel Islands take you across more than 20 miles of open water and involve a quite different set of variables, which differ from port to port. Careful advance planning will make even a windward passage a pleasant experience, so here are some thoughts on strategy.

The key elements in passage making in the Santa Barbara Channel are the strength of the westerly in Windy Lane, off the northern shores of the Channel Islands, described in Chapter 7, and the likelihood of being able to use an evening or early morning land breeze or southeasterly. The strategies which follow take account of these factors.

Southbound Passages

Much depends upon where you are bound. If your destination lies in the Los Angeles area or at Catalina Island, I strongly advise staying inside the Channel Islands, riding the prevailing westerlies down the north shore of Santa Cruz Island, then passing through the Anacapa Channel and then south. In this way, you take advantage of the predictable stronger winds closer to the islands. Use the additional wind power of the Anacapa Channel, where the westerlies funnel between Anacapa and Santa Cruz. Once clear of the Channel, you are some distance off the mainland, with a slightly lower, but by no means fail-safe chance of being becalmed at night. Most people who sail south outside the Channel Islands complain of lighter winds and sometimes long periods of calm. A more conservative course takes you inside.

When bound for Channel Islands or Ventura Harbors at the eastern end of the Santa Barbara Channel, or for any of the islands, shape a course to pass within 3.0 miles or so of the northern shore of Santa Cruz Island. With luck, you'll carry the westerlies at Point Conception along Windy Lane, then ride the afternoon wind which funnels between Anacapa Island and the mainland. If your destination is Ventura, you are best off staying close to Santa Cruz Island, and reaching off to the mainland on the fastest angle possible, knowing the wind will lighten as you sail inshore. Generally, the westerlies blow stronger at the eastern end of the Channel than they do close to the mainland W or near Santa Barbara, enabling you to sail right to your destination most summer afternoons.

Santa Barbara lies 40 miles to leeward of Point Conception, on a direct course which takes you fairly close inshore. Chances of light winds or flat calm increase along this course, especially E of Gaviota. You are almost certain to be becalmed by sunset and all night. As you clear Conception, stay offshore, keeping in Windy Lane until Santa Barbara is on the port bow. On many summer days, you'll make a fast passage along the islands, then haul your wind onto a comfortable reach to your destination. This may seem like an indirect course, and it is, but your chances of significant wind are much higher, with an added bonus. If the westerly drops as you approach the mainland, you may pick up the light SE wind, which sometimes fills in toward sunset and blows until the small hours. As your brethren inshore slat in oily calm, you will ghost softly to your destination feeling disgustingly smug! With no more certainties in the Santa Barbara Channel than elsewhere along the coast, this strategy often works.

These strategies give you the option of stopping at an island anchorage if becalmed. You can catch up on needed sleep while waiting for the winds to fill in the next day.

Northbound passages

During summer, the afternoon westerlies fill in by noon with such regularity they have been called the California trade winds. Unless you like long hours on the wind, plan your passages to windward ports for the night and early morning hours. Once you have made the long run from the Los Angeles area to Santa Barbara Channel or the islands, you can harbor hop your way along the islands or mainland in easy day passages, ending up at Cojo for the next long leg. Much of this windward work will be under power, but the enterprising skipper can squeeze in some sailing by careful observation of local conditions. For example, a delightful offshore breeze sometimes blows at Ventura and Channel Islands Harbor at night and in the early morning hours. Get up early, set your spinnaker, and enjoy a wonderful sunrise passage to somewhere like Pelican Bay on Santa Cruz Island. You can then work your way from cove to cove as far as San Miguel Island over the next few days. Alternatively, sail across to Santa Barbara on the afternoon westerly, then make a 40-mile passage to Conception. Though such winds are unpredictable, if you happen upon one, then take advantage. They make all the difference.

Cross-Channel Passages

Bound from Santa Barbara Harbor to Santa Cruz Island, you will be hard on the wind near the mainland if sailing to somewhere like Pelican Bay. Plan to leave early in the morning, motor for one or two hours, steering to windward of your destination. By mid-morning, the westerly should be filling in and you can bear off comfortably. Be prepared to tuck in a reef in Windy Lane, as the afternoon summer wind regularly blows at 20 to 25 knots close to the islands.

Channel Islands Harbor and Ventura are to leeward of the Channel Islands. Most people power up to the islands in the calm hours, on the grounds that a few hours of motoring will give them more time in paradise. Avoid a late start, which put you in Windy Lane during mid-afternoon. Beating your brains out against steep wind waves is not a sailor's idea of heaven.

Whatever your destination, avoid approaching the islands at night unless you have local knowledge and there is at least a half moon. The Channel Islands are effectively unlit on their north side and even the major anchorages are hard for a stranger to identify in the dark. Above all, take care not to be benighted on your first visit to the islands. My very first passage took me from Santa Barbara Harbor to Prisoner's Harbor on Santa Cruz Island on a beautiful fall afternoon. The sun set when we were still seven miles off. Fortunately we had a good wind and were able to identify the warehouses behind the Prisoner's pier in the twilight. But we anchored in complete darkness with the aid of a depth meter and little else. I remember the gentle crash of small wavelets on the beach close astern, and a wonderful smell of eucalyptus leave wafting offshore in the dark. Had we been an hours later, we would have had to spend the night at sea.

Sailing directions for the Santa Barbara Channel are divided into two chapters. This chapter covers the mainland, Chapter 12 the northern Channel Islands.

Mainland Sailing Directions

Cojo Anchorage to Santa Barbara (Charts 18720 and 18721)

At Point Conception, the mainland trends sharply E for 12 miles. Low, yellow-brown cliffs lie along the beach, with deep gullies extending up to the mountains inshore. The Southern Pacific railroad follows the coastline and the trestles are conspicuous from seaward. This remote coast is well worth exploring. Details of local anchorages can be found in the *Cruising Guide To Southern California's Offshore Islands* (hereafter referred to as the *Cruising Guide*).

Gaviota Canyon forms a large gash in the Santa Ynez Mountains which can be clearly identified from some distance. A large railroad trestle and a pier mark Gaviota State Park. A series of large oil storage tanks and a processing plant lie 1.5 miles E of the pier. Strong down-canyon winds can sweep over the coast between Gaviota and Point Conception even on calm days. Exercise caution under sail and be prepared to reef down in a hurry.

Dense kelp beds line the coastline between Gaviota and Goleta, 20 miles E. The Santa Ynez Mountains provide an imposing backdrop to the coast all the way to Ventura. Rolling foothills and steep canyons slope down to the low coastal bluffs, normally between 50 and 100 feet high. Both the railroad and US 101 run parallel to the coast. You can anchor at Refugio State Beach (oil platform Hondo is offshore) and El Capitan Bay (see *Cruising Guide*).

Once past the oil pumping facilities at Ellwood, you come on the Goleta-Santa Barbara urban sprawl at Coal Oil Point, a low, sandy promontory with shallow water and kelp extending some distance offshore. Keep at least 1.5 miles off, to avoid a kelp-infested rock (15 feet) 0.9 mile off the point. Oil platform Holly lies 1.5 miles SW of Coal Oil Point. It makes a conspicuous landmark, even on foggy days. A natural oil seep off Coal Oil Point emits a petroleum smell on the afternoon wind.

Anchorage may be obtained off Goleta pier, which lies in the lee of lowlying Goleta Point in a shallow indentation just E of the highrises and bell tower of the University of California at Santa Barbara campus (see *Cruising Guide*). The bay makes a good berth in moderate westerlies, and a wonderful place for a lunch stop. The University bell tower is an excellent landmark from a long distance offshore.

The coast from Goleta to Santa Barbara Harbor rises to a moderate height, with cliffs reaching an altitude of about 150 feet. Many expensive homes lie on the bluffs overlooking the ocean. A sandy beach runs along the cliffs and a sometimes dense kelp bed mantles the coast in a depth of about 35 feet.

Santa Barbara Point, capped with trees and houses, slopes steeply into the ocean. Santa Barbara light(Lat. 34 deg 23.8 min N; Long. 119 deg. 43.4 min W) (Fl. W 10 sec. 25 miles) is exhibited from a small tower and is relatively inconspicuous until you are within a mile or so of the headland.The light is a much better landmark at night, because the flash stands out against the city lights. E of Santa Barbara Point, the coast slopes down toward Santa Barbara Harbor, whose artificial breakwater runs parallel to the shore. You can identify the harbor from the yacht masts behind the breakwater, which tends to merge with the land. When approaching from W, give the point a wide berth, as dense kelp beds lie close offshore.

Santa Barbara Harbor (Chart 18725)

A prime destination for Southern California sailors Santa Barbara harbor, so much so that it's often hard to obtain a visitor's slip in July and August. The harbor's a friendly place, with every facility close to hand. It is an ideal place to recuperate after a long passage from north or south, and a convenient base for exploring the Channel Islands less than four hours offshore.

The harbor was paid for by Colonel Max Fleishmann of the margarine family to shelter his private yacht in 1929. A century ago, visiting small craft anchored in the open roadstead with their anchors ready to slip at a moment's notice. Thick kelp beds lay close inshore. The uncomfortable anchorage almost invariably meant a landing on the beach and a dousing.

Approach

From W. Identify Lavigia Hill, the 142-foot-high hill overlooking the harbor 0.6 mile NE of Santa Barbara Point light. Maintain a course about 0.75 mile offshore until Santa Barbara light is well astern and the white buildings of Santa Barbara City College and the stadium built into the cliff appear on the port bow. The harbor breakwater with its yacht masts runs parallel to the shore. Keep close with the breakwater, staying 0.5 mile off, until the Santa Barbara Harbor approach buoy (Fl. G. 4 sec.) and the fairway buoy (Fl. G 2.5 sec.) are in sight. Steer to pass close offshore of the latter, by which time Stearn's Wharf, which forms the E end of the harbor, will appear inshore. Once well clear of the end of the breakwater, alter course to port and enter the harbor channel between the sandbar to port and Stearn's Wharf to starboard.

From E. Lavigia Hill with its twin summits can be seen from at least ten miles off. Steer for the saddle between the two peaks until you pick up the white buildings of City College and the harbor complex, which lies to starboard of the hill. As you approach, you will identify some white condominium buildings and the Spanish Mediterranean

Hotel 3.2 miles E of the harbor. Stearn's Wharf projects clearly from the land. You will know when you are approaching the harbor by the anchored boats lying in the lee of the wharf. Once close in, pick up the approach buoys, then join the harbor channel.

From Offshore: Santa Barbara Harbor can be somewhat hard to find on hazy days. When coming in from Santa

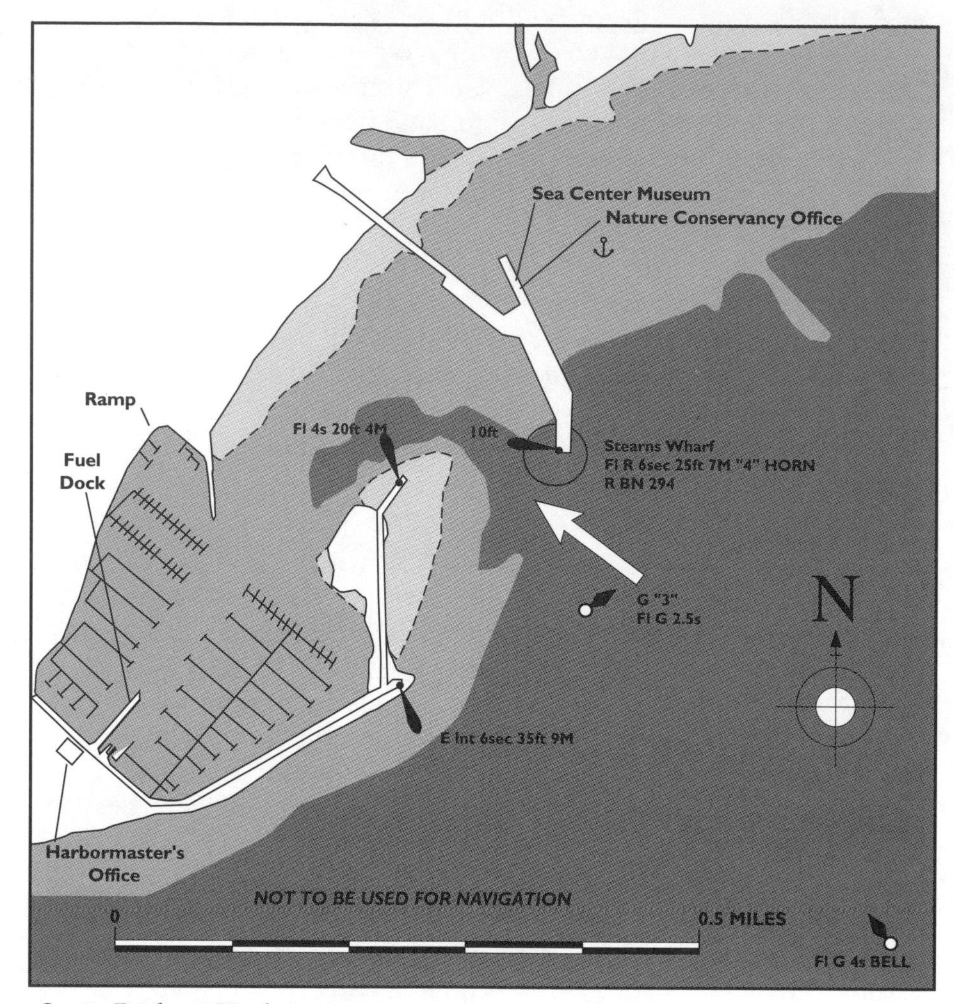

Santa Barbara Harbor

Cruz Island, your best mark is a grey-colored cleft in the Santa Ynez Mountains known as "Larco's Dip," after a well known Italian fisherman of the 1920s. Larco will bring you in past the oil rigs which lie 5.5 miles SSE of the harbor until you can pick up Lavigia Hill, the buildings of City College, and the white Bekin's Moving and Storage building which lies directly behind the entrance. A course for the City

College buildings will suffice and keep you slightly to windward until the approach buoys and Stearn's Wharf come into sight to lead you into the channel.

At night, Santa Barbara light is a useful guide from offshore if you keep it well on the port bow until you pick up the lights on the harbor breakwater (Iso. W 6 sec. 9 miles) and Stearn's Wharf (Fl. R . 6 sec. 7 miles).

Santa Barbara Harbor entrance is subject to shoaling and can be very dangerous in strong SE winds, when the sandbar which protects the harbor is a lee shore. A buoyed channel is maintained, which curves sharply to port as you near the tip of the sandbar to starboard. If you follow the channel buoys you will have no problem with the entrance. Under SE and other rough conditions you can raise the harbor patrol on VHF Channel 16 for advice on the channel. At certain times of the year, a dredge operates in the channel, which restricts the space available for navigation. A first time night entry can be tricky, for the small channel buoys are hard to see against the city lights and the flashing light on the critical green buoy by the sandspit is often hard to see. Once round the sandbar, which is also lit (Fl. W 4 sec.), a 225-foot-wide channel leads to the head of the harbor.

Moorage and Facilities

Anchoring in the harbor is forbidden. Visiting yachts should secure to the float at the head of the harbor and apply to the Harbor Director's office nearby for a berth. Visitors are limited to a 14-day stay. If the harbor is full, anchorage may be obtained E of Stearn's Wharf in 35 to 60 feet (soft sand). This anchorage is reasonably smooth in summer, but suicidal in SE gales. You can land your dinghy at Stearn's Wharf.

All facilities are available at or near the harbor, including showers. There is a boatyard, a small boat launching ramp, and a fuel dock. The Chandlery below the harbor director's office is an exceptional marine store which offers outstanding service. Provisions can be obtained a short distance from the harbor. Ask for directions or call a cab.

There is much to see in Santa Barbara, including a late eighteenth-century Spanish mission and Presidio, well-known art and natural history museums, and the Sea Museum on Stearn's Wharf. Old Spanish Days Fiesta in early August offers an orgy of parades, dancing, parties, and general good times. The Santa Barbara to King Harbor race coincides with Fiesta. More than 150 boats take part, filling the harbor to the limit for two or three days before the start.

Harbormaster: 132A, Harbor Way. (805) 564-5520.
Weather recording: (805) 962-0782.

Santa Barbara to Ventura Harbor (Chart 18725)

Traveling E from Santa Barbara with the prevailing winds, you may benefit from an eastgoing current, which sometimes flows at between 0.25 and 0.50 knots close inshore. Monitor the current by looking at the wash created by the harbor approach buoy.

Once you clear the urban sprawl of Santa Barbara and Montecito, the cliffs rise sharply to a 250-foot high yellow bluff, Ortega Hill. The small village of Summerland lies immediately E of the hill, fronted by a sandy beach which runs all the way to Carpinteria, another small town which boasts of the safest beach in the world. It may be safe for swimmers, but keep at least a mile offshore to avoid breakers on isolated sandbars and reefs. All the way to Ventura, US 101 follows the low lying shoreline, backed by foothills of the Santa Ynez Mountains. The white buildings of Carpinteria and Santa Claus Lane E of the town are visible from a long way offshore, even in hazy weather.

E of Carpinteria, low lying Rincon Point forms a slight indentation popular with surfers. Four-and-a-half centuries ago, Juan Cabrillo landed at this very uncomfortable berth. The Rincon has distinctive yellow-brown, contoured bluffs inshore of the freeway. The bluffs can be seen from a long way off. From here, the mountains now press on the shore, with 2,000-foot peaks behind the beach. Punta Gorda, E of the Rincon, stands out because of the oil piers and artificial island 0.5 mile offshore. This island displays a light (Fl. W 5 sec.) at night and should be given a wide berth. Bright lights from the oil facilities in this vicinity are a useful landmark at night. Pitas Point 5.5 miles NW of Ventura is a low spit running seaward from a steep slope. Keep at least a mile offshore along this coastline to avoid kelp and occasional offlying rocks.

The coastal mountains fall away into the Ventura River Valley, with a large freeway bridge 4.4 miles E of Ventura Harbor.

Ventura Harbor (Chart 18725)

Ventura Harbor is an attractive and friendly harbor, often missed by visitors from Northern California because it is a little off the direct course to Catalina Island and the Los

Ventura Harbor © Geri Conser 1994

Angeles area. Unfortunately, the entrance can be very dangerous in strong westerly winds, but improvements will be made in the near future. Ventura is an attractive alternative to Channel Islands Harbor except in bad weather.

Approach

From W: Once opposite the freeway trestle 4.4 miles E of the harbor, look for the prominent highrise Holiday Inn building, which lies close to shore 0.5 mile E of the green- and yellow-roofed buildings of the Ventura County

Fairgrounds. Then identify the fishing pier just E of the hotel, by which time you should see the harbor breakwaters and the Ventura harbor whistle buoy "2," (Fl. R 2.5 sec.) 0.5 mile from the entrance.

From S: Identify the Mandalay Bay power plant with its high smoke stack 3 miles SE of Ventura Harbor. Approach the coastline with care, until you see the tall Channel Islands National Park building behind the harbor entrance.

The entrance lies between the S end of the detached breakwater (Fl. G 2.5 sec., 5 miles) and a rock groin, the channel carrying 20 feet into Pierpoint Basin. Do not enter from the N end of the detached breakwater, where there is only 3 feet.

Warning. Do not attempt Ventura Harbor entrance when high swells are running and strong W or NW winds blowing. Shoaling can make the channel extremely hazardous. Under these circumstances, divert to Channel Islands Harbor.

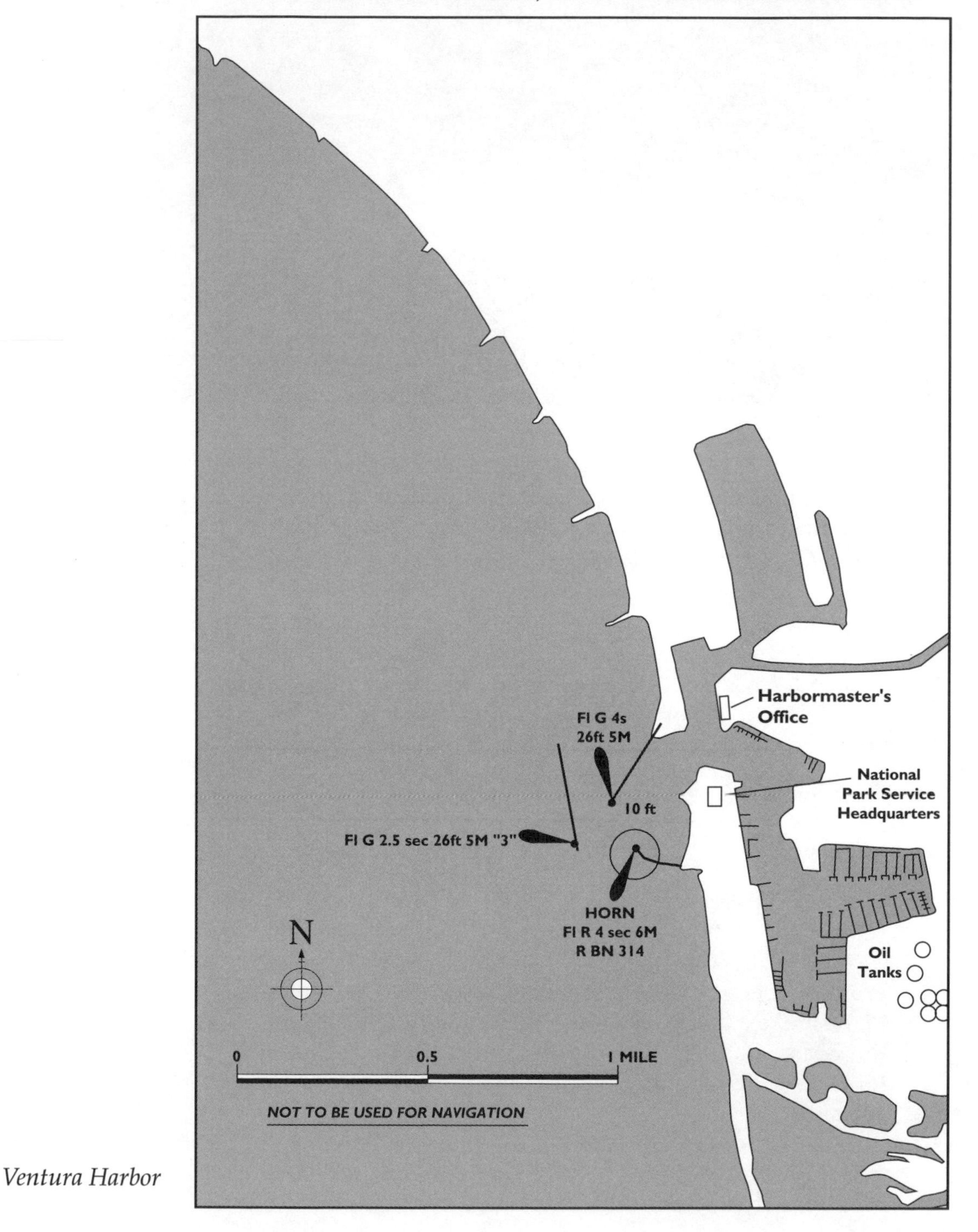

Ventura Harbor

If in doubt about conditions in the entrance, raise the Harbormaster on VHF Channels 16 or 12.

A first-time night visit is best made with local knowledge, as the entrance lights are hard to spot against the blazing city lights ashore.

Berths

All three harbor marinas have guest slips and full facilities for the visitor. Anchoring in the harbor is prohibited. You can anchor in Pierpoint Bay W of the harbor entrance, but the berth is uncomfortable and rarely used. George Vancouver spent a day recovering a fouled anchor here.

Facilities

Excellent facilities for repairs and marine supplies. Provisions are a short cab ride away. A visit to the Channel Islands National Park headquarters and to Ventura's excellent Maritime Museum is strongly recommended.
Harbormaster: Ventura Port District, 16033 Anchors Way Drive. (805) 642-8538.

Ventura to Channel Islands Harbor (Chart 18725)

A low lying, sandy beach stretches SE to Point Hueneme, then E to Point Mugu, the ocean extremity of the Santa Clara plain. The five miles of coastline between Ventura Harbor and Channel Islands consists of low sand dunes and a yellow, sandy beach, with few features of interest ashore. The single, 225-foot red and white smokestack of the Mandalay Bay powerplant is a superb landmark, visible from miles offshore. When approaching this coast, identify the powerplant, then stay well offshore until you have identified the harbor which is your destination. Large swells than roll onto the beaches here, and you should give the beach a wide berth. The low lying coastline ends at low, sandy Point Hueneme a mile E of Channel Islands Harbor. Point Hueneme light (Lat. 34 deg 08.7 min N; Long. 119 deg. 12.6 min W) (Gp. Fl. W (5) 30 sec. 20 miles) is exhibited from a 52-foot-high light with a fog signal, a useful landmark when entering or leaving the Santa Barbara Channel at night.

The prevailing westerlies tend to blow stronger at the E end of the Channel. You are almost guaranteed a nice sailing breeze most afternoons.

Channel Islands Harbor (Chart 18725)

Channel Islands Harbor is a large modern yacht harbor, with every facility imaginable. The entrance is safe in all but the roughest weather, and the port has ample space for

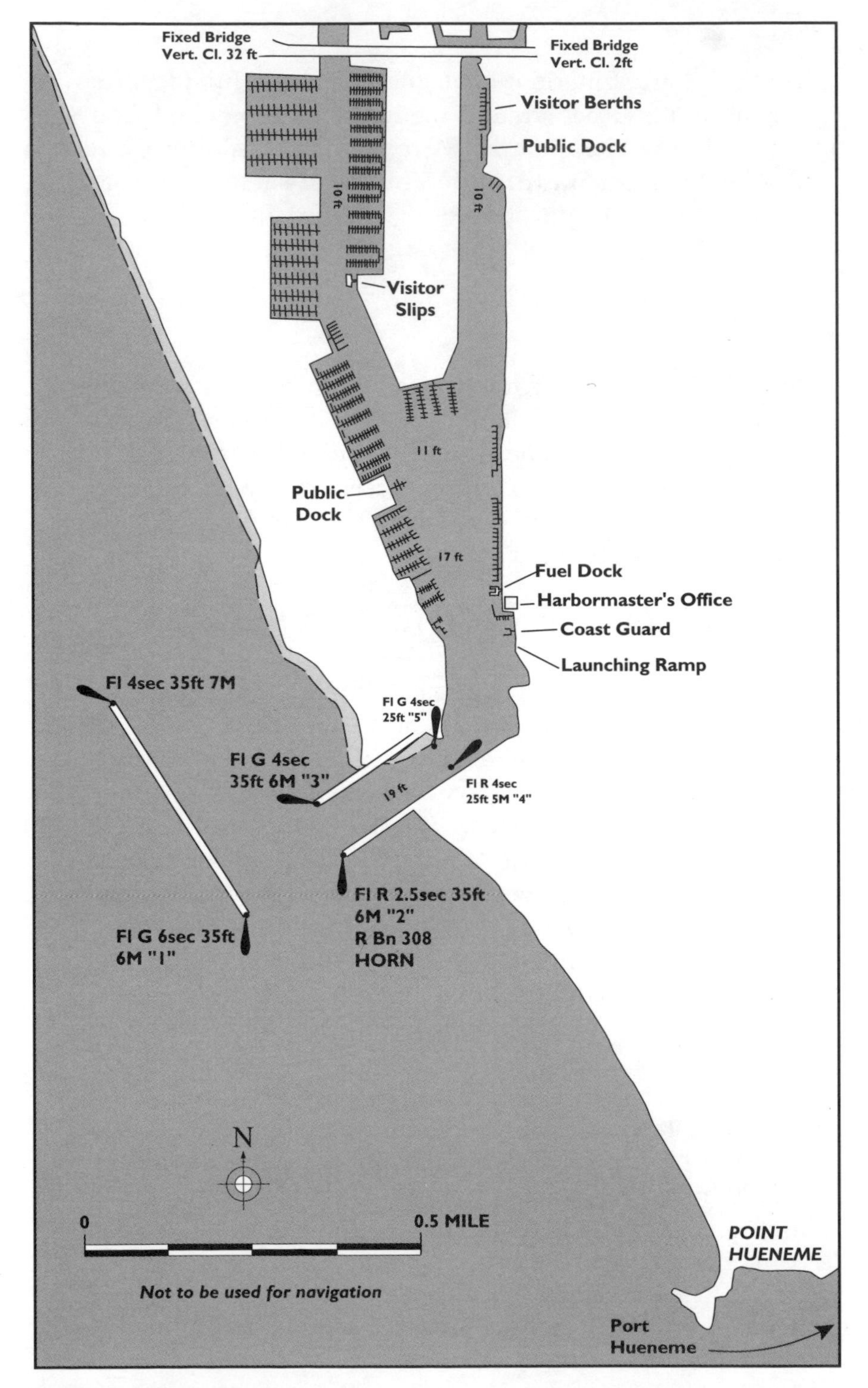

Channel Islands Harbor

visiting yachts. Channel Islands is an ideal stopping off point both north-and south-bound because it lies close to Point Hueneme and the direct course from the Santa Barbara Channel to Southern California ports.

Approach

Channel Islands Harbor can be difficult to identify, for there are no conspicuous landmarks at, or behind the breakwaters.

From W: Identify Point Hueneme and Mandalay Bay powerplant, then shape your course one mile N of Hueneme. A large square building at the point is a good landmark. Channel Islands Harbor breakwater lies about 1.0 mile SE of the N end of a row of beach houses which extends along the coast from Point Hueneme. The detached 2,300-foot breakwater of the harbor can usually be spotted about 2 miles offshore on a clear day. Once the breakwater is in view, alter course for its S end.

From SE: Round Point Hueneme, staying 0.75 mile off the land while keeping a look out for commercial traffic leaving Port Hueneme. Follow the coast N and you will see Channel Island breakwater a mile ahead. Shape a course offshore of the breakwater, but close to the S end, where the entrance lies.

The harbor entrance lies between the S end of the detached breakwater and two rock jetties 300 feet apart. At night the jetty lights can be seen at a distance 0of about 5 miles (Fl. R and G. 4 sec). The entrance channel is dredged to 13 to 20 feet. After 0.5 mile, the channel trends N. The harbormaster's office and dock and Coast Guard docks will be seen on the starboard bow. A shoal extends from the N shore of the channel immediately seaward of the Fl. G light marked on the chart.

Do not use the northern entrance channel between the shore and the detached breakwater without local knowledge.

Berths

Apply to the harbormaster's office for a visitor's slip. Forty bare available. Channel 16 is monitored on a 24-hour basis. Guest berths are also available at the privately-owned marinas in the harbor. You cannot anchor in Channel Islands harbor. There is a launching ramp on the E side of the harbor.

Facilities

Three boatyards offer all repair facilities, while ample fuel and water can be obtained. Small grocery stores are near the harbor, and Oxnard is a 2 1/2-mile cab ride away, where all provisions and other needs will be found. People planning a long passage can avail themselves of a large Wal-Mart and Price Club/Cosco within cab distance.
Harbormaster: 3900, Pelican Way. (805) 985-5544.

Port Hueneme (Chart 18725)

Port Hueneme, a mile from Channel Islands, is a commercial harbor maintained and operated by the US Navy and Oxnard Harbor District. Large commercial vessels and oil boats use the harbor day and night.

Since Channel Islands harbor is so close, and there are no facilities for pleasure craft, use the former except in extreme emergency.

Point Hueneme with Channel Islands Harbor entrance to N © Geri Conser 1994

CHAPTER 12

Northern Channel Islands

When we neared Fry's Harbor the vision changed to one of extreme beauty. The harbor was surrounded by high rocky cliffs, which were covered with scrub oak, cactus, and many succulent plants. These were in full bloom, making masses of yellow, red, lavender and magenta color...The water in the bay was so blue and so transparent that I could see the rocks on the sandy ocean bottom.

Margaret Eaton, *Diary of a Sea Captain's Wife* (edited by Jan Timbrook, McNully and Loftin, Santa Barbara, 1980).

The Channel Islands are a favorite destination for skippers from British Columbia to Mexico. The unspoiled islands are a superb cruising ground, ideal for a weekend visit or for a cruise lasting several weeks. Many Northern California sailors make the long passage down from the San Francisco Bay area just to spend time in Santa Cruz Island's remote coves. With dozens of anchorages large and small at the Channel Islands, we cannot hope to describe them all in this book. Our main concern deals primarily with passage-making and the coast as a whole. Anyone contemplating a leisurely exploration of the islands should acquire the companion volume to this book: *Cruising Guide to Southern California's Offshore Islands.* The smallest coves are described in detail. Here, we touch on the highlights and give directions for a handful of major anchorages which you might use when making a transit of the Santa Barbara Channel, or during a short visit.

General Comments

Four islands protect the Santa Barbara Channel. Windswept San Miguel Island guards the western end, separated by the San Miguel Passage from Santa Rosa Island. The Santa Cruz Channel allows you to pass between Santa Rosa and Santa Cruz Island, at 20.5 miles long the largest of the four islands. The Anacapa Passage separates Santa Cruz from Anacapa Island, only 11 miles from Point Hueneme. San Miguel and Santa Rosa are relatively low lying islands, while mountainous Santa Cruz and Anacapa with steep cliffs and deep water lying close inshore offer more spectacular anchorages. The winds tend to blow stronger out at the islands. San Miguel Island's notorious westerlies remain localized and come at highly unpredictable velocities. Strong winds also funnel through the island passages, sometimes blowing 10 to 15 knots stronger than offshore. "Windy Lane," a 7-mile-wide belt of rough seas and stronger winds, sweeps along the northern shores of the Channel Islands from Point Conception. Windy Lane makes a wonderful asset for sailors bound for leeward ports, for you can ride the tail wind and shoot through the Channel in fine style. Crossing from the mainland, you can sometimes encounter winds 10 to 20 knots stronger than those closer to the mainland. Be prepared to reef and batten down the hatches in short order. On no account venture offshore when the wind blows 30 knots close to the mainland. The same northwesterly may be howling at about 45 to 60 knots near the islands.

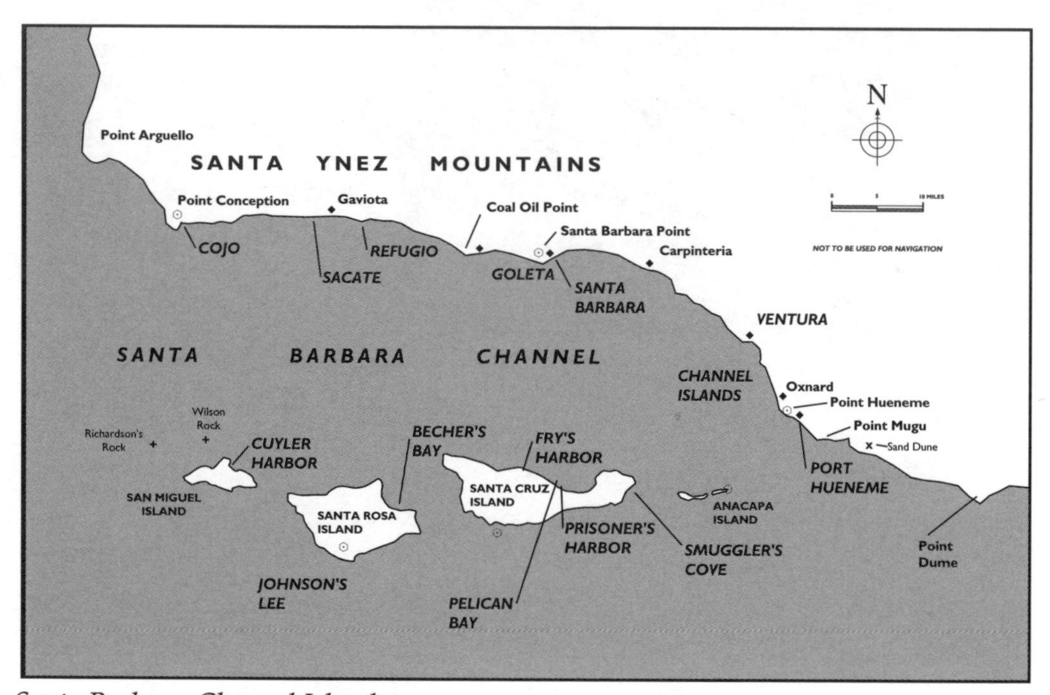

Santa Barbara Channel Islands

Landing on the Channel Islands

Anacapa Island, Santa Rosa, and San Miguel Islands belong to the Channel Islands National Park. Information on access, landing, and appointments for excursions on San Miguel can be obtained from the Channel Islands National Park, 1901 Spinnaker Drive, Ventura, CA 93001. (805) 644-8262. Santa Cruz Island's eastern portion is in process of coming under Park Service jurisdiction. The same source will give you information on access.

The Nature Conservancy controls the old Stanton Ranch property on Santa Cruz Island, from Coche Point to Sandstone Point west. You need a permit to land, the necessary document being obtained in advance from: The Nature Conservancy, PO Box 23259, Santa Barbara, CA 93121. (805) 962-6591. You can obtain application forms from the Conservancy, harbormasters' offices, yacht clubs, or chandleries. The Conservancy charges a modest fee and does not issue permits at the island. Allow at least a week to ten days for permit processing. Please do not land without a permit. The Conservancy polices their part of the island and may ask to inspect your landing document.

Santa Barbara County sheriffs, the Department of Fish and Game, also National Park Service rangers patrol the Channel Islands. The Park Service also supervises the Channel Islands National Marine Sanctuary, which surrounds the islands.

Channel Island Anchorages

San Miguel Island (Chart 18727)

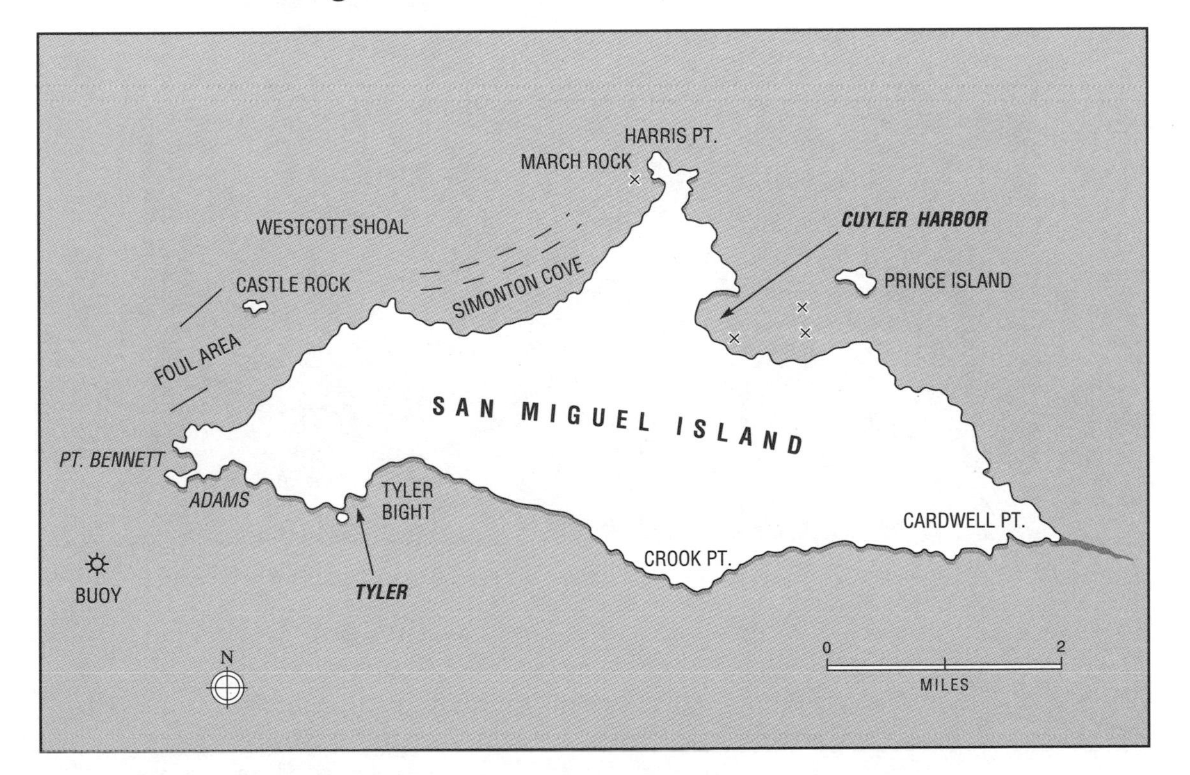

San Miguel's elephant seal colonies are famous. For this reason, anchorage around its shores is controlled. But I strongly recommend a visit in the company of a Park Service ranger as a full-day excursion.

Approach

Offlying rockers and breakers make San Miguel's W and NW shores dangerous to approach. Swells can run high in this vicinity. Eastbound from N of Point Conception, aim to pass at least 5 miles N of the W end of the island, keeping a look out for Richardson Rock, an isolated 53-foot-high rock 5.5 miles NW of Point Bennett, the western end of San Miguel. A lighted whistle buoy (Fl. R. 2.5 sec) lies 0.5 mile NW of the rock. Identify bold and precipitous Harris Point, which is visible from a long distance before closing the island. A saddle connects the point to a 485-foot-high peak 1.0 mile S of the headland. 19-foot-high Wilson Rock projects from an extensive reef 2.2 miles NW of Harris Point. Except in unusually clear visibility, either head close inshore to pass well inside Wilson Rock, or stay out until Harris Point is on your quarter before steering toward shore.

Point Bennett and the western end of San Miguel Island. You should give this area a wide berth.

Graham Pomeroy

Approaching from Santa Barbara or points E, San Miguel Island appears as two gentle peaks. Once again, Harris Point will be the prominent landmark, visible at least 5 miles off. Steer for a point just inshore of the promontory until the landmarks of Cuyler Harbor can be identified.

Effectively unlit, I do not recommend approaching San Miguel Island's shores without local knowledge, and even then only on a moonlit night.

Cuyler Harbor is the only all-weather anchorage on San Miguel, and is a dangerous place in SE winds. Named after a nineteenth-century surveyor, it offers excellent shelter and holding in the strongest of NW winds.

Approach

Harris Point is your initial landmark from all directions. Once E of the point, identify 288-foot high Prince Island at the E side of the anchorage. This huge rock lies 0.4 mile offshore. Entrance to the anchorage lies one-third of the distance between Prince Island and Harris Point cliffs. Steer inshore when about 300 yards off the cliffs, clear of the kelp and foul ground off Prince Island. Maintain a straight course toward the beach until you clear a reef which extends over 300 yards E of the NW extremity of the anchorage. Once your depth meter tells you are clear, turn W into the main anchorage.

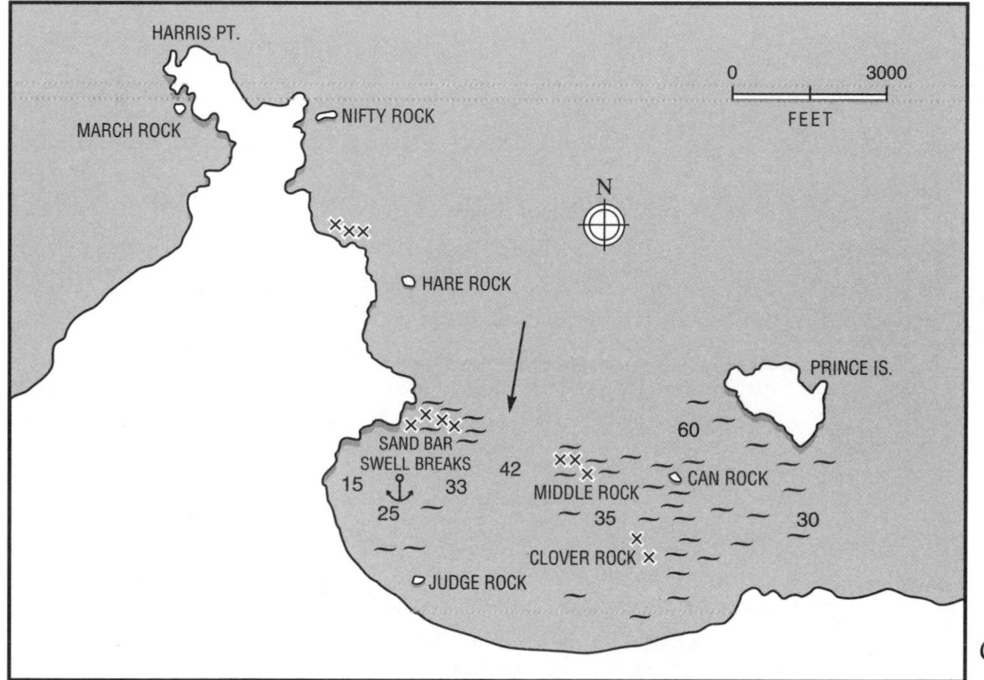

Cuyler Harbor

Anchorage

Anchor according to draft, wind conditions and surge. 20 feet will be found up to 200 yards offshore in places. Many people lay two anchors at 45 degrees to the bow here, on account of the strong winds.

Facilities

None. You need an appointment with the Park Ranger to venture further than the beach. For appointments, contact the Channel Islands National Park headquarters at Ventura Harbor (Chapter 11).

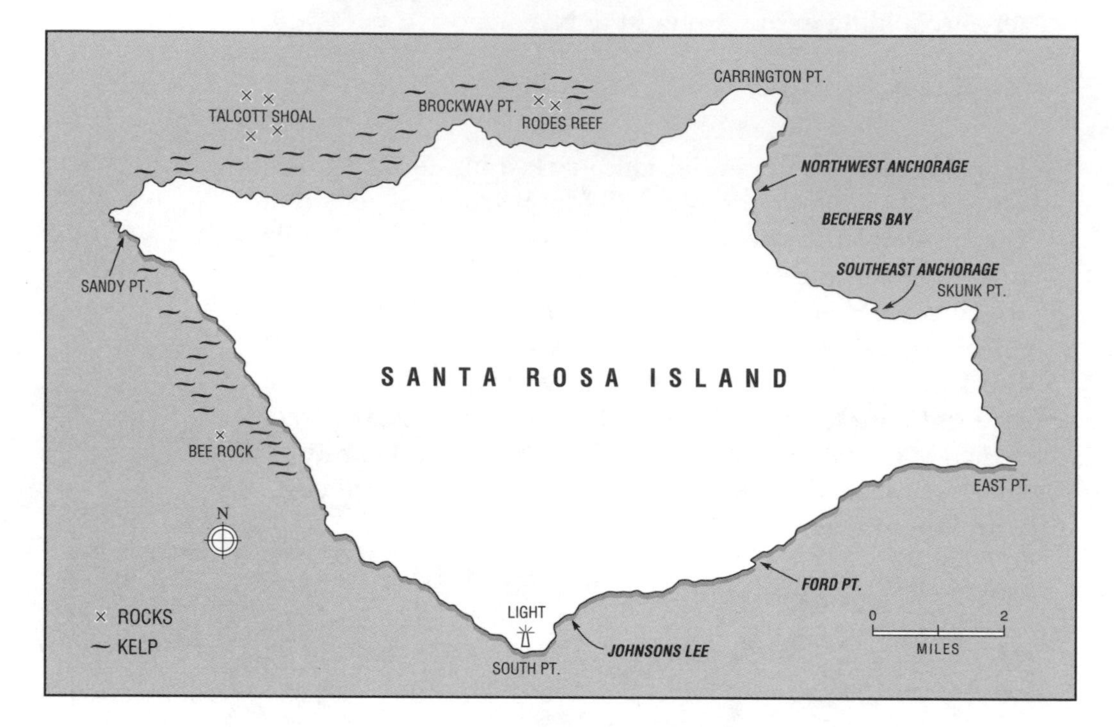

Santa Rosa Island (Charts 18727 and 18728)

Rocks and kelp obstruct the northern shores of Santa Rosa Island. Give this coastline a berth of at least 2 miles. Many small craft pass through San Miguel Passage, giving a wide berth to the sand spit at Cardwell Point, which breaks even in calm weather. A course outside offlying Bee Rock will take you past South Point and into the calmer water along the southern shores of Santa Rosa and Santa Cruz Islands.

Becher's Bay on the E side of Santa Rosa Island is a large bight, well sheltered from prevailing northwesterlies. I have ridden out 45-knot gales here in comfort. The anchorage is an excellent staging point when bound W to San Miguel Island, or for catching up on your sleep when on a long passage. Becher's has the advantage of being easy of approach, even at night. The Vail and Vickers Ranch has a pier here and you can pick up the lights of the ranch house ashore from a considerable distance offshore on a clear night.

The bold cliffs of Carrington Point, the NE corner of Santa Rosa Island are a good approach landmark. Once clear of the point, head for the low ground in the center of the bay, when you will sight the pier. Anchor under the cliffs about 0.5 mile N of the pier, in an opening in the kelp. The anchorage off the end of the pier has 16 feet, but is less comfortable.

Santa Cruz Island (Charts 18728 and 18729)

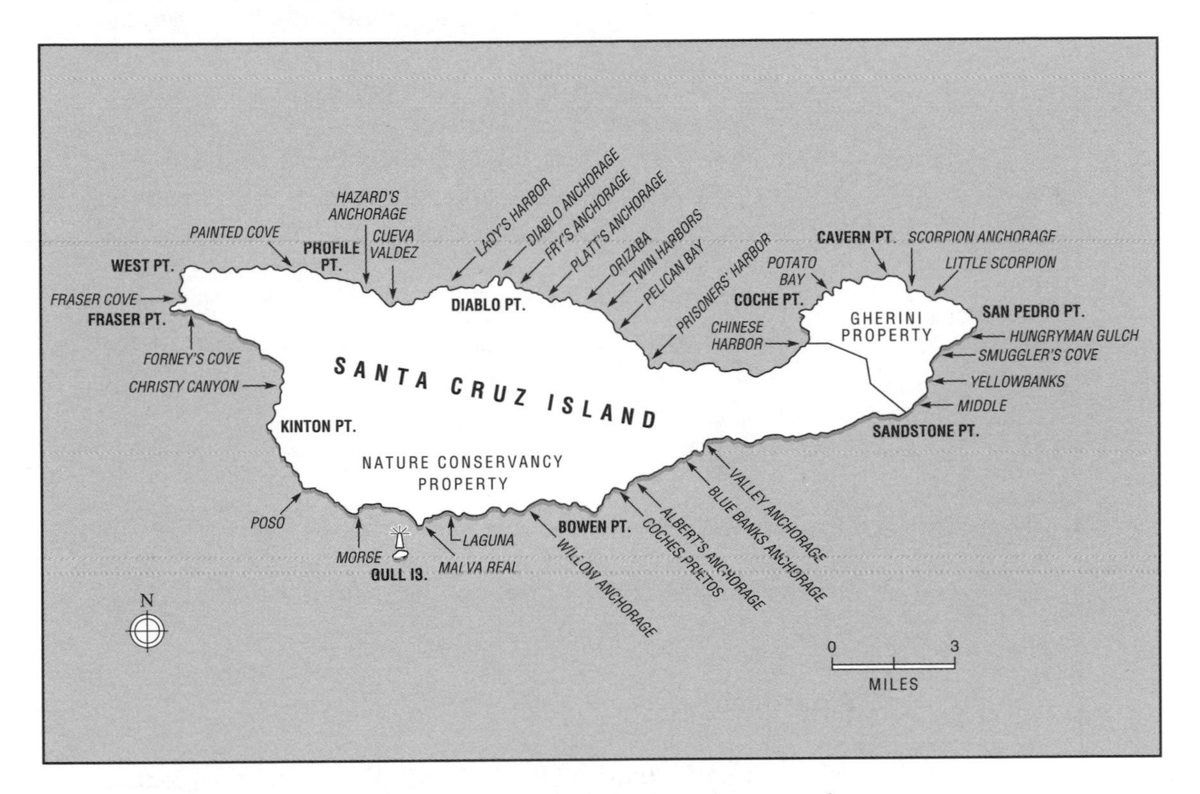

Santa Cruz Island offers a great choice of anchorages large and small, most of them on the north coast, convenient to Windy Lane. We describe five of the major anchorages here.

North Coast

The Santa Rosa Passage leads between Santa Rosa and the western coast of Santa Cruz Islands. The wind can blow strongly through here. Give the W end of Santa Cruz ample room, as seas can be disturbed in this vicinity.

Forney's Cove lies just E of West End, a shallow bay named after a government surveyor of the 1850s. Forney's is a delightful anchorage in calm weather, but the surge can be troublesome at high tide. In any sea, you will be more comfortable in Becher's Bay across the Passage. I use it as a convenient sleepover spot when bound for San Miguel or either coast of Santa Cruz. The anchorage lies E of table-like Fraser Point, behind a rocky outcrop connected to the mainland by a sand spit and rocks. Pass E and offshore of the outcrop before shaping your course into the anchorage. Anchor according to draft, with about 15 foot throughout much of the bight. Forney's is suicidal in strong NE winds.

From the precipitous West End, the north coast consists of steep cliffs with deep water so close you can almost touch the rocks from your boat, part of a massive raised beach more than 3 million years old, which looks like an elevated shelf from a distance. If you have the time, moter or sail slowly along the cliffs close inshore. The scenery is spectacular and you will sometimes encounter sea lions, even whales close offshore. The celebrated Painted Cave lies near the E end of these cliffs (see *Cruising Guide*). The cliffs end in a large bight, which ends in Diablo Point, the most prominent headland on the north coast. Fry's Harbor lies on the E side of Diablo Point.

Fry's Harbor

Fry's is famous for being the quarry for the rock for Santa Barbara Harbor breakwater in the 1920s. Although relatively small, the cove offers excellent shelter in all but NE winds.

Approach

From E or W, identify Diablo Point, the most conspicuous headland on the N coast of the island. It lies directly below the highest, 2,434-foot, peak on Santa Cruz, a good landmark when approaching from the mainland. Fry's forms a conspicuous indentation 0.5 mile E of the point, easily identified by following the cliffs from the promontory. Enter the anchorage midway between the two sides.

Anchorage

Tuck in under the W cliff (kelp and sand), as close to the beach as your draft allows, 20 to 45 feet, but any berth in the cove is adequate. Larger vessels often lie just outside in about 60 feet. Use two anchors in this often crowded spot.

Facilities

As elsewhere on Santa Cruz Island: None. Landing by permit only.

Pelican Bay and Prisoner's Harbor

The coast between Fry's Harbor and Pelican contains some fascinating small anchorages, also long slopes where you can walk and enjoy spectacular views. The coast is still steep-to, so you can pass close inshore.

Pelican Bay was once the site of a small resort hotel where Hollywood stars played in the 1920s. Sailors from all over Southern California flock to this beautiful spot during the summer months.

Approach

Pelican Bay is about 4 miles E of Fry's, behind a low bluff with several clumps of trees on its west side and a distinctive notch in its base. Use this bluff as a useful landmark from either direction. You can locate the anchorage from offshore by steering just W of the lowest ridge on the island until the high cliffs behind the cove stand out against the shore. The roofs of the warehouse buildings at Prisoner's bay also show up far out to sea. Steer for the bluff until the anchorage opens up, then steer into the middle of the bay. Pelican Bay's eastern side forms a low promontory adorned with several century plants, once landscaping for the resort which flourished above the cove in the 1920s.

Anchorage

The best anchorage lies under the western cliffs in 25 to 35 feet, avoiding loose rocks on the bottom. Grass and kelp patches litter the sea bed, so dig your anchor well in, especially when lying in the middle of the bay or on the eastern side. Pelican is sheltered, except in SE winds. Two anchors are almost obligatory, as many small craft anchor here, even in mid-winter.

Facilities

None. Hiking trails ashore. Landing by permit only.

Prisoner's Harbor, the main landing for the Nature Conservancy, lies a mile E of Pelican. Anchorage may be obtained W and offshore of the pier in 25 to 35 feet grass and sand. An uncomfortable surge often rolls in here. Pelican is a better anchorage except in very calm conditions.

From Prisoner's Harbor E, the north coast forms a large bay known as Chinese Harbor, then curves NE to Coche and Cavern Points. Beyond Cavern Point the cliffs become lower, the topography more rounded. The Scorpion area offers excellent anchorage (see *Cruising Guide*).

Smuggler's Cove lies at the extreme E end of Santa Cruz Island beyond San Pedro Point. A large open roadstead, Smuggler's offers shelter in strong NW weather, but the wind funnels off the land and two anchors at the bow are advisable

South Coast (west to east)

Santa Cruz Island's south coast has attractive anchorages, which are popular with Southern California sailors. These coves are somewhat out of the way for vessels on their way to the Los Angeles area or bound for San Francisco Bay.

Offlying Gull Island light (Fl. W. 10 sec. 73 feet, 16 miles) marks the eastern boundary of strong winds which often funnel through Santa Rosa Passage during the afternoon hours. Light air conditions often prevail along the south coast.

The southern shore is still rugged and precipitous, but is easy of approach once you are E of Gull Island. Pass offshore of the island and its kelp beds, then steer inshore toward Bowen Point (for details see *Cruising Guide*).

Coches Prietos Anchorage

Coches Prietos, "black pigs," is a delightful cove, ideal for families with small children and a perfect place to recover from an arduous offshore passage. It lies just over half way down the south coast.

Approach

From W, once past Gull Island, identify precipitous Bowen Point with its small, white offlying rock, and the brown-yellow headland with sloping strata just over half a mile

E, which forms the eastern arm of the anchorage. The narrow entrance to the anchorage will open up to port as you near this feature. The same point makes a prominent landmark from E. A semi-circular beach at the mouth of a valley extending inland forms the cove. To enter, head for the beach, keeping the headland cliffs about 40 yards to starboard, keeping an eye for kelp. You are inside once the curving point at the W side is abeam.

Anchorage

Anchor in 15 to 15 feet (sand) off the beach, keeping outside the low tide breaker line. Tuck in behind the kelp and western cliffs as much as possible, using two anchors to keep you head to surge. Alternatively, you can anchor outside in 40 to 60 feet, with limited protection from Bowen Point. Before entering, monitor the beach for surge. In rough conditions, best head for another cove.

Albert's anchorage E of the headland offers excellent protection in strong NW winds.

Facilities

None. Landing by permit only. Excellent walking ashore. You may see an elusive island fox here, a species unique to Santa Cruz Island.

E of Albert's the cliffs turn yellow and are slightly less precipitous, with extensive kelp beds off the SE corner of the island. Strong downslope winds sometimes blow in this vicinity, forcing sail boats to reef at short notice.

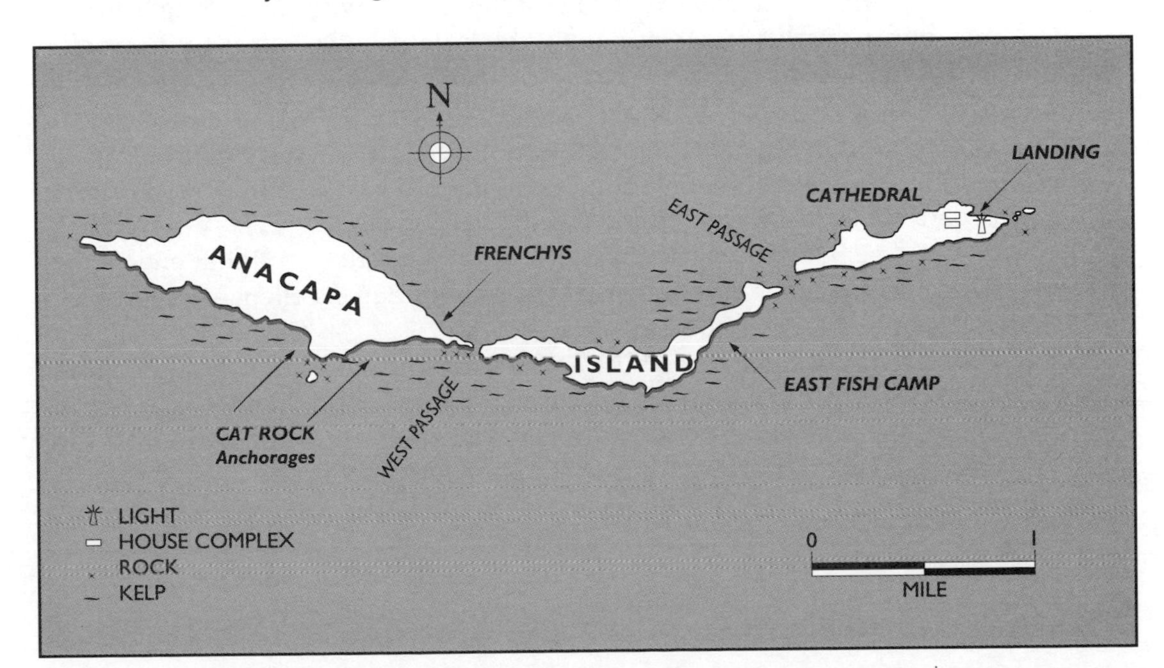

Anacapa Island (Chart 18729)

The Chumash Indian word *anyaoah,* meaning "mirage" has become Anacapa Island. Its distinctive profile has been likened to a freight train and locomotives, with the highest part, the locomotive, at the W end. Like Point Conception, once seen Anacapa is never forgotten. Precipitous and without water, Anacapa has never been settled permanently. Only government personnel manning the light and Park Service rangers have lived on the island.

On December 2, 1853 the mail steamer *Winfield Scott* struck the island in a dense fog. All the passengers and $800,000 of gold bullion were rescued safely. A young artist named James Whistler sketched the island for the pilot books. Anacapa light (Lat. 34 deg. 01.1 min N; Long. 119 deg. 21.6 min W) (Gp. Fl. (2) 60 sec. 277 feet, 20 miles) was established as a result of the Winfield Scott disaster, but for all the fuss about the wreck, the lighthouse was not built until 1912, 56 years later. Anacapa Island makes a wonderful day excursion for the family, with interesting exhibits and nature walks. Unfortunately, thick kelp beds and offlying rocks make the island hard to land on, although deep water extends inshore. Every time I have anchored off the island, I have spent an uncomfortable night because of the surge, even in calm weather.

Graham Pomeroy

Arch Rock and Anacapa light from SE, distant 0.5 miles. The lighthouse is 277 feet above sea level

The lighthouse landing lies at the NE island, but leave someone aboard when anchoring off for a visit.

The Santa Barbara Channel ends at Arch Rock at the E end of the island. Point Hueneme and Anacapa lights offer excellent signposts for entering and leaving the area at night.

This chapter gives but the sketchiest account of this fascinating cruising ground. Again, consult the companion *Cruising Guide to Southern California's Offshore Islands* for complete information on the Santa Barbara Channel and its many ports and anchorages.

CHAPTER 13

Mainland: Point Hueneme to Newport

It was like...coming to anchor on the Grand Banks; for the shore, being low, appeared to be at a greater distance than it actually was...The land was of a clayey quality, and as far as the eye could reach, entirely bare of trees and even shrubs; and there was no sign of a town—not even a house to be seen. What had brought us into such a place, we could not conceive.

Richard Henry Dana on San Pedro Bay,
now Los Angeles and Long Beach Harbors, 1840.

South of Point Hueneme you enter true Southern California waters, home to thousands of pleasure craft large and small. In contrast with the Channel Islands and the Big Sur coast, humankind has left a massive imprint on the coastline here. At Point Dume, you enter Santa Monica Bay and the world of artificial harbors and marinas with every service for the small boat sailor imaginable. Anchorages, few and far between, attract more private moorings every year. Nevertheless, Catalina and Santa Barbara Islands offshore offer many interesting attractions with much to see and to do here.

Passage Making Strategies

Channel Islands Harbor to Marina del Rey 42 miles S can be done in an easy daytime passage, especially if you take advantage of the afternoon westerlies. Northbound, most people motor to windward at night, either skirting the shore on their way to Channel Islands Harbor, or aiming to pass outside Anacapa Island while cruising the islands. As we said in Chapter 7, timing your passage to be between Santa Cruz and Anacapa Islands in late morning when bound for Santa Barbara Harbor, you can enjoy a nice afternoon sail. Your sailing vessel can pick up the afternoon westerly for a long board inland to her destination.

Santa Ana winds blow very strongly below the canyons along this stretch of coast, especially between Points Mugu and Dume. Exercise extreme caution when passage making under such conditions.

Point Hueneme to Point Dume (Chart 18740)

Between Point Hueneme and Point Mugu, the low lying Santa Clara Plain peters out into the sea in sand dunes and a long sandy beach. The only outstanding landmark is the Ormond Beach power plant, which has two smoke stacks, in contrast to Mandalay Bay's one; Point Hueneme light (Gp. Fl. (5) 30 sec. 20 miles), 52 feet above sea level flashes from a white, square tower. The other buildings belong to Port Hueneme base and Point Mugu Naval Air station.

The Pacific Missile Range extends for 170 miles SW from Point Mugu and may be in use any day. The Navy broadcasts the dangers portions of the firing area daily, Monday through Friday at 0900 and 1200 on 2638 kHz. You can also call them at (805) 982-7209. Also, a launch patrols the shoreline and stops passing vessels until the danger is over. Normally, you can pass without delay, but a call ahead of time makes for peace of mind.

The main runway of the Air Station extends out to the coast. Sometimes, fast-flying Navy jets will pass low overhead, leaving a deafening noise behind them. Be aware of a small-arms firing range that extends about 2 miles offshore just N of Point Mugu, so stay at least that distance offshore during daylight hours. A large sign on shore says "Live Firing," leaving you in no doubt of the range's location.

On summer afternoons, prevailing westerlies funnel between Anacapa Island and the mainland, making for stronger winds between Point Mugu and Point Hueneme. These westerlies can make for a strenuous beat to windward compared with conditions further south.

The Santa Monica Mountains terminate at Point Mugu. Aluminum-colored fuel tanks and a white radar structure (marked by flashing red lights) on the summit of Laguna Peak close inland can be seen from a long distance offshore. Mugu itself appears like an isolated rock, because highway 1 cuts right through, separating the point from the natural slops inshore.

14 miles of rugged coastline lies between Point Mugu and Point Dume, with no outlying dangers. Highway 1, condominiums, and other structures N of

Zuma Beach, a mile N of Point Dume can be easily identified. When making landfall on the mainland from Catalina Island, your first landmark may be a prominent, 140-foot high sand dune, marked on the chart as a "prominent slide," about 2 miles E of Point Mugu. I have found this to be a wonderful reference point on moonlit nights.

200-foot high Point Dume forms a distinctive flat top. Its summit a casualty of World War II, when a gun emplacement adorned the peninsula, Dume has a reddish color, with a lighted bell buoy (Fl. R. 4 sec.) 0.5 mile off the point. Pass outside the buoy to avoid offlying reefs and kelp.

Point Dume to Marina del Rey (Chart 18744)

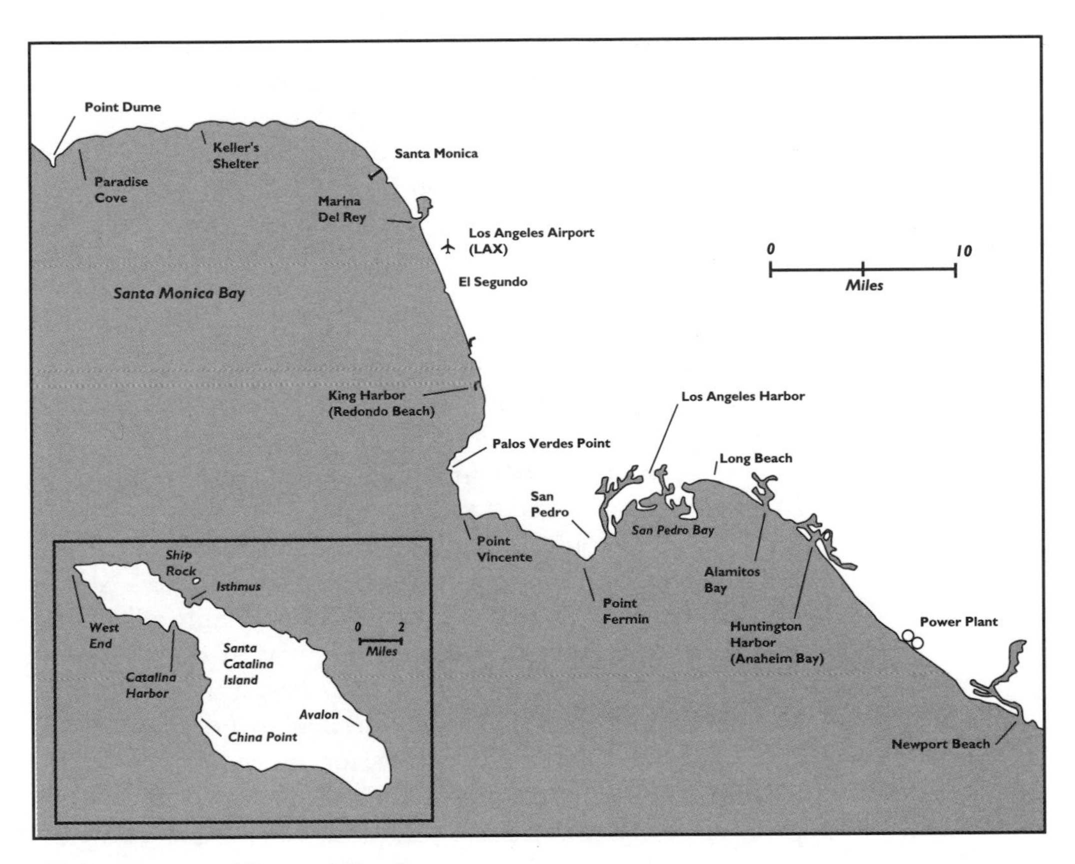

Point Dume to Newport Beach.

Point Dume marks the western extremity of Santa Monica Bay, a large bight backed, for the most part, with low lying coastal plains and dense urban sprawl from the Los Angeles area. The 10-fathom line lies about a mile offshore in relatively shallow Santa Monica Bay. Moderate weather prevails most of the year, except when Santa Ana winds blow from ENE or post-frontal northwesterlies kick up in outer waters. Coastal fogs persist from July through October.

Because the shore lies inside the direct course for Marina del Rey and points E, most people stay outside the western bight of Santa Monica Bay. When sailing inshore in light air, look out for a gently S-flowing current, which induces a slow, counterclockwise eddy inshore.

Two anchorages offer limited shelter. **Paradise Cove,** 2 miles NE of Point Dume, is the best berth in the lee of the headland. When round the point, identify the 300-foot fishing pier on the NW of Paradise Cove, then anchor opposite the fourth arroyo in the cliffs counting from Point Dume, in 35 to 45 feet (sand), with the peninsula bearing about 240 deg. I have used this anchorage overnight in moderate conditions, but it is untenable in Santa Anas. Anchor outside the kelp to avoid fouling your anchor.

Kellers Shelter offers equivalent anchorage 9 miles W of Santa Monica at Malibu Beach. The 700-foot fishing pier, with two prominent white buildings at its end, makes the best landmark for Kellers. A kelp-marked reef and a shallow bight offer protection from W and NW winds. Anchor about 0.5 mile E of the reef in 15 to 40 feet (sand). Look out for private moorings just E of the pier. I prefer Paradise Cove to Kellers. The noise from passing cars and surge make Keller an uneasy berth.

Keep about 0.75 mile offshore when approaching Malibu from W, to avoid a kelp reef close inshore.

Santa Monica's highrise buildings stand out from far offshore. With to attract the cruising sailor here, a stone breakwater protects the city pier and small craft moorings inside it. Both were damaged heavily in the El Ni§o storms of 1983. You will find about 22 feet at the end of the pier. Santa Monica is an uncomfortable anchorage at best. You must obtain advance permission by calling the Santa Monica Harbor Patrol on VHF Channels 12 or 16. Better proceed to Marina del Rey, 3.5 miles E, where you can berth in complete shelter in any weather.

A Word of Caution

One of the densest concentrations of sailing yachts in the world lies between Marina del Rey and San Diego. Most harbors are home to major yacht racing programs, and sometimes international regattas. Exercise caution when passage-making inshore, especially on weekends and midweek evenings when races are in progress off many ports.

Marina del Rey (Chart 18744)

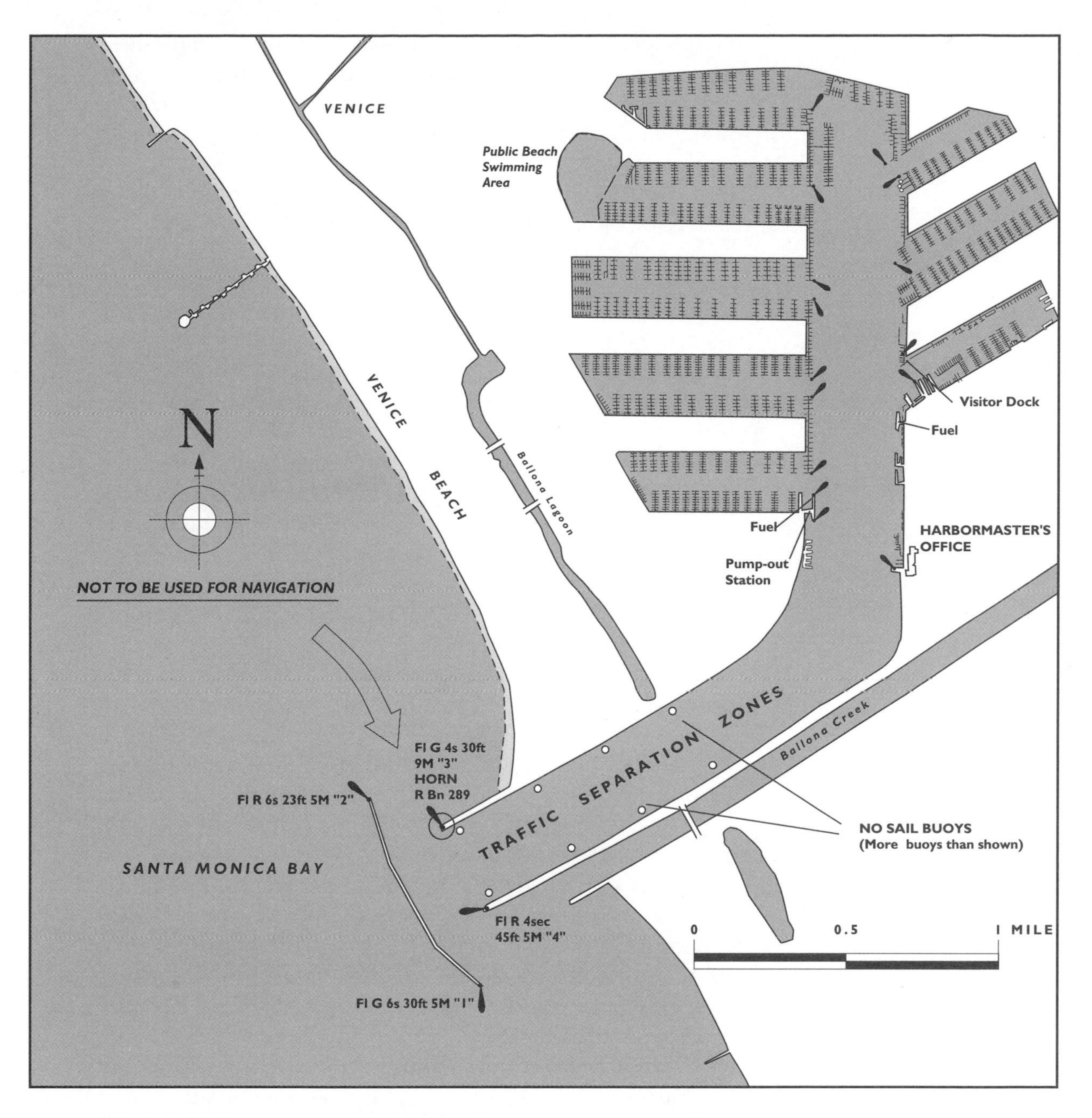

Marina del Rey

Marina del Rey, the largest humanly-constructed yacht harbor in the world, is home to over 6,000 pleasure craft. The congested entrance is so busy it requires separation zones to control traffic in the dredged channel. Entry for a newcomer on the weekends can be an ordeal. Try and enter first time on a weekday if you can.

Approach

Los Angeles International Airport lies immediately SE of Marina del Rey. Huge 747s rush out at you over a low ridge. A tract of barren land E of the harbor entrance matches the flight path. Two prominent, striped smoke stacks at El Segundo, 3 miles S of the entrance, are an excellent marker. From W, identify Venice pier with its characteristic rounded end. Marina del Rey entrance is a mile E. A northbound vessel should identify bell buoy "2ES" (Fl. W 4 sec.) which lies 3 miles, about 344 deg. M from the breakwater. A detached breakwater parallel to the shore protects the two harbor jetties. You will have trouble identifying it even in hazy weather.

In thick weather you may confuse Ballona Creek jetty SE of the breakwaters with Marina del Rey, so approach with caution. A night approach can be confusing because of the many city lights. Identify the flight path of aircraft taking off from LAX, then look for the harbor lights. The most conspicuous is light "3" (Fl. G 4 sec.) on the N jetty, visible for 9 miles. The ends of the outer, detached breakwater are lit by flashing lights (Fl. R and G respectively 6 sec. 5 miles).

Enter Marina del Rey between at the N end of the detached breakwater. The southern entrance is shoaled. The entrance channel between the jetties carries 14 to 15 feet in the center, but is shallower near the edges. Unlighted buoys marked "No Sail" delineate the traffic lanes inside the jetties. You MUST leave these to port and pass along the outer sides of the entrance channel if you are under power. Vessels under sail use the central lane. I strongly recommend you not sail into Marina del Rey, especially if you are in a larger vessel, or on a first time visit. During the weekends, use caution and watch out for aggressive skippers. I have been set aground here by inconsiderate captains.

A speed limit of 8 knots in the entrance, 5 knots in the harbor, is strictly enforced. You cannot anchor or stop in the channel.

Berthing

Once inside the harbor, you will find the harbormaster's office on the starboard side. During the busy month, I always call ahead on Channel 16, then 12 or 73, or telephone (818) 823-4571 for a reservation. The visitors' berths are in Basin H (Chace Park), to starboard in the first marina area. Stays over 7 nights are difficult to arrange. Transient berths can sometimes be arranged with one of the 9 local yacht clubs and 16 marinas. No anchoring, except in an emergency, when you can lie to bow and stern anchors in the northern part of the main channel, with the harbormaster's permission.

Facilities

Marina del Rey has every facility you can possibly need within easy reach, and hundreds of unique and fascinating yachts. If you want to splurge, spring for afternoon tea at the Ritz-Carlton, Marina del Rey, which overlooks the harbor. There is even a measured mile, marked with triangular markers just W of the entrance.

Redondo Beach (King Harbor) (Chart 18744)

King Harbor (Redondo Beach) © Geri Conser 1994

King Harbor lies 7.6 miles SSE of Marina del Rey. El Segundo's oil refinery and then the residential communities of Hermosa Beach and Manhattan Beach occupy the low lying coastline back of the sandy beach. Give a wide berth to the pipeline and tanker mooring area off the refinery, where large tankers often lie. I keep in at least 60 feet of water off the coast here, to avoid underwater obstructions. Fishing barges often operate offshore in the summer. When approaching King Harbor, the public fishing piers at Hermosa Beach and Manhattan Beach, though conspicuous landmarks, pale into insignificance compared with the enormous power plant with eight large smoke stacks, which lies behind King Harbor. The four northern stacks, especially prominent by day, look positively futuristic when lit at night.

Approach

Identify the Redondo Beach power plant, then the long breakwater, which protects the harbor area. The yacht masts in the inner basins will be prominent. From N, pass 0.5 mile offshore and parallel to the breakwater until the entrance opens up at the S end. Lighted bell buoy "I" (Fl. G 2.5 sec) lies about 230 yards SSW of the outer breakwater. Give the S end of the outer breakwater a wide berth when turning N into the entrance. Boats sometimes leave the harbor at speed. The jetty ends are lit (Fl. R and G 4 sec. respectively). The lights can be seen from about 5 miles away

The entrance channel is straightforward, with an area of mooring ports on the W side of the channel.

Berths and Anchoring

Visitors berths are available in the privately owned marinas. The harbormaster has no berths to allocate. You can anchor inside the S end of the outer breakwater with the harbormaster's permission (the office is opposite the fuel dock midway up the entrance channel, to starboard). Fore- and aft- anchors are obligatory and you cannot stay longer than 72 hours.

Facilities

The King Harbor Yacht Club is exceptionally hospitable, one of two clubs in the harbor. All facilities and repairs are close to hand.

King Harbor to Point Fermin (Charts 18744 and 18746)

The coast trends SW and the coastal topography changes at Flat Rock Point, just over 2 miles S of King Harbor, a spur, which protrudes from a rounded point, with two detached rocks off its end. Bluff Cove immediately S of the point does not offer adequate anchorage. Palos Verdes Point 1.7 miles SW marks the S extremity of Santa Monica Bay, a 120-foot high bold point, which rises to the W end of the Palos Verdes hills. Extensive kelp grows inshore, so keep at least 0.75 miles off shore, passing outside the bell buoy off the point (Fl. R 4 sec.). Lunada Bay under Palos Verdes point forms a small bight and an unsatisfactory berth even in calm conditions.

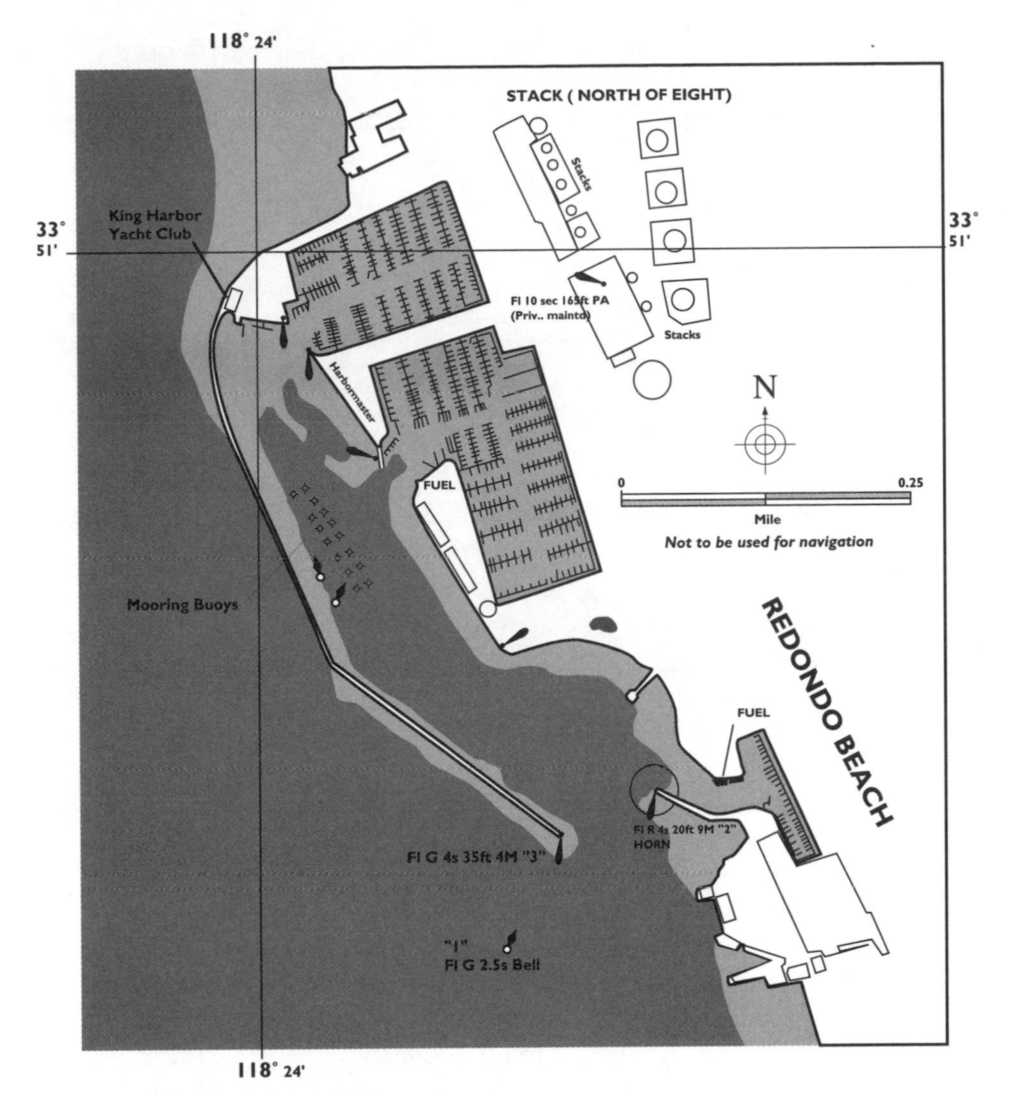

King Harbor (Redondo Beach)

Point Vicente, 2 miles SSE, is steep and rocky, with distinctive red and white cliffs rising 120-feet above the ocean. The light (Lat. 33 deg. 44.5 min N; Long. 118 deg. 24.6 min W) (Gp. Fl W (2) 20 sec. 185 feet) is visible at a distance of 24 miles. Keep well clear of the land, for a rock lies 250 yards SW of the point. Extensive kelp lies outside this rock, which breaks even in calm conditions.

At Point Vicente, the buildings of the Marineland Oceanarium with their white observation tower come into view 0.7 mile SE on Long Point. Keep clear of the ruined pier in this vicinity. The coastline trends SE past the radar dome on San Pedro Hill and into the outskirts of San Pedro. Point Fermin, a bold headland, is easy to identify with its prominent pavilion, "The Korean Bell of Friendship," which lies on high ground about 0.3 mile N of Point Fermin light (Lat. 33 deg 43 min N; Long 118 deg. 17.6 min W) (Fl. W 10 sec. 120 feet 16 miles). Point Fermin marks the W extremity of San Pedro Bay. Pass outside the whistle buoy (Fl. R. 4 sec.) which lies off the point.

San Pedro Bay: Los Angeles and Long Beach Harbors (Chart 18751)

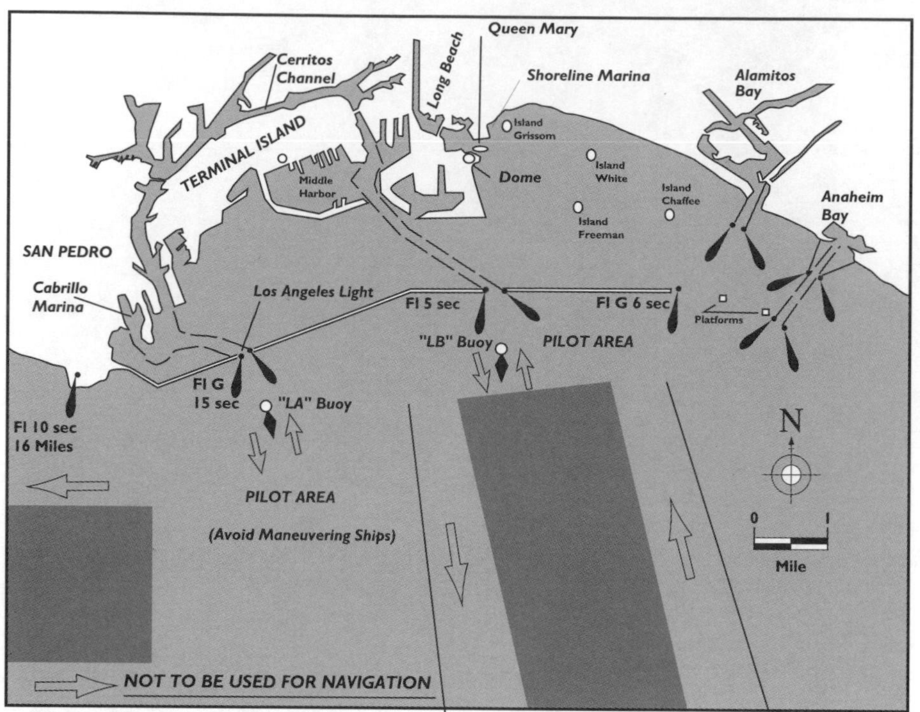

San Pedro Bay

The deserted bay described by Richard Henry Dana is now one of the major commercial harbors along the West Coast. I would be dishonest if I said San Pedro Bay and its busy commercial harbors was one of my favorite cruising grounds, though there is plenty to do and see, especially in Long Beach.

George Davidson was not effusive: "This bay is well protected in every direction, except against the winter gales from the southeast round to the southwest. During the spring, summer, and winter, it is an excellent roadstead...Vessels must anchor a mile off to get five fathoms...In winter anchor further out, and more to the southward, in order to be able to slip the cable and go to sea should a strong southeaster spring up...Wood and water are not readily obtained, and the charges are high. The beef raised here is remarkably tough." Today, long breakwaters protect Long Beach and San Pedro harbors from severe gales, but such is the area of open water inside the breakwaters that quite rough seas can build up in strong winds.

Traffic Separation Zones and Commercial Shipping

Merchant ships rule in San Pedro Bay. Container ships, tankers, warships, and ocean-going fishing boats are on the move day and night. Quite apart from the Rules of the Road, any vessel displacing over 300 tons is under a pilot's direction in the restricted waters of the approach to San Pedro Bay and inside the breakwater and deep water fairways. Your responsibility is obvious. Keep clear of all commercial shipping, even vessels at anchor waiting for a berth.

Two Traffic Separation Zones converge in the approaches to San Pedro Bay. The westerly scheme is a continuation of that running through the Santa Barbara Channel and Santa Monica Bay. The lanes turn E 4 miles S of Point Vicente, running toward the Los Angeles Approach Lighted Buoy (Mo (A) W), where pilots board and disembark, sometimes as much as 3 miles offshore. The north-south separation scheme passes E of Catalina Island and ends in the same general area. Exercise extreme caution when crossing the traffic lanes, and especially in the approaches to the harbor entrances. If possible pass inshore, or cross the traffic zones at near-right angles, as you are required to do under law.

Approaches to San Pedro Bay and its breakwaters

Two breakwaters protect the enormous harbor area. San Pedro breakwater extends in a bight E from Point Fermin, with Los Angeles Light (Fl. G. 15 sec. 73 feet. 20 miles) at its extremity. The detached Middle Breakwater runs for 3 miles, providing most of the protection for the harbors inside. The W end (the Long Beach entrance) is lit (Fl. R 2.5 sec. 42 feet. 5 miles) with a fainter light than Long Beach light at the E extremity (Fl. W 5 sec. 50 feet, 24 miles), which is a major light by any standards. Long Beach breakwater runs for a further 2 miles, also lit at both ends with lights visible about 5 miles away (Fl. R 2.5 sec. W end; Fl. G. 6 sec. E end). A pair of markers provide you with a measured mile on a course of 090 deg. T in the middle of this mole.

San Pedro Bay.

From offshore, as I mentioned earlier, San Pedro Hill with its two white radar domes 3.5 miles NW of Point Fermin provides the best landmark, but is sometimes obscured on hazy. days. However, the Korean "Bell of Friendship" at Point Fermin is usually visible from some distance, even on foggy mornings. High rise buildings in Long Beach appear to the S of these landmarks as you approach land, by which time the long, grey breakwaters should be in sight.

You can enter San Pedro Bay by three routes, two of them through the main breakwater entrances, a straightforward matter provided you time your entry when no commercial vessels are entering or leaving. Most small craft arriving from the N or Catalina Island and bound for Los Angeles Harbor or Long Beach use these entrances. The Southern entrance, between the Long Beach breakwater and the mainland, offers a convenient route from Newport Beach or leeward ports. When entering from S, pass well outside the breakwaters of Huntington Harbor and Alamitos Bay. Oil platform Esther is a convenient landmark in the approaches. You can pass on either side of oil island Chaffee, with its lighted markers.

Once inside San Pedro Bay, you have plenty of water until you approach shore. Be sure to have chart 18751 in front of you as you navigate these congested waters. Much of the central part of the bay is a busy merchant vessel and commercial anchorage. Adjust your course to avoid resident ships as necessary and keep clear of the main entrance fairways unless you must cross them, or use them to enter a commercial port area.

Los Angeles Harbor and Cabrillo Marina (Chart 18751)

Los Angeles Harbor is a commercial port, but also an important recreation center. Over 4,000 yachts are berthed within the administrative confines of the harbor, and there are long waiting lists for permanent slips. Visiting yachts can have trouble finding berths here, even in private marinas. You can sometimes use a slip on an overnight basis if the user is away, but you are probably best advised to try Long Beach or Alamitos Bay.

Most visiting yachts head for Cabrillo Marina, at the SW corner of San Pedro Bay. Immediately after entering the W breakwater entrance, identify the marina breakwater, which lies beyond some moorings off Cabrillo Beach, where

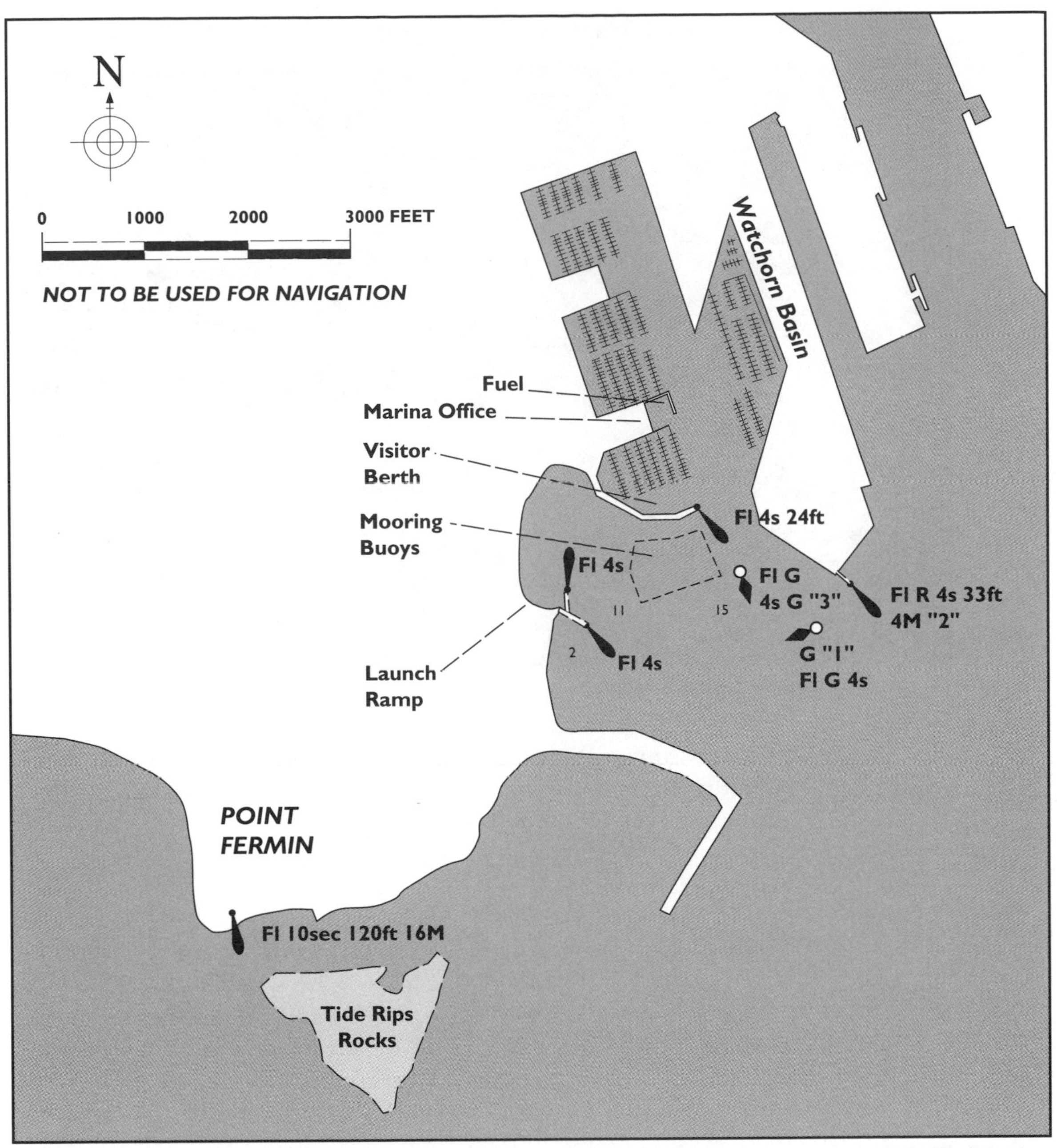

Cabrillo Marina

there is a boat launching ramp. The marina channel is dredged to between 30 and 35 feet, but there is only one transit berth on the outer finger of the marina, just inside the entrance. The Marina Office is at the head of the first slip basin. You can also use the moorings in the outer basin area, but you must call the harbormaster on Channel 16 for permission.

Facilities

Fuel, water, showers, and other facilities readily available.

Port of Los Angeles Administrative Office, 425 South Palos Verdes. (213) 519-3566.

Long Beach Harbor (Chart 1875)

Queen Mary, Long Beach Harbor.

Long Beach is a far more attractive proposition for the visitor, if nothing else because of the excellent shops and restaurants near the harbor, as well as the *Queen Mary*.

Approach to Downtown Marina

From N and offshore: Long Beach Harbor lies 4 miles E of Los Angeles Harbor entrance, E of the massive harbor facilities of Terminal Island. The most direct access is through the entrance between the Middle and Long Beach breakwaters, avoiding entering and leaving commercial shipping. (This can be interesting. The last time I entered, we were competing with two inbound and one outbound container ships!) Once inside, steer NE out of the main channel, which leads toward Terminal Island, passing between Pier J (to port) and Island Freeman (to starboard). The ***Queen Mary*** and the white dome which once housed the legendary Howard Hughes flying boat, the ***Spruce Goose,*** will come into sight as you steer outside a row of lighted buoys (Qk. Fl), which lead to the Queensway Bay area. The breakwaters of the Downtown Marina and Island Grissom will now appear ahead, perhaps slightly on the starboard bow.

From S: Enter San Pedro Bay between the Long Beach Breakwater and the mainland, then steer to pass 0.25 mile inshore of Island Chaffee. Once Chaffee is abeam, set a course

Long Beach Downtown Marina © Geri Conser 1994

0.3 mile offshore of Island White. By the time White is close, you will have picked up the *Queen Mary* and Island Grissom, which forms part of the Downtown Marina.

Enter the Downtown Marina between the curved breakwater which forms the SW side of the marina and Island Grissom. The entrance lies between a short detached breakwater and curved jetty. I would advise going round the W end of the former. The detached breakwater is lit, but I sometimes find the light hard to see against the city lights in the background.

Do not enter through the eastern entrance between Grissom and the E breakwater, which is obstructed.

Berths

Visitors' berths are available on end ties, for a maximum of 15 days a month. Reservations will be accepted from visiting yachts berthed at least 100 miles away, with two weeks notice. You will have to pay the first night with your reservation. There are also private marinas in the Long Beach area, which can sometimes accommodate visitors.

The Queensway Bay Moorage offers 40 mooring buys, which are convenient for visiting the *Queen Mary.* Reservations can be made by contacting the Queensway Bay Marina, 700

Marina Drive, Long Beach, CA 90801. (213) 436-0411. There is a 30-day limit. Charges vary according to boat length.

Facilities

All facilities within easy reach. Long Beach is an exceptional tourist town, while a rental car will take you to Disneyland and other amusement parks, also to museums and other well known delights. Harbormaster: 450, East Shoreline Drive, Long Beach, CA 90802. (310) 437-0041.

Alamitos Bay (Chart 18749)

Alamitos Bay is 3.25 miles S of the Long Beach Downtown Marina opposite the end of the Long Beach Breakwater. The two harbor jetties can be seen from a considerable distance.

Approach

From S: Identify the end of the Long Beach Breakwater. The twin jetties of Alamitos Bay Harbor are a mile NE, and can be seen projecting from the mainland. The angled breakwaters of Huntington Harbor lie a mile SE, but are easily distinguished from Alamitos Bay's jetties, which run straight into the ocean. Pass inshore of Platform Esther, steering for Island Chaffee until the entrance is clear in sight. Then alter course to pass between the jetties.

From Offshore: Pass inshore a safe distance from the end of Long Beach Breakwater, then identify the harbor jetties a mile ahead.

From Long Beach and other San Pedro Bay locations: Pass between Island Freeman and Island White (the islands are named after NASA astronauts who died in a launching accident), aiming to pass close inshore of Island Chaffee. The coast is heavily built up, but you will see Belmont Pier 0.5 mile E of Island White. The Alamitos Bay jetties will be clearly seen slightly on the port bow as you come up on Island Chaffee.

The Alamitos Bay entrance channel (17 to 20 feet) leads straight into the harbor, which contains Long Beach Municipal Marina. The harbormaster's office is on the NE side, just inside the entrance. A fuel dock lies slightly further inshore.

A night approach is straightforward, once the Long Beach breakwater light is identified. The jetty ends are lit (Gp. Fl (2) G. 6 sec. 5 miles; E jetty Fl. R. 2.5 sec. 5 miles). I have confused the Anaheim Bay lights for those of Alamitos Bay when tired and in the small hours. Remember that red and green flashing entrance lights mark Alamitos Bay.

Berths

For transit berths, apply to the Harbormaster's Office. Reservations can be made up to 14 days in advance. The first night's rental is payable in advance.

All facilities are within a reasonable distance. Repairs can be undertaken. Harbormaster: (310) 498-1391.

Huntington Harbor (Chart 18749)

Seal Beach pier lies 0.5 mile SE of Alamitos Bay, with 9 feet at its outer end. The twin, angled jetties of Huntington Harbor are 1.5 miles S of Alamitos. The jetties protect Anaheim Bay, site of the US Naval Weapons Station. You enter the harbor through restricted waters. State registered and documented vessels may enter under power, subject to special military controls when the Navy moves explosives. The Commanding Officer, US Naval Weapons Center, Seal Beach, CA 90740, can provide further information. A speed limit of 5 knots is in effect.

A fixed bridge with a vertical clearance of 23 feet crosses the channel inside the harbor leading to the private marinas and housing developments with private docks inshore. The harbormaster's office lies on the NE side of the channel once you are above the bridge and have turned to starboard into the main channel.

Huntington Harbor is best avoided, unless you are in a power boat and have compelling reasons to visit.

Approach

Two lighted buoys ("I" (Fl. G 4 sec.); "2" (Q.R.) mark the approaches to Anaheim Bay and the entrance channel between the jetties. The channel itself is well marked, with a lighted range for day and night use. An explosives anchorage lies within the breakwater.

Berths

Berths are only available beyond the bridge. Anchoring in Anaheim Bay is forbidden. Fuel and other facilities readily available.

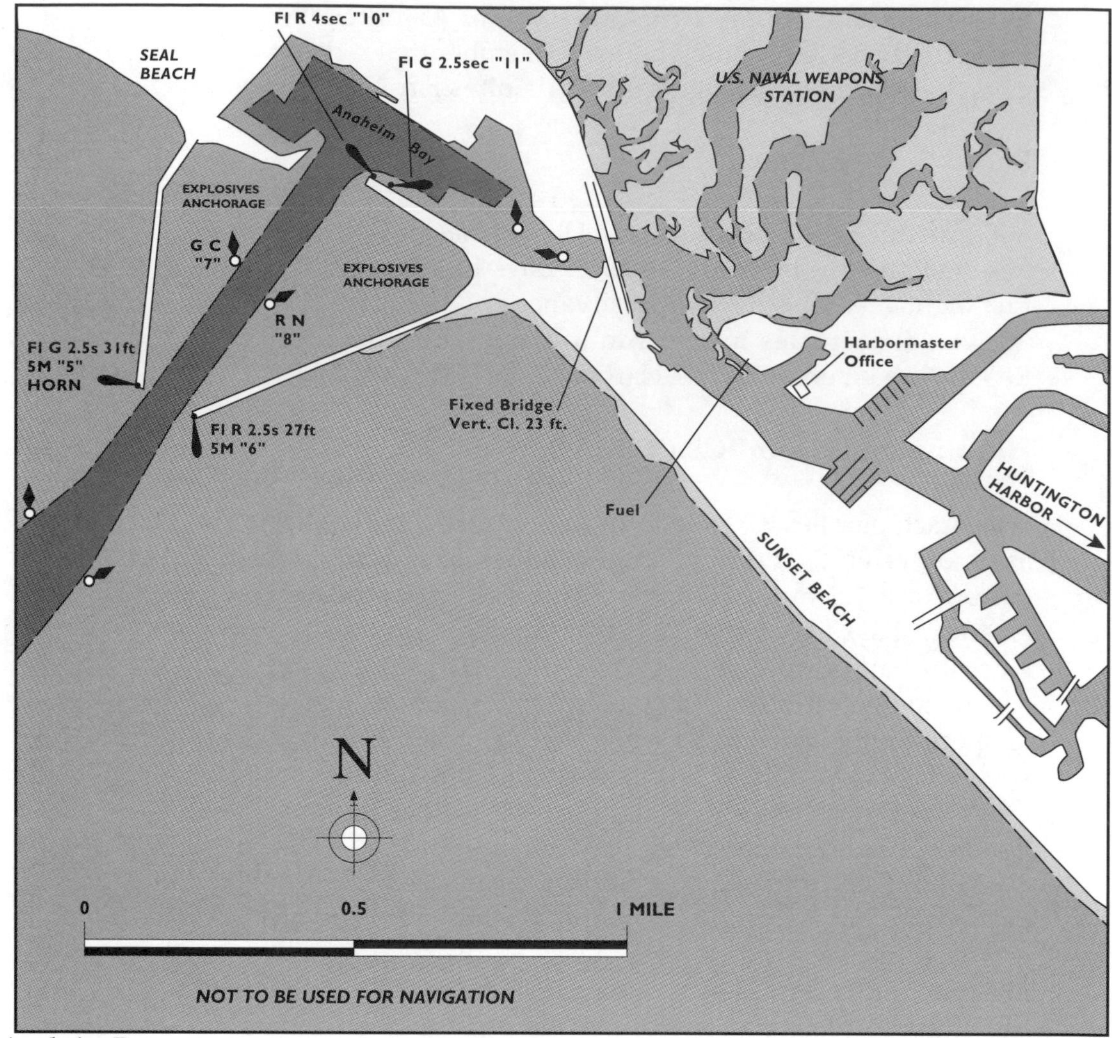

Anaheim Bay

Huntington Harbor to Newport Beach (Chart 18749)

Anaheim Bay lies 14 miles NW of Newport Beach, the major yacht harbor between Los Angeles and San Diego. The intervening coast is low lying, with highway 1 passing behind the sandy beach. A more-or-less continuous ribbon of urban development backs the beach. Keep outside the 10-fathom line along this stretch of coastline to avoid tanker moorings and other industrial paraphernalia. There is nothing to detain you along the shoreline, but I remember a fast passage hard on the wind against a strong Santa Ana. *Chabuka* heeled to strong gusts, a double-reefed main and storm jib carrying us effortlessly through the smooth water close inshore. The air was crystal clear. You could see Catalina Island far offshore, the only sound the creak of the rigging and the hiss, hiss of the hull coursing through the blue water.

The following landmarks are of use:

- An elevated water tank at the E end of Sunset Beach, 5 miles NW of Huntington Beach.
- Oil rig "Emmy" lies a mile offshore about 1.5 miles W of Huntington Beach, a city remarkable for its many oil derricks.
- Huntington Beach fishing pier.
- The twin smoke stacks of the Southern California Edison power plant 5.5 miles NW of Newport Beach Harbor.
- A highway trestle at the mouth of the Santa Ana River 4.5 miles N of Newport Beach Harbor.
- The highrise buildings of Newport Center, 1.4 miles N of the harbor entrance,
- Newport Beach and Balboa Beach piers immediately W of the Newport Beach Harbor entrance.
- Newport Beach Harbor breakwaters extend into deep water, sheltering the dredged entrance (about 15 to 20 feet). I describe this important harbor in Chapter 15.

CHAPTER 14

Southern Channel Islands: Catalina Island and Neighbors

It was wild. I couldn't hear anything except the howling wind. Clouds of dust blew over the deck in the dark as we sheered wildly in the gusts. I thought we were in hell's kitchen

Anonymous California sailor under the lee of the cliffs at Catalina in a fierce Santa Ana wind, 1991.

The southern Channel Islands are more widely separated than their northern neighbors, with only two of them, Santa Catalina and Santa Barbara Islands being popular destinations. San Clemente and San Nicolas come under military control and effectively are off-limits for pleasure craft. This chapter gives sailing directions for Catalina and Santa Barbara Island, but provides minimal coverage of the more offshore islands, as relatively few yachts visit them.

For passages to any of the islands in this chapter, use Chart 18740.

I have described the southern Channel Islands in more detail in *Cruising Guide to Southern California's Offshore Islands.* In this book, I give more general descriptions aimed at the short-term visitor.

San Nicolas Island (Chart 18755)

San Nicolas Island lies 54 miles W of Point Hueneme and 24 miles SW of Santa Barbara Island. Juan Cabrillo in 1541 visited the outermost of the Channel Islands, San Nicolas. The U.S. Navy took over the remote and windswept island in the 1930s. San Nicolas has become part of the Pacific Missile Range. Few yachts visit its coasts, but fishing boats often make the long trip to its rich fishing grounds.

From a distance, 8-mile long San Nicholas has a gently rounded profile, rising to 905 feet at its highest point. A prominent aerobeacon (Rot. W&G) can be seen from a long distance at night. The western end of the island is mantled with drifting sand. Deep arroyos cut into the higher ground. The airstrip and Naval buildings are concentrated at the eastern extremity. Dense kelp beds surround the entire island, up to 3 miles offshore at the W end. Strong northwesterlies sweep over the summit and around the shores of the island, especially when the Catalina Eddy is blowing.

Approach San Nicholas with great caution from N, as Begg Rock, a 15-foot-high rock rises abruptly from 300-foot-deep water 8 miles NW of the west end. Reefs associated with the rock extend for 100 yards N and S. A red buoy (Fl. 4 sec. 4 miles) lies 500 yards, 330 deg M from the rock. You can come on the rock suddenly in thick water, as the good ship **John Begg** did on September 20, 1834, striking it with great force. A lighted target ship lies 6.5 miles NW of Begg Rock and exhibits Fl. W lights at bow and stern and a Fl. R at the masthead. I always leave the mainland for San Nicolas in the evening hours, motoring across overnight, so I arrive before the northwesterlies kick up. Be sure to check with the Pacific Missile Range authorities about firing schedules before departure (Chapter 11). If you do not, you may find yourself pursued by a loud-hailing aircraft, always a disconcerting experience.

San Nicolas is a Naval Restricted Area. You are only allowed in certain designated areas of the coastline. The Commander of the Pacific Missile Range at Point Mugu must give you written permission to land. You can only anchor with written permission, or in grave emergency with the permission of the senior officer on the island. The best anchorage is at Dutch Harbor on the S side of the island, 1.0 mile W of South Side light (F. 6 sec. 50 feet 6 miles). Enter the bay through a gap in the kelp. Anchor in 30 feet (sand) as close in as convenient.

Santa Barbara Island (Chart 18756)

Santa Barbara Island lies 42 miles SW of Los Angeles Harbor, and in the outer approaches to the Santa Barbara Channel. The small and desolate landmass of Santa Barbara Island is part of the Channel Islands National Park.

For more information, contact the Channel Islands National Park (Chapter 12). And before departing from Channel Islands Harbor or the Santa Barbara Channel, check firing schedules for the Pacific Missile Range. In typical summer conditions, you can pick up a nice afternoon wind for the second half of your passage. Time your departure to ensure you reach the island before dark. The only anchorage is unlit.

Santa Barbara Island is an easy day sail from Catalina Harbor on Catalina Island, but plan to leave early, unless you plan to beat to windward all day with a 20-mile passage in front of you.

Approach

Santa Barbara Island affords a relatively small offshore target, being only 1.5 miles long and about a mile wide. Your first sight of the island will probably be one or two prominent peaks. The lower lying land will only come into sight less than 10 miles out. In thick weather, approach the island with caution, as surrounding shoals shallow rapidly from about 60 feet.

A night passage is straightforward, for Santa Barbara Island light (Lat. 33 deg 29.2 min N; Long. 119 deg 01.8 min W) (Fl. W 5 sec. sec. 195 feet 15 miles) is easily visible. It is, however, obscured by high ground from 342 deg. to 053 deg, M. The main island lies 700 yards W of the light. Do not attempt to close the land or anchor without local knowledge, and then only on a moonlit night.

The island cliffs rise steep-to, bold, and dark-colored. Arch Rock, the NE corner, is lowlying. Steep cliffs on the island's E side merge with the higher ground's dry slopes, which drain into the ocean. The main anchorage lies off these cliffs.

To approach the anchorage, identify Arch Rock and shape your course to the headland until just outside the kelp beds. Then look for the Park Service structures on the summit of the island. The main anchorage lies N of the structures and the landing spot below them. Sometimes you will find a gap in the kelp. Otherwise you'll have to make a make through.

Anchorage

Anchor off the landing in 30 feet or more, but look out for solid rock on the bottom. Lay a second anchor if there is surge or restricted space. Not a particularly sheltered anchorage, I have ridden out a 35-knot post-frontal northwesterly here. Once, I had to leave in a hurry when a fierce Santa Ana turned our comfortable berth into a suicidal lee shore.

Facilities

Santa Barbara Island is a fascinating place with abundant wild life, including sea lion rookeries on the NW side of the island. I think the best time to visit is in spring, when the wild flowers are in full bloom. The new Museum/Interpretative Center is well worth a visit.

Santa Catalina Island (Chart 18757)

Southern California's favorite cruising destination, a quiet paradise, a comfortable day's sail from the urban sprawl of Los Angeles, even at the height of the summer, life seems to move slower at Santa Catalina with space for everyone.

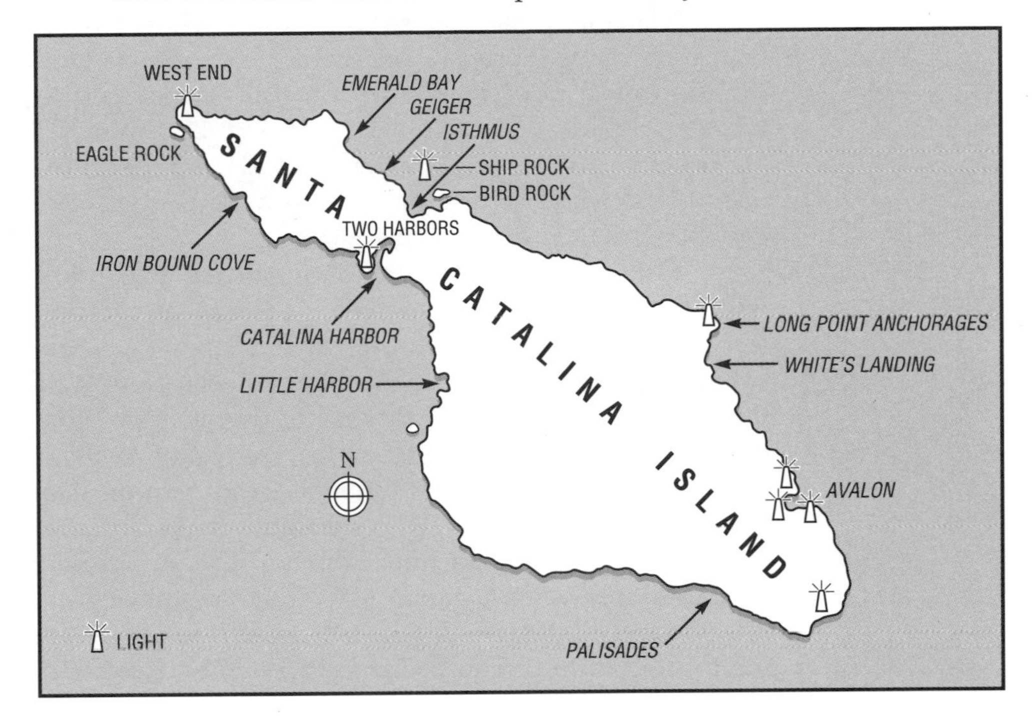

Catalina lies 18 miles S of Point Fermin, within easy reach of all the major yacht harbors between Marina del Rey and Newport Beach. Cabrillo in 1542 visited the island. Sebastian Vizcaino named it Santa Catalina in the seventeenth century. When Cabrillo first arrived, a flourishing Catali§o Indian population lived on the island, but exotic disease soon decimated them and the survivors were transported to the mainland. Now Santa Catalina Island Conservancy owns and controls most of the island except the incorporated city of Avalon.

Approach

With the exception of winter frontal conditions or during a Santa Ana, or in dense fog, a passage to Catalina Island is straightforward. Keep a close lookout for shipping when you cross the traffic lanes approaching San Pedro Bay.

Catalina is 18.5 miles long and 7 miles across at its widest point. The rugged peaks of the highest points of the island can be seen from a long distance on a clear day, reaching their greatest elevation of 2,125 feet near the middle of the E end. A deep canyon about six miles from West End nearly severs the island. Two coves, forming the Two Harbors area, almost divide Catalina, their bights being only 0.5 miles apart. Like Santa Cruz Island, Catalina is precipitous, with steep cliffs falling into deep water. There are few outlying dangers, except off Isthmus Cove on the NE coast.

Catalina is hard to see when approaching from N on a hazy day. You will probably be within five miles before seeing the high ground of West End. At night, West End light, a white pyramidical structure (Lat. 33 deg. 28.7 min N; Long. 118 deg 36.3 min W) (Fl. W 10 sec. 76 feet, 16 miles) provides a useful landmark, but is surprisingly faint. You may be quite close to the island before you see it.

The approach from the mainland is straightforward, with the Two Harbors region being prominent because of its low topography. A radio tower on Blackjack Peak, midway between Long Point and Avalon can be seen from some distance. The flashing red light on the tower is invaluable at night. Once you are within ten miles, the city of Avalon is easily seen, with its huddle of buildings, condominiums, and the circular casino building. The city lights make an admirable marker at night. Approaching from San Diego, a rock quarry 1.5 miles E of Avalon Bay may be seen before the city.

Once at the island, you can circumnavigate it at about 0.5 to 0.75 mile offshore, for kelp beds and rocks do not extend far offshore.

Catalina has numerous anchorages, some familiar and congested with moorings, others mere fair weather refuges when everything else is crowded. Catalina has become such a popular cruising ground, it's almost superfluous to give more than a general account of the most important stopping points.

Important Warning. Catalina Island is extremely hazardous in strong Santa Ana wind conditions with effectively no shelter in island anchorages or ports. Avoid cruising these waters when such weather is forecast.

Readers requiring more complete information should consult the readily available *ChartGuide for Catalina Island,* which provides commentary on all the coves. *Cruising Guide to Southern California's Offshore Islands* also offers a convenient summary.

The first-time visitor or short-term visitor will probably call at Two Harbors or Avalon Harbor. At either, you enter a highly organized world of moorings and relatively high fees for overnight stays, quite unlike anything you will encounter elsewhere on the West Coast.

Two Harbors

The Two Harbors area is operated by the Catalina Cove and Camp Agency, headquartered at Isthmus Cove. Their address is P.O. Box 1566, Avalon, CA 90704. (213) 510-0303 or (213) 510-2683. The Agency operates the private moorings in the coves. Everything is on a first come-first served basis. Those who own moorings have until 24 hours before arriving to notify the Agency that they'll be using their moorings. After that, the early bird gets the worm!

Two Harbors has two components: The Isthmus on the NE coast and Catalina Harbor on the NE.

The Isthmus

The Isthmus is everyone's favorite, a relaxed place where life seems to jog along at 1920s pace. On high summer weekends, the place is mobbed, but quietens down considerably mid-week. The best time to visit is off-season, between mid-September and late-May, when there are usually moorings available.

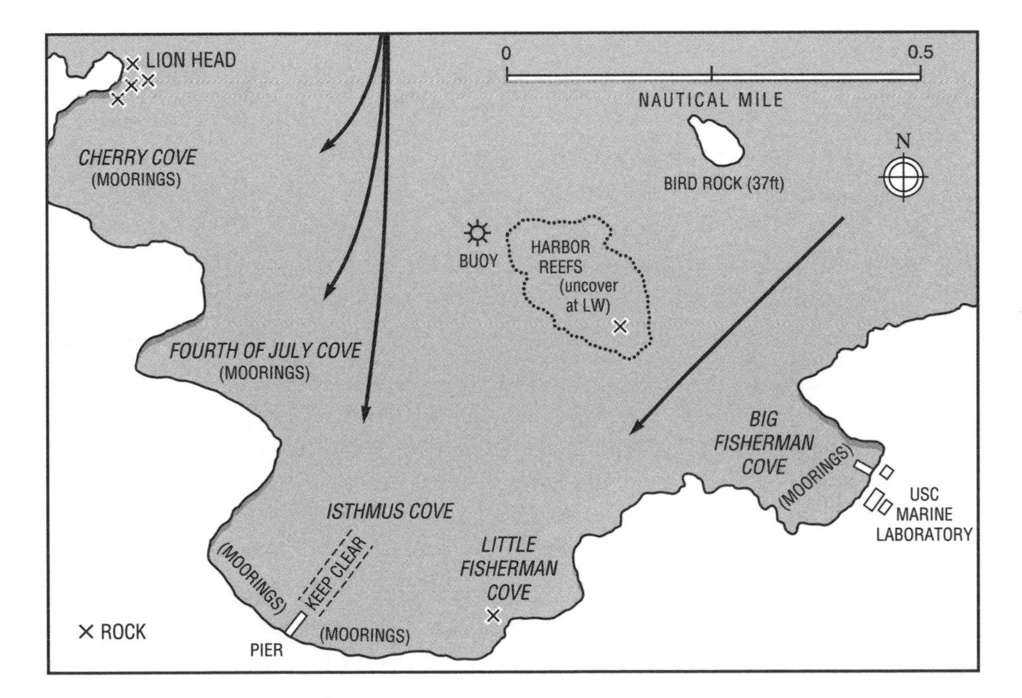

Approach

The low isthmus of land between the Two Harbors is your best mark offshore. Steering for it will bring you into the general area. Once 2 to 3 miles offshore, identify the following:

- Ship Rock (66 feet), 1.0 mile N of the cove, which is lit (Fl. 4 sec. 75 feet. 6 miles),
- Bird Rock (37 feet), a rounded, white-topped outcrop 150 yards long SE of Ship Rock, some 500 yards off the E coast of Isthmus Cove,
- USC Marine Laboratory Buildings, conspicuous ashore SE of Bird Rock,
- Isthmus Pier at the head of the cove.

Once you have identified these landmarks, steer to enter the cove, leaving Bird Rock and the green buoy marking the NE end of Harbor Reff well to port.

Approaching from E, you can pass between Bird Rock and the mainland, leaving the red buoy at the SW end of Harbor Reef to starboard.

A nighttime approach is straightforward. Identify Ship Rock light, then the green flashing light of the Harbor Reef buoy. Also, the lights from the resort area stand out and are easily identifiable. A speed limit of 5 knots blankets the area.

Moorings and Anchorage

Rows of private moorings lie off the pier area, with a fairway leading down the center, which must be kept clear. A patrol boat or the harbormaster's office on the pier will direct you to a mooring if one is available. Note they have bow and stern ties. The harbor authorities monitor VHF Channel 9. You will be charged a mooring fee even if you raft alongside another moored boat.

Anchorage may be obtained in deeper water outside the moorings, in depths of 60 feet or more. The anchorage is relatively exposed and is some distance from shore facilities. I recommend laying two anchors to hold you head to surge. Fortunately, summer weather conditions are usually calm and waves are not a major problem here. But it's a long dinghy ride ashore and you may prefer a mooring if one is available.

The Isthmus is a busy place, and can be very noisy with outboards at the weekend.

Fourth of July and Cherry Coves, Little Fisherman Cove, and Big Fisherman Cove are crowded with private moorings and are subject to club and other leases. Unless you have connections, you are best off at the Isthmus, where the action is.

Graham Pomeroy

Catalina Harbor

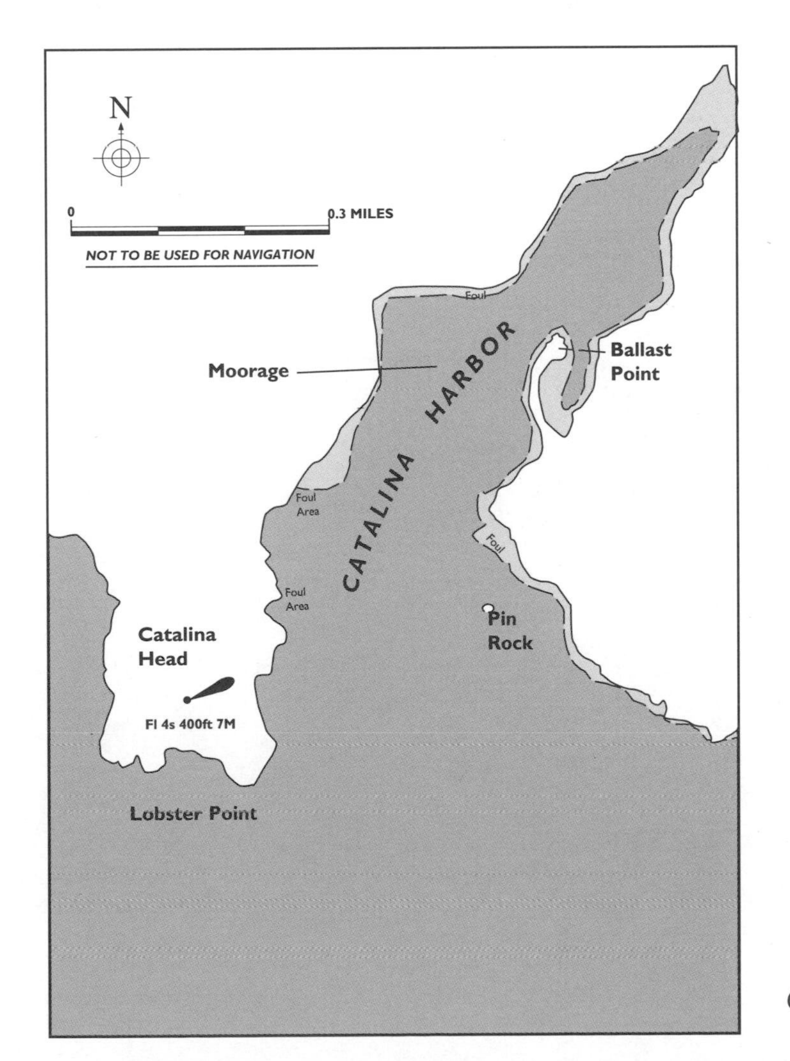

Catalina Harbor

Facilities

Fuel and water available at the pier, and a wide range of provisions can be purchased. Very limited repair facilities. Most visitors try to be self-sufficient as far as food and drink are concerned, although there are restaurants and bars ashore. Shore boats operate in summer, which is a convenience.

Catalina Harbor

The south side of Two Harbors is quiet, with a rugged beauty all it own. The narrow, well-sheltered inlet provides protection in all weather. 99 moorings lie in the harbor, but there is space for about 300 boats, most lying at anchor. I prefer Catalina Harbor to the sometimes frenzied atmosphere at the Isthmus, but it's a longer journey unless you have arrived from the north.

Approach

From N, follow the coast 6.5 miles SE to the deep indentation which marks the entrance to Catalina Harbor. You can approach the coast within 0.25 mile as you enter the 800-yard wide entrance between two steep headlands.

The Isthmus, Catalina Island

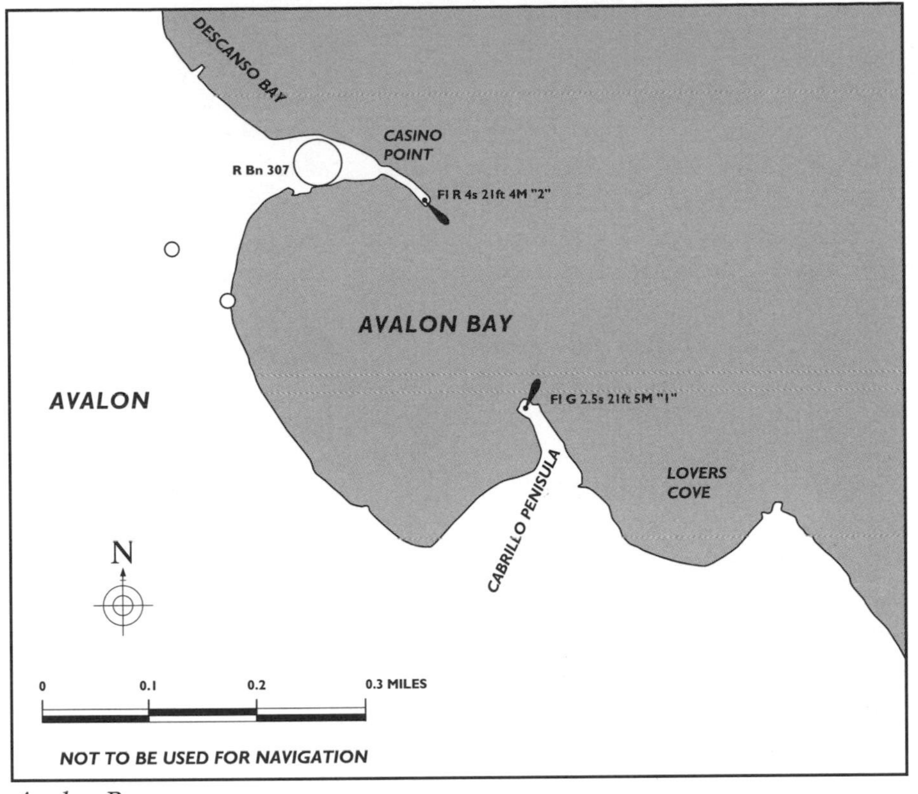

Avalon Bay

From SE, follow the outer edge of the kelp as you round China Point, then identify the Two Harbors area and the indented Catalina Harbor entrance.

Enter the harbor midway between the two headlands, giving Pin Rock, 100 yards offshore just inside the east point a wide berth. Sound your way toward the head of the harbor and obtain permission to pick up a mooring or anchor outside them according to draft and available space.

Facilities

As for the Isthmus. Catalina Harbor is a half mile walk to the main restaurant and store area on the north shore.

Avalon Harbor

Avalon, a pleasant resort town, which has, unfortunately, become a port of call for weekend cruise ships, has a charm all of its own, especially during the off-season.

Approach

Identify the buildings of the town, especially the Wrigley Mansion on the E side of the harbor, the major condominium development on the same side, and the circular casino building at the root of the Casino Point Breakwater.

Once these landmarks are in sight, steer to pass midway between the harbor breakwaters. Keep a sharp lookout for fast-moving ferries and seaplanes.

Avalon Harbor can be entered at night using the two harbor lights (Fl. W 2.5 sec. on Cabrillo Breakwater; Fl. R. 4 sec. on Casino Mole), which are visible about 5 miles out.

Anchorage and Moorings

The Harbormaster (VHF Channel 16, then 12) allocates visitor moorings when available. A harbor boat will meet you when you arrive and assign you a mooring. You may be asked to move each day, the request coming between 0730 and 0900. Anchoring in the harbor is impossible, but you can lie in Descanso Bay NW of Casino Point in 65-85 feet (rock and sand), clear of the moorings. This is a bumpy spot even on calm days. Anchor lights are required. You cannot leave your vessel unattended here.

Facilities

A shore boat and garbage service operate in Avalon Harbor. A fuel dock lies close to the Casino. Avalon Marine Service provides engine and underwater repairs, while provisions and marine hardware can be purchased in town. Place your garbage on your stern for collection. Toilet treatment systems are mandatory and the city checks on this. Harbormaster: (213) 510-0535.

The definition of an anchorage seems to change at Catalina Island, for many minor coastal indentations are dignified with the status of a safe overnight anchorage, when they would never be considered as such in less benign cruising grounds. This redefinition is due in part to a rapid expansion of moorings in island coves. Every year, anchoring safely becomes even more of an impossible dream at Catalina. Identification of the various coves is easy, provided you have a large-scale chart aboard. Your judgements as to suitable anchoring spots must be conditioned, as always, by prevailing weather conditions.

San Clemente Island (Charts 18762, 18763, 18764)

The Federal Government owns San Clemente, which lies 43 miles SSW of Point Fermin and 19 miles beyond Catalina across the outer

Santa Barbara Channel. San Clemente is 18 miles long and 4 miles wide, and 1,1965 feet high. Like San Nicolas, the island is off-limits to the public. From a distance, San Clemente looks like a table mountain. The NE coast is bold and precipitous. A white radar dome stands on the highest point of the island and can be seen from both sides of San Clemente. The SW shore is more irregular and has gentler slopes. Kelp beds extend out to the 10-fathom line, masking outlying rocks for several hundred yards offshore. George Davidson was unenthusiastic: "Very few trees were found and the aspect is sterile."

The approach is straightforward, even in grey weather, for the island's bold topography stands out from a considerable distance. San Clemente is well lit by the Pyramid Cove Anchorage light (Fl. R 4 sec. 4 miles) exhibited at a height of 886 feet at the S end. You will spot the light on 900-foot high Pyramid Head (Fl. W 10 sec. 226 feet 16 miles) at the SE corner of the island when about 10 miles out and approaching San Clemente from 132 deg to 080 deg. M. China Point light is a good marker from SW (Fl. W 5 sec. 112 feet 15 miles), when on a course between 245 and 113 deg. M. Wilson Cove North End light identifies the NE corner (Fl. W 10 sec. 125 feet 17 miles), when approaching between 124 and 315 deg. M.

Although the fishing is good, San Clemente has little to offer the visitor, for it is a military restricted area. There are two major anchorages:

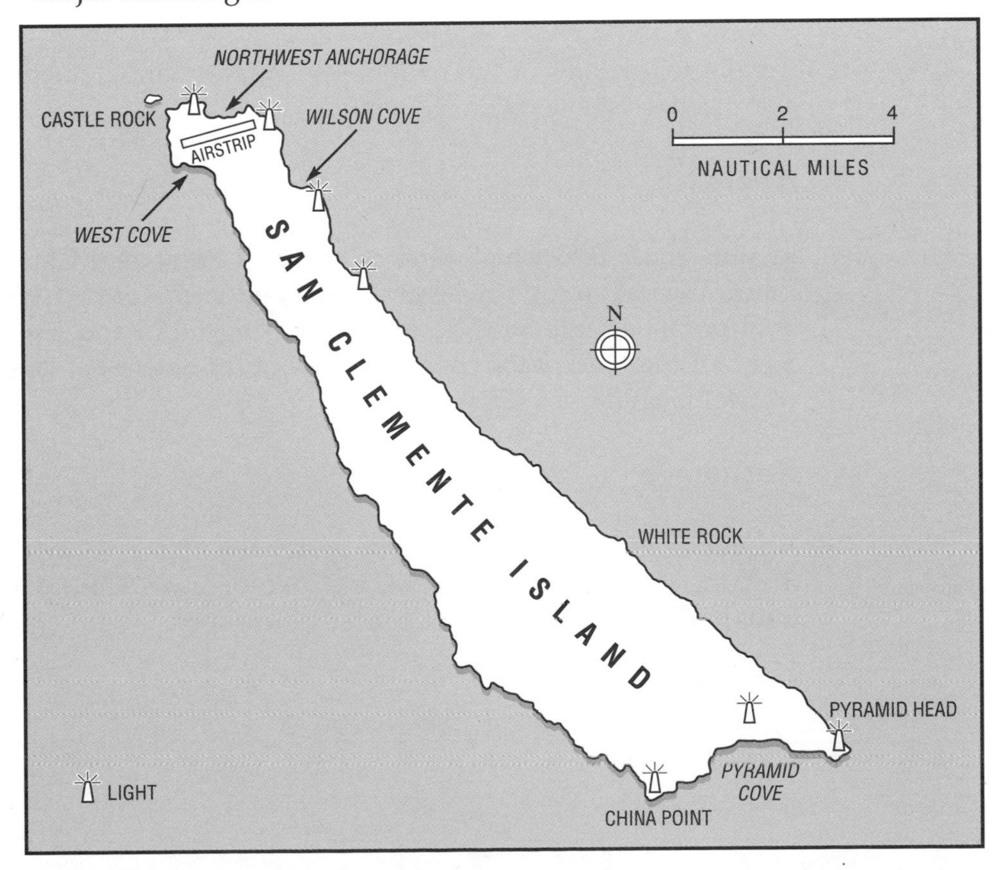

Wilson Cove

The major military anchorage, Wilson Cove has a 550-foot Navy pier extending seaward from the center of the bay. You may anchor here if military activity is not in progress.

Approach

Steer for the NE corner of the island until the buildings on the hill above the pier can be seen. Approach the cove from NE, as there are numerous military buoys N and S of the cove.

Anchorage

Anchor up to a mile NW of the pier in 30 feet or more (sand). The surge can be uncomfortable, but you will find some shelter from W winds. Strong downslope winds can blow in the afternoon.

Facilities and Landing

No facilities. You may not land without special permission.

Pyramid Cove

Pyramid Cove lies at the extreme SE end of San Clemente and provides shelter from NE winds.

Approach

Identify the 900-foot high bluff of Pyramid Point, and China Point, lower lying with several detached rocks of it. Give both points a wide berth to avoid off lying rocks and kelp. Steer for the head of the cove, looking out for patches of kelp which may hide sub surface dangers.

Anchorage

Anchor at the W end of the cove under the cliffs and away from the beach in 25 to 40 feet (sand). Observe the wind patterns and local currents to establish the best spot.

Facilities and Landing

No landing without special permission. You can use Pyramid Cove except when firing exercises are in progress. Contact The Commander, Amphibious Force, Pacific Fleet, North Amphibious Base, Coronado, CA 92118, (619) 437-2231, for information on firing schedules.

Other anchorages on San Clemente offer but limited shelter from prevailing winds or are under anchoring restrictions. Relatively few cruising boats make their way to this remote and somewhat unattractive island.

Courtesy of Gene's Rock and Gem Shop, Avalon

Avalon Harbor during Santa Ana conditions.

Chapter 15

Newport Beach Harbor to Ensenada, Mexico

San Diego is decidedly the best place in California. The harbor is small and landlocked; there is no surf; the vessels lie within a cable's length of the beach, and the beach itself is smooth, hard sand, without rocks or stones.

Richard Henry Dana
Two Years Before the Mast (1840).

Back on the mainland, I now describe the coast between Newport Beach and Ensenada, Mexico, the final stop on our California coastal passage.

Newport Beach Harbor (Chart 18754)

Newport Beach Harbor was once a coastal lagoon, a quiet place where passing ships occasionally collected hides and grain. The peace and quiet did not last long, for efforts to dredge the shallow entrance began as early as 1876. The present harbor with its two jetties and well dredged channel and turning basin dates to 1936. Over 9,000 pleasure craft make their homes here. Newport Beach is now a major yachting center with seven yacht clubs and every facility for the sailor imaginable.

The annual Newport to Enseñada yacht race is one of the great spectacles of the Southern California sailing year. Hundreds of yachts large and small charge across the starting line off Newport in a frantic dash for Enseñada. The fastest racing catamarans and ultralight sleds often arrive at the finish in early evening, if the winds oblige. In other years, the entire race is a drifting match past the Coronado Islands. A hard core of competitors take the racing seriously, but many boats just go along for the ride and the parties. Stories of pornographic movies shown on mainsails and multi-course gourmet dinners served at midnight abound. The parties in Enseñada are famous. An Enseñada Race is a worthwhile experience at least once, although the long motor homeward can be excruciating, especially with a hangover.

Approach

From N: Identify the Southern California Edison power plant 5.5 miles NW of Newport Beach, then follow the coastline at a distance of 0.75 mile until the harbor breakwaters are sighted.

From offshore: The SCE power plant N of the harbor and the highrise buildings of the Newport Center, 1.4 miles inland from the harbor, are excellent landmarks, even in poor visibility. Steer for the Newport Center buildings until the harbor entrance comes into view.

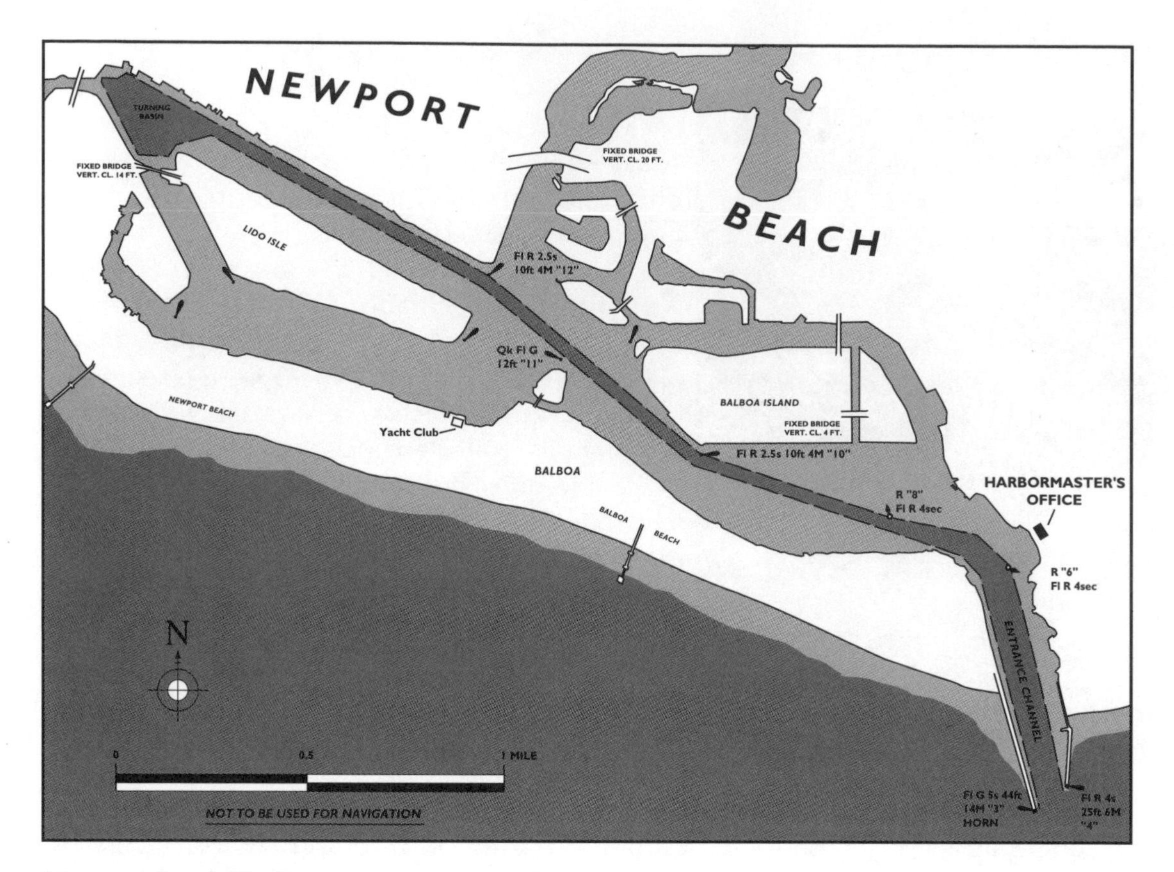

Newport Beach Harbor

From S: The dense urban sprawl of Newport Beach and neighboring communities offers the best general landmark until the highrise structures of the Newport Center come into view. Thereafter, stay 0.75 mile offshore until the harbor entrance is sighted.

Enter the main channel (15 to 20 feet) between the two jetties, which are 825 feet apart. Both are lighted (W jetty: Fl. G. 5 sec 44 feet 10 miles; E jetty: Fl. R 4 sec. 25 feet 6 miles). There is a speed limit of 5 knots, which is enforced. Newport entrance is very congested during summer weekends, especially in the early evening, when everyone wants to get home for the evening cocktail. Try and avoid rush hours during your first visit and exercise caution because of aggressive skippers.

A night approach is straightforward, confused only by the bright city lights which blaze out from the coast. The harbor lights can usually be spotted from two or three miles away, and the SCE power plant is a good general landmark.

Berthing and anchoring

Newport Beach Harbor is enormous and confusing to the first-time visitor. Affluent, well manicured houses crowd to water's edge everywhere, many with private docks. Thousands of yachts lie to fore-and-aft moorings here, so a dinghy is essential. For details of the various channels, governing depths, etc, consult Chart 18754. Our plan gives a general impression of the harbor layout.

The Orange County Harbor Patrol will assign you either a guest slip at the Guest Dock near their office (on the starboard side on the turning basin, by the Coast Guard station) or a mooring elsewhere in the harbor. Members of recognized yacht clubs can often obtain berths at the California Yacht Club and other clubs. You can spend 20-days on a visitor's mooring.

You can anchor west of Lido Island in a free designated anchoring area for no longer than 5 days with the permission of the Harbor Patrol. If you anchor here, one member of the crew must be aboard at all times and you must anchor in such a way as not to swing out of the anchoring area. The Patrol enforce these rules strictly. The anchoring area is far from convenient for provisioning, or even getting ashore, as most of the surrounding shore is privately owned. You may be able to get permission to land at a club dock. Most waterside restaurants have dinghy docks where you can tie upon whilst eating for your convenience.

Facilities

All supplies and facilities are available locally, or within a cab ride's distance. However, a dinghy is near-essential.
Harbor Patrol: (714) 726-7330.

Newport Beach to Dana Point (Chart 18746)

Twelve miles separate Newport Beach from Dana Point, named after Richard Henry himself. Dana Point itself juts out from the coastline consisting of low bluffs and sandy beaches fronting on low hills which roll down to the cliffs. The houses of Laguna Beach finger toward Dana Point. The Spanish Mediterranean structures of the Ritz-Carlton Hotel are prominent on a coastal bluff just N of Dana Point. From offshore, Santiago Peak, 17.5 miles NE of Dana Point has an unmistakable double-headed peak.

Dana Point lies at the seaward end of a long ridge, ending in a 220-foot high sandstone cliff with a precipitous face. Rocks and ledges extend at least 350 yards offshore. Pass outside the lighted buoy (Fl. R. 2.5 sec.) 0.5 mile off the point. A rock covered 2 fathoms 2.4 miles SE of the point sometimes breaks in strong winds.

The point is famous for its associations with Dana and the crew of the **Pilgrim.** Dana wrote that "no animal but a man or a monkey could get up it." They loaded hides by the simple expedient of throwing them one by one over the cliff. "As they were all large, stiff, and doubled, like the cover of a book, the wind took them, and they swayed and eddied about, plunging and rising in the air, like a kite when it has broken its string." The men at the bottom picked the hides up and carried them to the boat on their heads. When a hide caught on the cliff, they threw others at it to dislodge it from its perch. On another occasion, Dana himself was lowered down on a pair of topsail studding-sail halyards to free stubborn hides. Thus—Dana Point.

Dana Point Harbor (Chart 18746)

Dana Point Harbor lies in the lee of this famous point. Only built in the 1970s, it is the epitome of a modern small boat harbor: Efficient, comfortable, and thoroughly sanitized. I recommend it as a stop on the long transit up and down the coast.

Approach

From all directions, identify Dana Point, then shape a course immediately to its south. The main harbor breakwater runs parallel to the land, running out S from Dana Point. A light (Fl. G 4 sec.) marks the S end and the harbor entrance, which is also protected by a shorter breakwater from land (Fl. R. 4 sec.). Give a wide berth to the rock 300 yards NE of the southern breakwater light, marked by a buoy.

Enter the harbor midway between the breakwaters, taking care not to swing too close too the seaward breakwater, to allow for departing traffic.

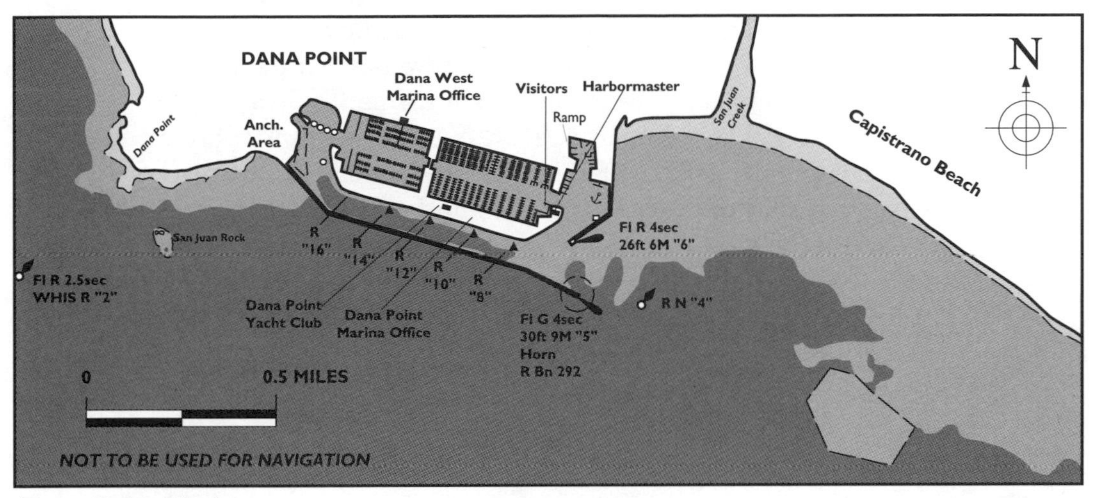

Dana Point Harbor

Berths

The Harbormaster's Office lies at the head of the inner breakwater protecting the marina area, where transient docks are to be found. Apply to the office for a slip (VHF Channel 12 and 16), or you can try the two private marinas in the harbor. Each has an office, the two marinas being separated by a low fixed bridge. Dana Point Marina has regular visitor slips for boats under 28 feet. You can also anchor in two designated areas, the one at the head of the main channel, the other in the East Basin, on the breakwater side of the yellow buoys. Obtain the permission of the harbormaster before anchoring.

Facilities

All facilities, with excellent shopping both at the marina and in Dana Point itself, with a shuttle between the harbor and downtown. Good waterfront restaurants.
Harbormaster: (714) 748-2222.

Dana Point to Oceanside Harbor (Chart 18744)

S from Dana Point to San Mateo Point 6.5 miles away, the rugged shoreline is still fairly high, with both the railroad tracks and the highway running close to shore. San Mateo Point, just south of San Clemente's red roofs, rises 60 feet high. Lit (Lat. 33 deg 23.3 min N; Long. 117 deg. 35.8 min W) (Fl. W 10 sec. 63 feet 16 miles), the point makes a fairly prominent landmark. But the most conspicuous signposts are the white domes of the San Onofre nuclear generating plant, 2.5 miles S. The plant, when brilliantly lit at night, stands out like a bright beacon on the coastline. Stay at least 1.5 miles offshore between Dana Point and Oceanside to stay clear of outlying dangers and kelp. The low-lying coastal plain between San Onofre and Oceanside is part of

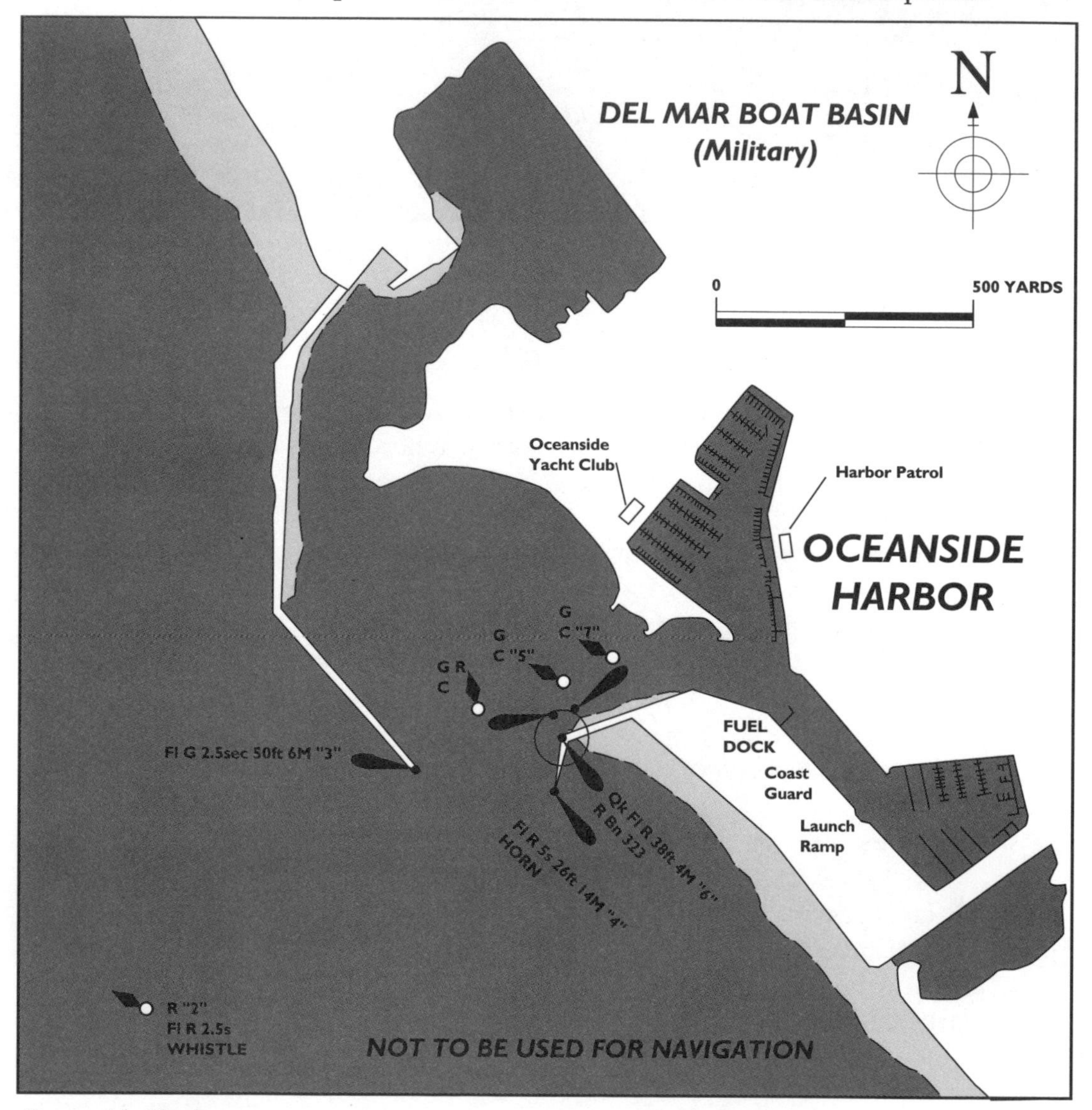

Oceanside Harbor

Camp Pendleton Marine Base. A military restricted area extends from San Clemente 3 miles seaward along the coast to Del Mar Basin in Oceanside Harbor. A busy US 101 runs parallel with the beach. *Local Notices to Mariners* gives details of exercise times, or you can call the Oceanside Harbormaster's office (714) 722-1418. If you pass outside the 3-mile limit, you have nothing to worry about. Keep outside the 10-fathom line on this 12-mile passage.

Oceanside Harbor (Chart 18744)

Approach

From N: Oceanside Harbor lies just S of the Santa Margarita River, marked from offshore by conspicuous freeway and railroad trestles. An elevated water tank lies 1.7 miles NE of the harbor. You can steer for this structure until you locate the breakwaters.

From S: Identify the city pier, which can be seen from some distance. The harbor entrance is 1.2 miles NW and located just SW of a 17-story apartment complex painted white with a blue trim. A lighted tower on the SE side of the harbor resembles a lighthouse.

Whichever direction you approach from, you have local help. Some considerate souls have placed a lighted sign saying OCEANSIDE on a grassy ridge behind the harbor, just in case you get lost!

A lighted buoy (Fl. R. 2.5 sec.) lies 1,000 feet SE of the entrance. The two breakwaters enclose the entrance, the E jetty bearing a light (Fl. R 5 sec. 26 feet. 14 miles) visible from a considerable distance. The western jetty is also lighted (Fl. G, 2.5 sec. 50 feet 5 miles).

The breakwaters protect two harbor basins: Camp Pendleton's Del Mar Basin and Oceanside Harbor itself. A bifurcating dredged and buoyed channel (20 to 24 feet) leads to the inner harbors. The Del Mar basin is government property and off-limits to private vessels. Follow the starboard fork to Oceanside Harbor. Stay well clear of the rock groin on the port side of the entrance. Both ends are obstructed or shallow at low water.

Warning: Oceanside Harbor approach is dangerous in rough SE conditions, because of wave action and shoaling. Do not attempt an entrance in such weather and call the Harbormaster on VHF Channel 16 for a report on the condition of the entrance. The channel buoys are moved according to shoaling.

Berths

Over 900 yachts lie in Oceanside Harbor. The harbor office lies by the turning basin in the northern marina area. Transients should report there for slip assignments.

Facilities

Excellent eating ashore, provisions, fuel, and water readily available, also a boatyard and launching ramp.
Harbormaster: (714) 722-1418.

Oceanside Harbor to Mission Bay (Charts 18744 and 18765)

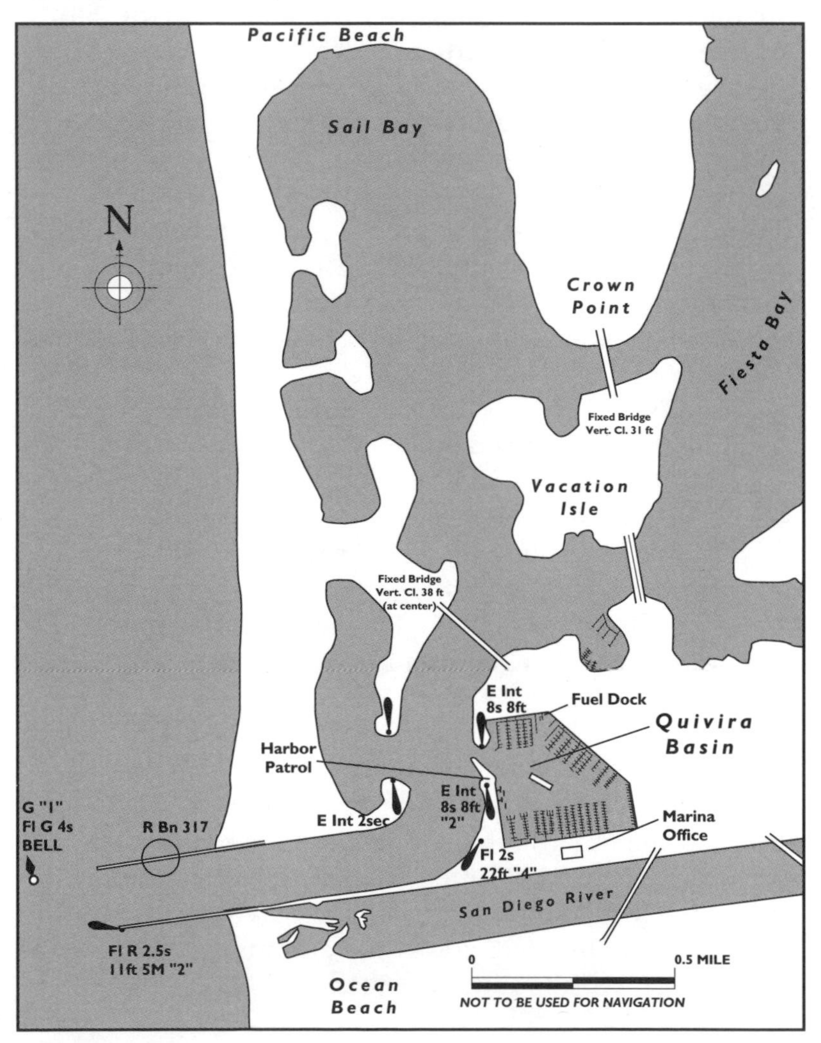

Mission Bay

I always find the next stretch of coast somewhat monotonous. From Oceanside you pass mile after mile of low tableland with steep and low, usually brownish cliffs that range between 60 and 130 feet high. Numerous canyons dissect the cliffs and break the monotony of the bluffs. The railroad and US 101 run parallel to, and just inshore of, the beach. You can hear the traffic for miles to seaward on a still night.

The few landmarks on this long stretch of coast are:

- Carlsbad, 30 miles N of Point Loma: a conspicuous power plant stack with fixed and flashing red lights at night. A lighted bell buoy (Qk. Fl. W) and a complex of mooring buoys lie about a mile offshore. Your course should pass well offshore of this buoy.

- Del Mar, 18 miles N of Point Loma, a conspicuous smoke stack, also resort buildings.

- A measured nautical mile 13.5 miles N of Point Loma, marked by two pairs of steel towers.

- Scripps Institution of Oceanography, 12 miles N of Point Loma. This famous institution is 5 miles S of where the coastal cliffs rise to about 300 feet and US 101 diverts inland. The Scripps buildings and its privately maintained pier are prominent from a considerable distance. A restricted area lies off the pier, and is clearly marked on the chart.

Point La Jolla is a ridge of Soledad mountain, a rounded, 822-foot high promontory that lies 9 miles N of Point Loma. Point La Jolla is the first high ground seen as you approach San Diego. The mountain has two TV towers on its summit. Buildings of La Jolla and Pacific Beach are prominent. When bound between Point La Jolla and Point Loma, keep at least 3 miles offshore to avoid extensive kelp beds that mask the rocky shoals inshore. A safe course along this 11-mile stretch takes you well outside the 10-fathom line.

Mission Bay

Mission Bay is a popular yacht harbor with extensive areas of shallow water where dinghy sailing is a delight. Unfortunately, the entrance is hazardous in rough weather.

Approach

Mission Bay entrance is 5.5 miles N of Point Loma. Approach from well to seaward, because of kelp, even when coming from San Diego.

From N: Locate the US Navy Electronics Tower a mile NW of the lighted entrance jetties (N jetty: Fl. G 6 sec. 36 feet 7 miles; S jetty: Fl. R. 2.5 sec. 11 feet 5 miles). By this time you should see the 338-foot Sea World tower 1.8 miles E of the entrance.

From S: The Ocean Beach fishing pier extends from the shore 0.3 mile S of the entrance and may be sighted before the Mission Bay jetties. So is the Hyatt Islandia Hotel on the N shoe of Quivira Basin inside the entrance.

Approach the jetties from seaward, and stay closer to the N jetty if any swell is running, as breaking can occur on the S side of the channel.

Warning: Swells can break in 20 feet even in moderately rough weather. Avoid Mission Bay in rough onshore weather and divert to the all-weather harbor at San Diego.

The dredged entrance channel carries 14 to 19 feet (shallower at the edges) and leads to Quivira and Mariners' Basins, on the E and W sides of the fairway. Mission Bay Bridge with a clearance of 38 feet crosses the main fairway 1.3 miles from the entrance above Quivira Basin, limiting access to the inner bay for larger vessels.

Berths and Anchoring

Contact the Harbor Patrol on VHF Channel 16 for berthing information, or call in at the office, just to starboard inside Quivira Dock. Three private marinas in Quivira Dock itself offer transient slips, with convenient access to fuel and restaurants. The Harbor Patrol will give you permission to anchor in Mariner's Basin, where you will find 9 to 12 feet (mud and sand). The best anchorage lies in the W part of the basin, opposite the entrance. You can remain here for 72 hours. I have spent hours exploring Mission Bay with my dinghy from this comfortable spot. There are public restrooms on the beach.

If you want to explore the inner reaches of Mission Bay, do so from your dinghy. Depths above the fixed bridge rarely exceed 6 to 6 feet. The three small boat marinas above the bridge in Dana and Perez Coves have no guest slips. An aerial tramway passes over the channel with a clearance of 42 feet at Perez Cove.

A surge can run into the harbor and the yacht basins in rough weather.

Facilities

Mission Bay is a wonderful place for family cruises. Most of the shoreline and all the islands are part of a large San Diego city park. The Bay makes a good base for visiting Sea World, also the San Diego Zoo and other attractions, but a rental car is essential.

Harbormaster: (619) 686-6272.

Mission Bay to San Diego Harbor (Chart 18765)

The 5.5-mile coast between Mission Bay and Point Loma is rocky, and heavily infested with kelp. Keep at least 3 miles offshore to enjoy clear water. Your first landmark will be the Y-shaped Ocean Beach fishing pier 0.3 mile S of Mission Bay entrance. From there, simply run along the land until Point Loma is clear ahead, an easy landmark to find, even in thick weather.

When approaching Point Loma from N, give a wide berth to the coast NW of the point, and approach at least 2 miles offshore to avoid kelp beds and New Hope Rock, 2.25 miles NW of the headland. Point Loma is a major landmark in clear weather. George Davidson: "Vessels bound from the northwest make the ridge of Point Loma as a long, flat-topped island when about 25 miles distant." The low lying ground behind the point will become apparent as you close San Diego. Point Loma is about 400 feet high, a rugged peninsula bare of trees but covered with sparse vegetation. *US Pilot:* "The tanks and buildings of a sewage treatment plant are conspicuous about 0.9 mile N of the point."

Point Loma light shines from a skeleton tower (Lat. 32 deg 39.9 min N; Long. 117 deg. 14.5 min W) (Fl. 15 sec. 88 feet 23 miles). The S approach will bring the lowlying coastline S of San Diego to starboard, and the higher ground of Point Loma between the Coronado Islands and the coast ahead. The highrise buildings of downtown San Diego are visible from S a long way offshore. A course toward the higher ground will enable you to identify the approach buoys from a comfortable distance. The powerful lighthouse and well-lit entrance channel ensures an easy night approach.

San Diego Harbor (Charts 18722 and 18773)

San Diego has been a favorite haven since Juan Rodrigues Cabrillo sailed into the entrance in 1542. The Presidio and Mission were founded as early as 1769. George Davidson waxed lyrical about the place: "Next to San Francisco, no harbor on the Pacific coast of the United States approximates in excellence to that of the bay of San Diego." A generation earlier, Richard Henry Dana spent several months living on the beach in a hide processing house. In his day, San Diego was just a quiet backwater. He described the back-breaking work of hide curing and wood cutting in the bush accompanied by a pack of howling dogs. It was a tough life, but there were barely broken horses to ride and occasional visitors to ease the monotony of the passing days. Early visitors to the bay, like Vancouver, anchored "in ten fathoms water, fine sandy bottom...The Presidio of San Diego bore N21E distant 3.5 miles, and the nearest shore north west, within a quarter of a mile of our anchorage." The entrance was first lit with a lighthouse on Point Loma on November 15, 1855, with a fixed white light of the "third order of Fresnel." San Diego is, quite simply, one of the finest natural harbors in the world, offering complete shelter in any weather, and minimal tidal streams into the bargain. Today, San Diego is a major Naval and commercial port, also a world-famous yacht racing center, where several America's Cup challenges have run their course.

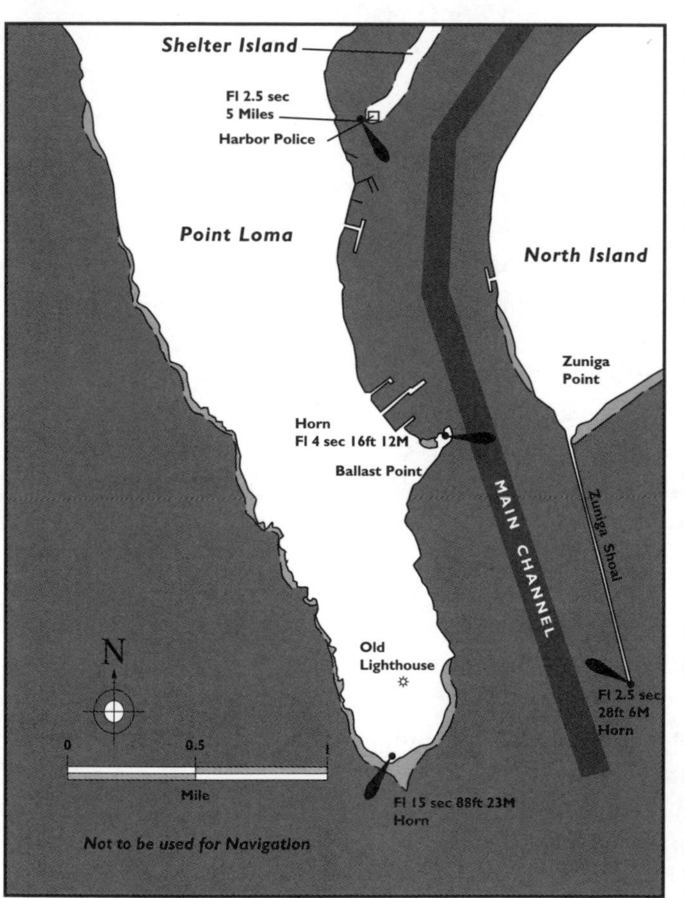

San Diego Harbor Entrance and Point Loma

Approach

From N: Give Port Loma a wide berth and aim to pass just outside the kelp, which can extend out as far as 2 miles. Whistle buoy "1" and bell buoy "3" mark the outer limits of the seaweed in normal conditions. Once past buoy "3," Ballast and Zuniga Points will open up, and buoys of the dredged entrance channel can be identified. The limits of the dredged channel are marked by red and green flashing buoys (see Chart 18773).

From S: Steer for the higher ground Point Loma, until less conspicuous landmarks come into sight. Then alter course for the entrance channel as the buoys come into sight and Zuniga Point is identified.

The entrance itself is straightforward. Tidal streams ranging between 0.5 to 3 knots set through the channel depending on the state of the tide. To time your entrance most effectively, make use of the Daily Current Predictions published annually in NOAA's *Tidal Current Atlas.* You can stay outside the channel buoys all the way up and down the channel, which will keep you clear of the largest ships. However, keep a sharp look out for traffic of all kinds and give the lighted jetty on the E side of the channel, which extends a mile S from Point Zuniga.

Warning: The Point Zuniga jetty is partially submerged at high tide. Give yourself plenty of room, for you may experience a set toward the jetty on the ebb. The jetty is a real hazard in foggy weather, when you can come upon it without warning when the set catches you without reference points on the land. I have nearly collided with it on two occasions in such conditions.

Watch, also, for a cross-current off Ballast Point that can deflect you into the channel. Steep swells can form in the channel during SE gales, but they are not life threatening.

In Davidson's day, the entrance was less developed. You entered watching the breakers on the shoals S of Zuniga Point. His sailing directions for a summer transit cannot be bettered for a yacht drawing 6 feet: "During the summer, keep as close to Point Loma as the draught of the vessel will permit, and lay on the wind up to Ballast Point, of which four fathoms can be carried within a ship's length, with ten fathoms in mid-channel."

Every Naval vessel needs protection against magnetic mines, so many are demagnetized on a degaussing range near Point Ballast. Look out for ships working the range in this vicinity and keep well clear.

Past Ballast Point, the entrance slowly trends to NE, with naval facilities to port and a measured mile to starboard. The channel is well marked day and night and presents no problems for small craft. At night, keep Point Ballast light (Fl. W 4 sec. 16 feet 10 miles) on the port bow and follow the channel buoy lights.

The main channel trends N and E , turning SE at buoy 21 (QG) past the highrise buildings of downtown San Diego, then under the Coronado Bay Bridge (clearance ranges between 156 to 195 feet). The channel narrows rapidly in South San Diego Bay, ending in a small dredged approach channel for Chula Vista SMall Boat Harbor.

I always have Charts 18722 and 18773 close to hand when navigating in San Diego harbor.

Berths and Anchoring

Shelter Island to the N of the entrance channel, lies well inside Ballast Point. You'll see the dredged channel to the marina area opposite channel buoy

"16." San Diego is a major Port of Entry for yachts returning from Mexico and further afield.You must go to the Police or Municipal Docks near their Office at the W end of Shelter Island, to starboard of the marina entrance, until all entry formalities (Customs, Immigration, Public Health, and Agricultural Inspection) are completed. You can moor at the Municipal Dock for up to 10 days, but this berth is usually crowded.

I recommend contacting the Harbor Police whether you have come from Mexico, or simply from a windward port. They will brief you on available transient berths, private marinas, and anchoring regulations. The latter are in a constant state of flux, and often controversy, to the point that anchoring is becoming a virtual impossibility.

Visitors' slips can be difficult to find in San Diego. The best advice is to contact a private marina, or to make arrangement with one of the yacht clubs. You must, however, normally be a member of another club to reserve a slip.

Port of San Diego Mooring Office: (619) 686-6227.

Harbor Police: (619) 686-651

San Diego Bay Marinas and Anchorages

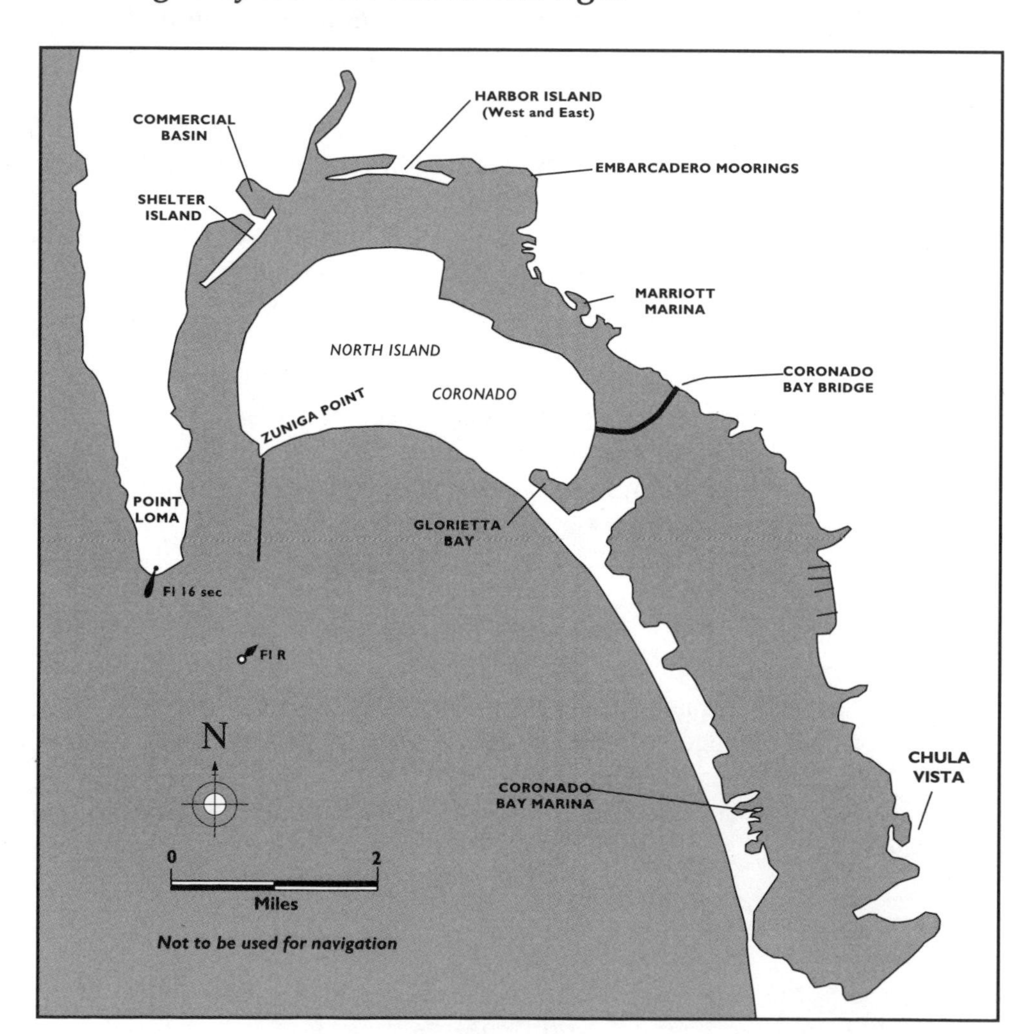

Controversy surrounds anchoring in this busy harbor, partly because the authorities want to control all activities in the commercial port. Before you anchor contact the Harbor Police (619) 686-6511 for the latest information. In this way, you can learn wherefree anchoring is permitted and avoid a ticket. Wherever you anchor, be careful to display an anchor light at night and a black ball by day. I would advise leaving someone aboard at all times, and locking your boat carefully. The current designated anchoring areas are:

La Playa Cove anchorage between the San Diego Yacht Club and Southwestern Yacht Club. This weekend-only anchoring spot requires not only a Police permit but a holding tank.

Glorietta Bay (See below.) Recommended.

South Bay 24th Street area. Apply to the Harbor Police for information.

Now some more specific information on San Diego yacht harbors:

Shelter Island

Shelter Island is the first marina facility, opposite buoy "16," where the channel trends NE. Prestigious, crowded, and expensive, it's an excellent base when preparing for a Mexican cruise.

Approach

The entrance channel lies opposite buoy "16." Identify the entrance marker, which delineates the starboard side of the entrance, then follow the 20-foot channel into the marina area.

Berthing

Five marinas and three yacht clubs form the nucleus of Shelter Island's elaborate infrastructure. Here you will find the San Diego Yacht Club, where many long distance cruising people congregate, and the base for occasional America's Cup competitions. Each competing team has a compound in this area. Transient slips are in short supply at most marinas, especially in summer, and, when available, they are expensive.

Facilities

Shelter Island has some of the best boatyards on the West Coast. Every kind of repair work can be carried out here. Provisions, restaurants, and other services are close by. You will need a rental car to explore the San Diego Zoo or other attractions.

Commercial Basin

Two private marinas occupy this basin E of Shelter Island. It has now been renamed the America's Cup Harbor and many activities surrounding Cup events will be held here. I have never been able to obtain a visitor berth here. I recommend going elsewhere.

Harbor Island

Harbor Island is a modern facility, close to the downtown area. This enormous marina area comprises two basins and four private marinas.

Approach

West Basin: Identify channel buoy "19" on the port side of the main channel, then inshore, leaving the Commercial Basin entrance to port and passing outside buoy "1." The entrance to the western basin lies straight ahead, with a least depth of 13 to 15 feet. A low fixed bridge lies at the head of the entrance, before which you turn hard a-starboard into the West Basin channel.

East Basin: The entrance lies opposite channel buoy "21," behind the eastern peninsula of Harbor Island. Steer for the end of the headland, passing 0.25 mile off, then turn to port into the buoyed channel.

Berthing

All four marinas have visitors' slips, much used in the summer. Charges vary considerably, as do services, so check carefully in advance.

Facilities

If using a marina, I prefer East Basin, as it is relatively close to downtown and seems less hectic than Shelter

Island. Nice restaurants and shops, with good marine repair facilities, fuel, and water.

Embarcadero Moorings

24 mooring buoys lie off the Embarcadero just upstream from Harbor Island, in a bight E of the large Coast Guard station. You can use these for up to a month, but the berth is a noisy one, owing to traffic and jet noise. Apply to the Wharfinger's Office at (619) 291-3900, extension 340 during business hours. After hours, call 291-1799. Rates double after the 15th day. I have never spent the night here, and would avoid it if there are other berths available. It's just too noisy.

The Laurel Street anchorage S of the moorings is usually crowded with permanent residents.

Marriott Marina

Marriott Marina has the advantage of being very close to downtown and Seaport Village close by.

Approach

The entrance lies opposite channel buoy 23, on the N side of the dredged fairway. There is 10 feet in the narrow defile between the breakwaters.

Berthing

Visitors are welcome if there is space available, especially off season. Apply to the dockmaster at the pump-out station, or call ahead (619) 230-8955.

Facilities

This is the berth for sybarites, with all the services of a top-quality hotel. Few marine facilities, but downtown with all its shops is close by.

Marinas above Coronado Bay Bridge

Glorietta Bay Marina lies S in the bay of that name on Coronado Island, at the end of a dredged channel (15 feet). A green buoy (Fl. G) just beyond the bridge on the Coronado side marks the port side of the entrance channel. Follow the markers into the bay (15 to 17 feet). The marina has visitors' berths and the Coronado Yacht Club is hospitable. I have been unable to obtain fuel at this marina.

An anchoring area at the NE corner of Glorietta Bay has 15 to 17 feet (mud and sand), but check anchoring regulations before using it.

Coronado Bay Marina is on the S side of South San Diego Bay. Identify a pair of red and white buoys opposite Sweetwater Channel, then steer SSW out of the dredged channel into shallower water (10 to 11 feet) for the pair of markers at the outer end of the entrance channel (10 feet). Keep well N of the two markers, as the water shallows rapidly S of them. Follow the entrance channel into marina area.Visitors berths sometimes available, but I would advise calling ahead before making the trek under the bridge: (619) 423-4982 or VHF Channel 16.

There are designated anchoring areas in the South Bay, but you should call the Harbor Police for the latest information on availability. They will be glad to give you specifics.

Chula Vista Marina is less than a decade old, a modern yacht harbor very close to the Mexican border. The entrance channel can be confusing to newcomers. You need Chart 18773 to hand. I always check off the channel markers here, to make sure I identify green buoy "7" (Fl. G. 2.5 sec.), which marks the port side of the dredged approach. Turn hard a-port and follow the pairs of markers into the harbor entrance. You have a least depth of 15 feet, but effectively no water outside the buoys, so be careful. The marina has some visitors' slips, but, again, call ahead on VHF Channel 16 or (619) 691-1860.

Many people spend a few days in San Diego and never really explore this most magnificent of harbors. With so much to do ashore and afloat you could spend six months exploring here and not see everything. Despite anchoring restrictions, the harbor is a wonderful place for a family vacation afloat. And if you're bound on a long cruise to Mexico or further afield, make sure you make contact with the people at Downwind Marine, 2804 Cañon Street, (619) 224-2733. They are famous for their service to both cruising and racing sailors and run both a VHF Radio Net and a parts-by-radio Single Sideband ordering service, which are invaluable to people in Mexican and local waters.

San Diego to the Mexican Border (Charts 18765, 21140, and 21021)

This is not a book about Mexican cruising, but many California yachts make a yearly pilgrimage to Enseñada as part of the annual Newport to Enseñada race each May, or make the harbor their port of entry for a longer cruise down Baja and into the Sea of Cortes. So I thought it appropriate to make some mention of the passage to Enseñada here.

The passage from San Diego to Enseñada is a pleasant downwind run that takes about 12 hours at 5 knots. Shape your course to pass inside the Coronados and follow the general trend of the coast to SE. Under normal conditions, you are unlikely to experience a wind of more than 20 knots. Most yachts tend to hug the coast past Punta Salsipuedes, enjoying the rugged scenery that leads to Bahia Todos Santos and Enseñada. Make the southbound 63-mile passage a day trip, planning to leave San Diego after an early breakfast. With normal winds, you will be enjoying margaritas at Hussongs that evening. The northbound passage is best executed during the calm night hours, under power. Stay at least 5 miles offshore and follow the coast, passing inside of the Coronados. If you leave after dinner, you should be in San Diego before the midday winds get up.

From the San Diego entrance, the coast forms a large, lowlying sandy bight as far as the border. The buildings of Imperial Beach are prominent, so is the city fishing pier located 1.5 miles N of the Mexican border. If you follow the coast closely, keep outside the 10-fathom line as far S as Punta Salsipuedes. The US-Mexican border is marked by a white marble obelisk 41 feet above the water near a low bluff, 200 yards from the beach. The obelisk is 10 miles, 127 degrees M from Point Loma, and is aligned with a stone mound 1 mile E to form a useful line bearing. The circular, concrete bull ring just S of the border is also prominent. As a matter of interest, bull fights are held every Sunday from May to September.

Coronado Islands

The Coronados lie 15 miles S of Point Loma. They are 7 miles off the coast and are Mexican-owned. The four islands make a fine landmark when approaching San Diego from the south. The celebrated British sailor Peter Pye was by here in the mid-1950s and described them as "round dry humps sticking steeply out of the water," an apt description. The Coronados are a favorite day excursion for San Diego yachts, and an underwater sports paradise. They extend NW for 4.5 miles and are surrounded by dense kelp beds. You have a choice of several fairly exposed anchorages:

Coronado del Norte. A deep water island, but anchorage is possible off a lobster shack on NE shore. Be prepared to move out in a hurry if the wind gets up.

Puerto Cueva on the E shore of Coronado del Sur, where there is 25 feet (sand), but considerable surge. The cove can be identified by the northern light (Gp. Fl. W (3) 15 sec. 19 miles) on its S shore.

Old Hotel anchorage on the E shore of Coronado del Sur offers shelter from NW winds off an abandoned hotel/casino, a low, 2-story building at the water's edge. Anchor in 35 to 50 feet (rock and sand). Lay plenty of scope.

All Coronado anchorages are dangerous in Santa Ana conditions. You must have fishing permits or official papers to land in the Coronados. Another word of caution: avoid approaching the islands at night. The only lights (which can be unreliable) are on the southern island, the S tip being marked by Gp. Fl. 5 sec. visible for 22 miles. A visit to these fascinating islands is best timed for quiet, NW weather in summer, when conditions are predictable. The seas can be quite rough off the Coronados in post-frontal winds, especially around the southern light.

The Coronado Islands to Enseñada

The mainland coast between the border and Punta San Miguel at the entrance to Bahia Todos Santos consists of barren hills and bluffs, with cliffs as high as 80 feet. Behind are low foothills and dry mountains rising to over 3000 feet above sea level. This stretch of coast is becoming more developed. Here are some useful landmarks:

- **Table Mountain,** a conspicuous, flat-topped hill, 25 miles SE of Point Loma and 6 miles inland.

- **El Rosarito,** a small resort community some 12 miles S of the border. A refinery with 13 storage tanks and a power plant with 4 smoke stacks are prominent just N of the town. The Rosarito Beach Hotel is also conspicuous.

Punta Descanso is the seaward end of a 392-foot high bluff, with an offlying 13-foot rock, Pilon de Azucar, 4 miles SE, sometimes referred to as Sugarloaf Rock. Although fishing boats anchor S of the rock in deep water, there is no reason to approach this stretch of coast closely.

Punta Salsipuedes is lower lying and is best identified by the large and well-lit mobile home park situated at the point. This is about the southern limit of coastal development.

Between Punta Salsipuedes and Punta San Miguel, the coast is barren and unlit, with higher rocky bluffs crowding on the shore. You can stay well inshore by day if you wish, and can anchor in 35 to 50 feet (sand), with some shelter from NW, behind El Pescadero if waiting for calm winds when northbound.

Punta San Miguel is bold and 150 feet high (Fl. W 4.5 sec. 17 miles). The N shore of Bahia Todos Santos is backed by 50- to 100-foot cliffs and high hills. El Sauzel is a small fishing harbor ESE of Puntas San Miguel, with an enclosed inner harbor behind a breakwater. The port is often crowded and I prefer Enseñada. Keep at least 1.5 miles offshore between El Pescadero and Punta del Morro to clear kelp beds, breakers, and off-lying dangers. A course of 118 degrees M from a position that distance off El Pescadero will take you clear of dangers. Do not try to pass inshore of the kelp off Punta Morro and give the shore a wide berth. By this time you will see Enseñada harbor ahead.

Punta Ensenada is 370 feet high, with a hexagonal house and mast on its slopes. The harbor breakwater extends SE from the point. A 150-foot chimney and a tank are conspicuous behind the town.

Enseñada Harbor

Enseñada is changing rapidly from a sleepy resort town into a sizeable commercial and tourist city. Many yachts bound for Mexico clear Customs and Immigration here before setting out for Cabo San Lucas.

Approach

S-bound: The Port is easy to approach from NW, once you have identified the major landmarks. Steer for a point about a mile off the end of the breakwater (about 256 degrees M from a safe point off Punta Morro), then shape your course inside the harbor, keeping a close lookout for departing traffic, especially at night.

N-bound: You approach from the vicinity of the Todos Santos islands, either passing outside San Miguel Shoal or S of this dangerous patch well clear of NW island. A short cut brings you between the Todos Santos Islands and the mainland, clear of off-lying dangers off Punta Banda, where strong N currents are reported. All these approaches should be taken with caution at night, as the lights are sometimes expunged. Todos Santos light (Gp. Fl. W (4) 12 sec. 18 miles) is reported unreliable. Punta Banda lighthouse is Gp Fl. WR (2) 9 sec. 7 miles, 10 miles.

The SW shores of Bahia Todos Santos are steep and rugged, but the land S of Enseñada is low-lying and sandy. A number of excellent anchorages lie on the E shore of SE island, but are outside the scope of this book. Enseñada harbor lies 8.4 miles E of this island.

The entrance is straightforward, between the breakwaters.

Berthing and Anchorage

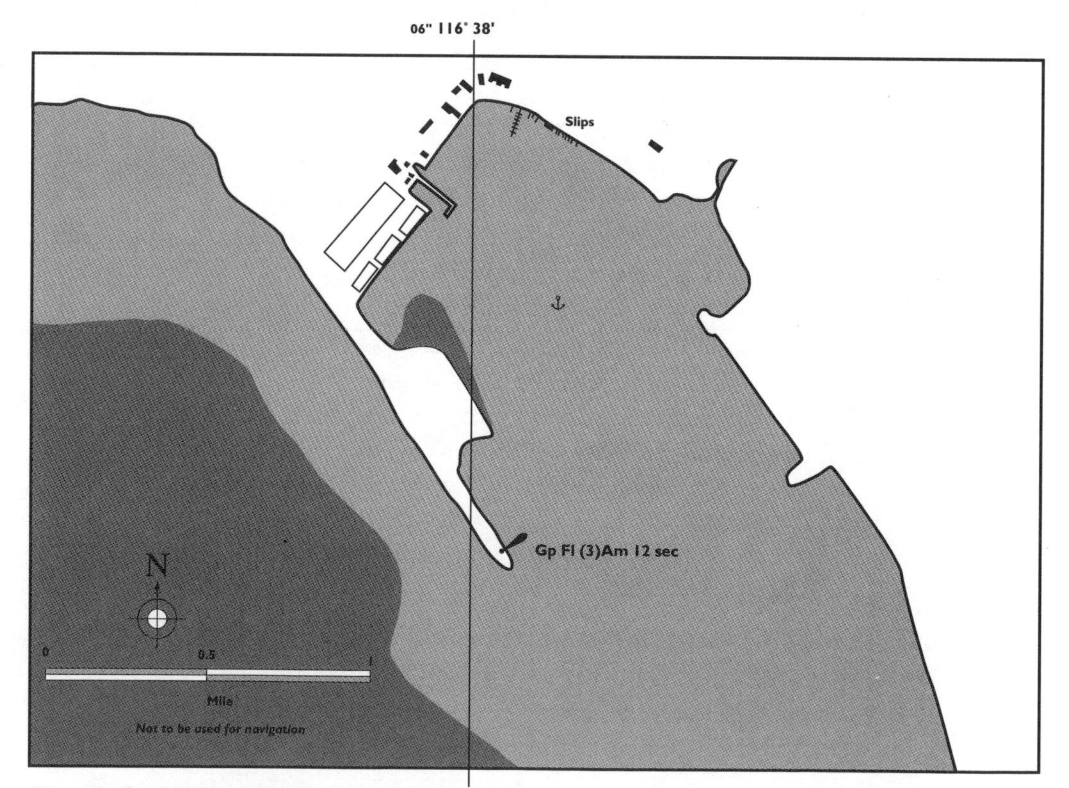

Enseñada, Mexico Harbor.

Enseñada is a port of entry and a commercial port, which has only recently developed facilities for pleasure craft. The Captain of the Port's office is on the NW side of the harbor, Immigration and Customs just N, in the town.

The 22 slips run by the Baja Naval yard can be recommended (call them on VHF channel 77). There are also somewhat delapidated visitors' slips along the waterfront, which are often full. If you rent one, be sure to rig spring lines and plenty of fenders, for the surge can make this an uncomfortable berth. You can also rent a mooring in the harbor, but they can not necessarily be relied upon in strong winds. I prefer anchoring off, in the shelter of the breakwater, in the area between the city waterfront and halfway to the breakwater in 15 to 30 feet (sand and mud). This berth can be crowded, especially at Enseñada Race time in early May. Lay plenty of scope, buoy your anchor, and look out for submerged objects.

If the harbor is too full, you can anchor in Granada Bay just E of Punta Morro in 15 to 18 feet (sand and kelp). Sound your way carefully into the cove, and expect some surge in prevailing summer conditions.

Anchorage may also be obtained on the S side of Bahia Todos Santos in SE weather, or in Bahia Papalote on the SW side of Punta Banda in NW winds.

Facilities

Fuel and water can be obtained, provisions in the town, while engine and other marine repairs can be arranged at the harbor. Land your dinghy at the waterfront, tying it to one of the docks. Tip someone to watch it if possible, and avoid unlit areas at night.

Entering Mexico

Enseñada is the normal port of entry for Baja cruises. Before you leave the US, arrange for a customs agent to obtain consular clearance papers for you. These papers, fundamentally a crew list, have to be processed at a Mexican Consulate before you leave. The agents charge a fee, but it is well worth the expense. You can, of course, do the paperwork yourself, obtaining the forms at the consulate. Some chandleries carry supplies for the asking. Make sure you obtain the correct insurance coverage and fishing license.

Anyone visiting Mexico for more than 72 hours must complete a tourist card, obtainable on production of a passport or birth certificate from a consulate, or at Mexican immigration at Enseñada or the border. These are validated on entry.

Yachts on a Baja cruise must take these documents to the Captain of the Port, Immigration, and Customs at Enseñada between 0900 and 1400 weekdays. Customs will issue a temporary cruising permit and stamp tourist cards.

You must get the same papers stamped when you leave Enseñada, whether bound for a US port or to another Mexican harbor. The same procedure is repeated at all Mexican ports of call, during office hours.

Of course you should take your State Registration Certificate or Federal Documentation papers with you at all times, together with your insurance policy. Note that most Southern California yacht policies end at Enseñada or Punta Banda.

Mexican consulates:

San Francisco: 870 Market Street, San Francisco, CA 94104 (415) 392-5554.

Los Angeles: 2401 West 6th Street, Los Angeles, CA 90054 (213) 351-6800.

San Diego: Central Federal Bldg, Suite 225, 225 Broadway, San Diego, 92101 (619) 231-8414.

Enseñada gives you a tantalizing sample of the fascinating cruising grounds that lie S of our familiar California waters. A beer at Hussongs, or a Mexican dinner and mariachi bands, are a delicious part of western cruising life, a life that can give you everything from ultra-modern yachting harbors to unspoiled anchorages that are unchanged since Richard Henry Dana's day. Fair winds, smooth seas and...enjoy...

RESOURCES

I compiled this book from months of sailing time on the water, also from a wide variety of sources, most of which are obscure, to say the least. The resources which follow are commonly available and deserve a space on your cabin bookshelf. Some of them are technical, others for pure enjoyment on those lazy days in port or at anchor in a quiet cove.

Official Publications

US Coast Pilot no. 7 Pacific Coast of the United States
Large commercial ships and fishing boats refer to the Coast Pilot frequently, for it contains all the regulations pertaining to safe navigation in California waters. The sailing directions in its pages change little from year to year and are superficial at best. It's still worth having a copy on board, if nothing else for browsing purposes on quiet

Ensenada Yacht Race © Geri Conser

watches. The Pilot contains an extraordinary range of esoteric information, which can be of use at the most unexpected moments.

Tide and Current Atlas
A vital aid, especially for San Francisco Bay sailors. You do not necessarily need the annual tide tables, as many marine stores hand out free copies at the counter. Again, the long-term information is invaluable.

List of Lights

If you plan extensive night cruising, I strongly recommend having the latest light list aboard. Light characteristics, even of major lighthouses, change frequently. You should double check everything you see on the chart against this list.

Charts

NOAA charts offer comprehensive coverage between Point Reyes and Ensenada, Mexico.The text of this guide is cross referenced to appropriate passage charts, which are also summarized in a text figure in Chapter 7. I strongly recommend acquiring a copy of NOAA's *Charts and Publications List number 2: United States Pacific Coast*, which is available free at all chart agents. This useful document lists complete chart coverage for our area, more, in fact, than you need.

Privately published navigational information

Caveat emptor—buyer beware! Every year sees more publications masquerading as pilot books or navigational directories, which do nothing but copy official sailing directions word for word. If you want the official word, buy the *Coast Pilot!* It's cheaper! The works mentioned here are designed specifically for small boat sailors and amplify the purple prose of anonymous government technical writers.

Chart Portfolios

Spirally bound chart portfolios have become popular items in recent years, as the cost of charts has risen sharply. These are good value, for you can obtain complete coverage for a fraction of the price of a complete portfolio. However, the commercial portfolios are clearly labeled "Do Not Use for Navigation," a US Government requirement of all chart copies. In fact, many people do use them on passage, without ill effects. I tend to use full size passage charts for maintaining Dead Reckoning plots, while using the portfolios for reference when concerned with harbor entrances rather than courses and bearings. Here are the major portfolios, all readily available in local marine stores:

Delta Yachtsman's Bay Area
Covers the Pacific coast from Point Reyes to Monterey Bay, San Francisco Bay, and Delta waterways. Little additional navigational information except for phone numbers of marinas and some details of facilities.

Chart-Kit for Southern California
Covers the waters from Point Conception to San Diego. Some aerial photographs, but little other navigational information. A high quality product with excellent printing.

Chart-Guide for Southern California
Covers the coast from central California to the Mexican border. The Chart-Guide contains much additional information on ports, facilities, anchorages, diving, and fishing, overprinted on the charts, and in summary form. This is sometimes superficial, but always accurate.

Chart-Guide for Catalina Island
Similar to the other Chart-Guide, but covers Catalina alone. Strongly recommended for Southern California weekend sailors.

Cruising Guides

Cruising Guide to Southern California's Offshore Islands.
(Caractacus Corporation, Santa Barbara, 1992).
The sister guide to this volume covers the Channel Islands of Southern California and adjacent mainland coasts in much great detail than is possible here. Strongly recommended for a Santa Barbara Channel cruise, also for Catalina and Santa Barbara Islands.

Sea Guide to Southern California by Leland R. Lewis and Peter E. Ebeling. (Sea Publications, Newport Beach, 3rd ed. 1973)
This large coffee table book is famous for its magnificent aerial photographs of the Channel Islands. Long out-of-print, it is somewhat superficial and outdated, but still worth owning if you can find a copy in a secondhand bookstore.

Weather

Marine Weather Handbook: Northern and Central California by Kenneth E. Lilly, Jr. (Paradise Cay Yacht Sales, Sausalito, 1985)
A technical book, but crammed with invaluable explanations of our weather systems. The local weather lore alone makes this book essential for any yacht. I used it extensively for this cruising guide.

Seamanship and Navigation

The Practical Pilot by Leonard Eyges. (International Marine Publishing, Camden, Maine, 1989) is the best primer on basic pilotage I have ever seen. It's one of the few books on the subject, which makes no concessions to electronics and has an intelligent perspective on such topics as identifying landmarks and estimating distance off. Keep a copy aboard and sharpen your navigational skills!

Staying Put by Brian Fagan. (Caractacus Corporation, Santa Barbara, 1993) is a short, to-the-point book on ground tackle and anchoring technique. An ideal quick reference source to have on board.

The Elements of Seamanship by Roger Taylor. (International Marine Publishing, Camden, 1986). Taylor is an elegant writer and a first-seaman, who covers the basics of seamanship in inimitable style. A classic work by any standards, and a book which keeps you honest!

Local History and Environment

Guide books to the ports and cities along the coast abound. A visit to the local Chamber of Commerce, Tourist Information Office, or a bookstore will provide you with the latest in a seemingly endless stream of such volumes.

In our over-published world, just about everyone has written some form of guide to outdoor activities along the coast. Few of these volumes are of lasting value.

Here are some of my lasting favorites:

Kimball Livingston, ***Sailing the Bay*** (Chronicle Books, San Francisco, 1981). Alas, Kimball Livingston's marvelous essay is out of print, but do all you can to find a copy in a secondhand store. Sailing the Bay may be outdated in places, but Livingston brings San Francisco Bay sailing to life as few authors ever have. A must for every boat!

Richard Henry Dana, ***Two Years Before the Mast.*** (Harpers, New York, 1841). The all-time classic of California history is as vivid and alive today as it was when first written. Never leave port without a copy: paperback reprints are in major bookstores.

Margaret Eaton, ***Dairy of a Sea Captain's Wife.*** (McNally and Loftin, Santa Barbara, 1980) (edited by Jan Timbrook). Life on Santa Cruz Island in the 1920s by the wife of a major waterfront character of the day. An engrossing read while on an island cruise.

Alma Overholt (updated by Jack Sargent), ***The Catalina Story*** (Catalina Island Museum Society, Avalon, 1989) is a useful source on this most visited of islands.

Notes

Notes

Notes

Notes